The Palestinian Resistance

Historical Documents of the Palestine Liberation Organization

The Palestinian Resistance

Historical Documents of the Palestine Liberation Organization

A Collection for Critical Organizational Study

ISKRA BOOKS
US | ENGLAND | IRELAND

Published by *Iskra Books* 2024

All rights reserved.
The moral rights of the author have been asserted.

Iskra Books
www.iskrabooks.org
US | England | Ireland

Iskra Books is an independent scholarly publisher—publishing original works of revolutionary theory, history, education, and art, as well as edited collections, new translations, and critical republications of older works.

ISBN-13: 979-8-3302-3691-6 (Softcover)

British Library Cataloguing in Publication Data
A catalogue record for this book is available from the British Library.

Library of Congress Cataloging-in-Publication Data
A catalog record for this book is available from the Library of Congress.

Cover Art by Ben Stahnke
Editing, Proofing, and Typesetting by David Peat

CONTENTS

EDITOR'S NOTE / vii

PUBLISHER'S NOTE
NOT A CAUSE FOR PALESTINIANS ONLY
David Peat & Ben Stahnke / xi

FOREWORD
A GUERRILLA HISTORY OF THE PLO
Adnan Hussein, Breht O'Shea, & Henry Hakamäki / xxxi

SECTION 1: THE PALESTINE LIBERATION ORGANIZATION

PROCLAMATION OF THE ESTABLISHMENT OF THE PALESTINE LIBERATION ORGANIZATION (1964) / 1

PALESTINIAN NATIONAL CHARTER: ADOPTED IN 1964 BY THE FIRST PALESTINIAN CONFERENCE (1964) / 2

PALESTINIAN NATIONAL CHARTER: ADOPTED IN 1968 BY THE FOURTH PALESTINIAN CONFERENCE (1968) / 7

10-POINT PROGRAM OF THE PLO (1974) / 13

SECTION 2: FATEH

THE POLITICAL STRUGGLE (1969) / 17

ABU LUTF ANSWERS QUESTIONS (1969) / 40

The Resistance: How Does it Think and Act? How Does it Face the Present? How Does it See the Future? (1969) / 50

Constitution of the Palestinian National Liberation Movement (Fateh) (1960s) / 108

Al Fateh: Towards a Democratic State in Palestine / 145

Section 3: Palestine at the United Nations

Text of United Nations Security Council Resolution 242 of 22 November 1967 / 169

Political Communique of the 19th Extraordinary Session of the Palestine National Council (1988) / 171

State of Palestine Declaration of Independence (1988) / 182

Address to the Security Council of the United Nations on the Situation in the Occupied Palestinian Territories (1990) / 187

Afterword

Disarming Empire
Paweł Wargan / 199

Appendix

Historical Documents of the PLO
Leila S. Kadi / 205

Editor's Note

In this book, *Fateh* is transliterated following the romanization in the historical documents included in this volume, whereas in modern non-Arab sources it is now typically romanized as Fatah. The organization's full name is *Ḥarakat al-Taḥrīr al-Waṭanī l-Filasṭīnī*, translated as the "Palestinian National Liberation Movement." Out of this, the reverse acronym FATAH was extracted, with the meaning of "conquering," or "victory."

The historical documents present in the text have been lightly edited for clarity, readability, and accessibility. The content and structure of the original documents has been preserved, with only the vicissitudes of translation and editing impacting the originals. Extra contextual information is provided throughout by footnotes beginning [**Ed. Note:**]. All other footnotes are from the originals.

A Critical Organizational Theory of Resistance: The 2023-2024 Zionist military assault on the Palestinians—the genocidal, ongoing *Nakba*—has, since the beginning of the onslaught, demanded the attention of organizers and peace activists the world over. Organizational theorists and radical organizers drawing from data-driven, historical, and real-world perspectives are well served by studying theories of organization drawn directly from oppressed peoples engaged in active revolutionary struggles under daily threat of violence, death, and displacement. As state repression

increases, both in the imperial core and beyond, so too does the need for critical organizational theory to incorporate more heavily the frameworks, concepts, and models of active revolutionary struggle under threat of state repression. Critical organizational theory drawn from the Palestinian struggle allows organizers and theorists to better serve and model the Palestinian Resistance by expanding public focus and academic attention while strengthening global anti-imperialist struggles.

Not a Cause for Palestinians Only

David Peat and Ben Stahnke

> *Who planted terrorism in our area?*
> *Some came and took our land,*
> *forced us to leave,*
> *forced us to live in camps.*
> *I think this is terrorism.*
> *Using means to resist this terrorism and stop its effects—*
> *this is called struggle.*
>
> Leila Khaled

An Opening Note

The events of October 7, 2023—the world-historic development in which fighters of the Palestinian people broke from a 17-year mass-incarceration in the open-air prison of the Gaza Strip—tore asunder myths of Zionist invulnerability, shattering accepted wisdoms of conventional geopolitics and fundamentally changing patterns of resistance in the region.[1] Subsequent responses from the Zionist entity[2] have been chaotic, genocidal,[3] and, necessarily, self-destructive. Desperately con-

---

1   To quote Nelson Mandela: "We choose peace rather than confrontation, except in cases where we cannot get; where we cannot proceed; or we cannot move forward. Then, if the only alternative is violence, we will use violence" (Mandela, Nelson. "Nelson Mandela and Palestine: In His Own Words," *Middle East Eye*, February 11, 2020. Accessed online at: https://www.middleeasteye.net/news/nelson-mandela-30-years-palestine).

2   In this foreword, we use "the Zionist entity" or simply "the entity" to refer to the occupying imperialist forces in Palestine, known otherwise as the State of Israel. Following Leila Shomali and Lara Kilani's call, writing in "Anti-Zionism as Decolonisation" (*Ebb Magazine*, vol. 1, no. 1, January 10, 2024), "anti-zionist formations should cut out language that forces upon Palestinian and non-Palestinian allies the violence of colonial theft." In the various historical and contemporary articles, as well as in direct quotations, the original appellations used have been preserved.

3   "Any small operation on our part will be answered by 10 in order to terrorize the Arab people and tell them that their endeavor is a hopeless one, and that the Israeli

fected public relations campaigns painting the Zionist entity as a liberal, "normal" state—a "Zionist image-making," as the Palestinian political party *Fateh* describes in the pages of the present volume—dissolved in the face of Israel's reactionary, genocidal response.

Since October 7, the wider forces of the Palestinian Resistance have engaged the military forces of Zionism on multiple fronts. First and foremost in Gaza, but also in the West Bank and in Lebanon, the Resistance has been engaged in qualitatively more pronounced and more effective activity. Resilient, well-coordinated forces in Yemen have fundamentally altered the flows of global trade, enforcing, in effect, a naval blockade against those supporting the Zionist entity's actions against the Palestinians.

Critical scholars, students, and workers the world over have rallied to Palestine's defense, standing in solidarity with the Palestinian Resistance and with victims of settler-colonialism worldwide—with wholehearted support for not only the moral right but the *legal* right of peoples to resist physical oppression and colonial occupation.[4] As Max Ajl noted, "Palestine crystallizes nearly every contradiction within the current order."[5] Palestine's highly organized forms of resistance, both directly against the military of the Zionist entity and within the Palestinian diaspora more generally—for example, in its actions against Zionism's ideological legitimators—not only lay bare the core contradictions of the modern era, but stand as an inspiration and a lesson for labor and peace organizers the world over, as well as for scholars and theorists of these organizations more generally.

The present text, *Historical Documents of the PLO: A Collection for Critical Organizational Study*, brings together important foundational

---

army is a legend which cannot be defeated" (present volume, "The Resistance: How Does it Think and Act? How Does it Face the Present? How does it See the Future? A Dialogue between Al-Fateh and Al-Talfah," p. 96).

4   United Nations resolution A/RES/37/43, passed by the UN General Assembly in 1982, endorsed, without qualification, the "inalienable right [of the Palestinian people to] self-determination, national independence, territorial integrity, national unity and sovereignty without outside interference," and, further, went on to recognize the legitimacy of their activities that upheld those rights "by all available means, including armed struggle." Accessed on March 14, 2024, online at: https://digitallibrary.un.org/record/40572?ln=en for the full text of the resolution.

5   Ajl, Max. 2024. "Palestine's Great Flood: Part I," *Agrarian South: Journal of Political Economy*, vol. 31, no. 1 Accessed on March 14, 2024, online at: https://journals.sagepub.com/doi/10.1177/22779760241228157

documents of the Palestine Liberation Organization (PLO), the driving political force of the Palestinian Resistance and *al-Filasṭīniyyūn* struggle for liberation, sovereignty, and statehood. The documents compiled in this book offer lessons in resilience and in strategic policy and practice—emphasizing the importance of aligning organizational structures with ideological goals. *Historical Documents of the PLO* is intended to illuminate Palestinian organizational contexts of resistance, as well as the importance of such structures of resistance under fire—under direct military threat, attack, and subversion. The book is thus a resource for organizational scholars as well as for organizers engaged in direct struggle with other, extant forms of settler-colonialism.

A Rationale for Palestinian Organizational Studies[6]

As of the writing of this foreword on April 25, 2024, the forces of Zionism continue in their genocidal campaign, underwritten fully by complicit Western governments. An unabated, ever-growing list of war crimes and inhuman atrocities have resulted so far in a death toll estimated to be well over 35,000—the blood of whom stains the hands of those occupying Palestinian lands, as well as those in Washington, Westminster, Berlin, and beyond.[7] An unending dissemination of video and still imagery of the martyrs—the innocent—deeply betray the Zionist narrative of "self-defense." There is, simply, no other way to view the ongoing acts of brutality; Zionists, in service of their national, colonial project of statehood—cheered on globally by fascists, reactionaries, and a pro-imperialist, religious zealotry, supported by a coordinated media push to legitimate the genocidal project—murder and displace Palestinians in an effort to 1. ethnically cleanse Palestine of the Palestinian people, and 2. make space for the encroachment of Israeli settlement. It cannot be danced around nor miscommunicated that Zionists, supported by allies in other core anglosphere states, are directly responsible for the system-

---

6   "If one has to refer to any of the parties as a terrorist state, one might refer to the Israeli government, because they are the people who are slaughtering defenseless and innocent Arabs in the occupied territories" (Mandela, Nelson. Qtd. in "Mandela Angers Australian Jews with Fresh Anti-Israel Rhetoric," *Jewish Telegraphic Agency*, October 25, 1990. Accessed on March 14, 2024, online at: https://www.jta.org/archive/mandela-angers-australian-jews-with-fresh-anti-israel-rhetoric.

7   Batrawy, Aya. February 29, 2024. "Gaza's Death Toll Now Exceeds 30,000. Here's Why It's an Incomplete Count," *NPR*. Accessed March 14, 2024, online at: https://www.npr.org/2024/02/29/1234159514/gaza-death-toll-30000-palestinians-israel-hamas-war.

atic murder of children, women, and other non-combatants of the Palestinian people.

Infrastructural attacks carried out by the Israeli Occupation Force (IOF)—the bombing of hospitals, mosques, and key points of Palestinian national infrastructure—are meant to punish a people whose only crime is to exist as targets of a Zionist manifest destiny; the unforgivable crime (for the imperialist) of regional Indigeneity.

The genocide presently underway in occupied Palestine is symptomatic of an ongoing Nakba. *An-Nakbah*—a term developed in reference to the violent 1948 displacement of the Palestinians—is a catastrophe of eugenic proportions that continues to be enacted in the face of the world in an unhinged, reckless, and brazen fashion. It is the sometimes-slow, sometimes-fast eradication of a people, their history, their infrastructure, and their genealogies—of their very memory.

Zionism, as a political project, is a European-originated ethno-capitalism supported by core anglosphere imperialist states united—and economically invested in—the existence of an Israeli state in the Middle East.[8] The State of Israel, given its historical illegitimacy and its lack of geographical precedent, requires, for its very existence, a subversion of history itself. As Christian Noakes observed, "[t]he Zionist cause of expansion requires legitimacy which it produces through a shifting and inconsistent memory of Israeli space. The continued colonization of Palestine is powered not only by the financial and military support of the U.S. and other imperialist nations but by a process of 'dispossession through amnesia.'"[9] Part of this inter-imperialist strategy of *dispossession through amnesia* includes not only highly-coordinated academic and intellectual attacks aimed at erasure and the delegitimization of Palestinian archaeological historicity,[10] but also surgical military attacks on research centers, universities, and libraries. These direct attacks have destroyed countless

---

8 Recall the words of U.S. President Joe Biden who has remarked: "I have long said: If Israel didn't exist, we would have to invent it. And while it may not feel that way today, Israel must again be a safe place for the Jewish people. And I promise you: We're going to do everything in our power to make sure that it will be" (Biden, Joe. "President Biden's Statement During his Visit to Tel Aviv," *U.S. Embassy to El Salvador*, 19 October 2023. Accessed online at: https://sv.usembassy.gov/president-bidens-statement-during-his-visit-to-tel-aviv)

9 Noakes, Christian. 2020. "The Sacred-Secular Dialectic: Zionist Superstructure in Palestine," *Peace, Land, and Bread*, vol. 1, p. 84.

10 See, more generally, Ibid., pp. 82-95.

important historical geographies, architectures, and archives necessary to the cultural survival of the Palestinian people.

Some of the writings from the present book were taken from an earlier 1969 text entitled the *Basic Political Documents of the Armed Palestinian Resistance Movement*.[11] The publisher of this text, the Palestine Research Center, was founded in 1965 and, at its height, employed over 40 dedicated researchers producing hundreds of translated works, as well as journals like *Shu'un Filastiniyyah* and *Al-Watha'iq Al-Filastiniyya*. The Research Center library held, in 1982, an astounding 25,000 volumes, "the world's largest collections of manuscripts on the question of Palestine,"[12] according to the Center's director.

In 1983, the Palestine Research Center was bombed by the Zionist, IOF-proxy, terrorist group, the Front for the Liberation of Lebanon from Foreigners (*Jabhat Tahrir Lubnan min al-Ghuraba*). After the bombing, in a naked display of Israeli collusion, the Center was quickly looted by IOF forces, who summarily stole, sequestered, or otherwise destroyed all of the Center's 25,000 documents.

Historical Documents of the PLO: A Collection for Critical Organizational Study is one very small attempt at a cultural stop-loss; an attempt at remembering in the face of dispossession by way of amnesia. It is the first in a series of indeterminate length from Iskra Books, to be quickly followed by *Historical Documents of the Popular Fronts: A Collection for Critical Organizational Study*. The resources in these books are meant to be in circulation for the sake of organizational and resistance studies of both present and posterity. They are, in fact, the legacy of the Palestinian Resistance itself and their publication is an effort to, in some small way, belay the Zionist entity's attempts at Palestinian erasure.

The books in this series are collections of primary sources, situated alongside relevant new writings, for the sake of studies in critical organizational theories of resistance. *Historical Documents of the PLO* is also a practical resource—a study guide, in a sense—for the labor organizer who seeks to apply organizational values, principles, and practices drawn from the Palestinian context. Organizational theories drawn from the

---

11   A new edition of this book has recently been published by Midnight Books, Los Angeles, 2024.

12   Hijazi, Ihsan A. 1982. "Israeli Looted Archives of P.L.O. Officials Say." *The New York Times*. Archived from the original on 17 July 2014; accessed on March 14, 2024, online at: https://www.nytimes.com/1982/10/01/world/israeli-looted-archives-of-plo-officials-say.html

operations of the PLO have much to offer both scholars and organizers in the imperial core, and it is in this spirit that Iskra Books publishes this collection.

While we aim to situate this series, *The Palestinian Resistance*, within the larger field of organizational studies—a field which has long been keen to adopt Marxist theories of organization and Soviet organizational sciences for the purposes of increasing capitalist productivity[13]—these works also lend their support to critical archival studies and "efforts to examine the ways in which records and archives serve as tools for both oppression and liberation."[14] Practically, the resources in the present text and series can support research in at least two distinct capacities: 1. to assist in academic and cultural study, preservation, and research in organizational studies drawn from the Palestinian context, and 2. to offer labor organizers outside of Palestine a way to engage in high-level—and *guerrilla*—organizational study for the purpose of enhancing and sharpening organizing efforts in anglosphere geographies, both within and adjacent to the imperial core.

In Palestine and elsewhere, it has always been the case that it is none other than the masses themselves who—rising up in organized resistance—overthrow oppressive systems. Each context has its own specificities, which those engaged in the struggle will know best—and each liberation movement will also have lessons for the wider movement. It is with that in mind that Iskra Books has put together this series of edited collections of works from the core organizations of the Palestinian Resistance.

The present volume covers the early years of the PLO—primarily the 1960s and 70s—and begins with the formative documents and statements of the organization. In the second section of the text, the reader will find resources from the largest organization that went under the PLO grouping: Fateh. Finally, spanning into the final decades of the 20th century, the reader will find documents and statements from the PLO's constituent organizations' engagements with the United Nations.[15]

---

13 Hatch, Mary Jo. 2018. *Organization Theory: Modern, Symbolic, and Postmodern Perspectives*. Oxford University Press, p. 26.

14 Caswell, Michelle, Ricardo Punzalan, and T-Kay Sangwand. 2017. "Critical Archival Studies: An Introduction." *Journal of Critical Library and Information Studies* 1, no. 2.

15 This last section's inclusion is not to suggest we should seek the solution for Palestine's liberation in appeals to liberal international institutions, when such libera-

The Spark That Started the Prairie Fire[16]

Thus far, the events of October 7 and the over-the-top reactions of the Zionist entity have brought about a variety of responses from progressive forces in the imperial core. Millions have been in the streets, occupying campuses, and marching in countless demonstrations in support of the Palestinian cause—protesters and organizers having long since been disabused of any remaining notions regarding their ruling classes' capacity for "supporting human rights," "upholding international law," or even the most basic level of human compassion.

Sustained, naked brutalities carried out by the Zionist entity, on the back of years of activism by Palestinians and their supporters, have brought about an enormous upsurge in support for the cause. Some have engaged in forms of direct action, such as Palestine Action's courageous occupations of weapons manufacturers and connected organizations. Likewise, other groups have engaged in the picketing of Zionist speakers and cultural figures, reinvigorating and expanding existing BDS campaigns. Such actions reveal the reality that the Palestinian struggle is tied tightly to the world-system[17] of imperialism. For example, drones built by

---

tion can only come through the organized actions of the Palestinian people and their allies in struggle. Instead, it recognizes that these interactions between the Palestine Liberation Organization and the UN form just one aspect of their struggle, and also recalls how, for better or worse, decolonization movements globally have looked to institutions like the UN to underpin their sovereignty (with, for example, the 1965 Afro-Asian [Bandung] Conference's "Ten Principles" for peaceful coexistence being based on the Charter of the United Nations). Such ambiguous engagements have continued into the present day with the "Group of Friends in Defense of the Charter of the United Nations" being established at the UN in 2021 by nations subject to Western sanctions, and economic, political, and military oppression by the Global North. Palestine holds an "observer" status in this grouping.

16 In the words of Mao Zedong: "Here we can apply the old Chinese saying, 'A single spark can start a prairie fire.' In other words, our forces, although small at present, will grow very rapidly. [...] When we look at a thing, we must examine its essence and treat its appearance merely as an usher at the threshold, and once we cross the threshold, we must grasp the essence of the thing; this is the only reliable and scientific method of analysis" (Zedong, Mao. 1930. "A Single Spark Can Start a Prairie Fire," *Selected Works of Mao Zedong*. Accessed on March 14, 2024, online at: https://www.marxists.org/reference/archive/mao/selected-works/volume-1/mswv1_6.htm).

17 Che Guevara wrote that, "imperialism is a world system, the last stage of capitalism and must be defeated in a world confrontation" and the response of the imperialist countries has hammered this point home, with Palestine a, or more likely 'the', key node of the world-system that oppresses people the world over. The technologies (both material and organizational) of oppression are 'battle-tested' here and will be rolled out on the rest of us as the 'polycrisis' of increasingly brittle neoliberal capitalism and

Israel-based weapons manufacturer *Elbit Systems* are deployed not only in Gaza, but also to police and border patrol agencies along the US-Mexico border, as well as to the English Channel, where they are used, in all cases, to oppressive ends.[18]

The small and relatively well-trodden activist responses in and of themselves are of course insufficient to take on the too-long established Zionist project, but their frequency, size, and wide range of targets are effecting a shift—evidenced by the hysterical reactions from the ruling classes and capitalist political elites. Responses that reflect the sacrifice of the Palestinian people have also occurred: on February 25, 2024, for example, organizers and peace activists around the world witnessed the heart-wrenching self-immolation of 25-year-old United States Airman, Aaron Bushnell. Dousing himself in a liter of clear, liquid fuel and setting ablaze a pant leg after a few missed clicks of the lighter, Bushnell stood tall, courageous, and immortal in his final moments—his last cries for a "Free Palestine!" echoing from behind a wall of orange and yellow flame.

The video of Bushnell's final act spread quickly. A brilliant sun in the midwinter sky, the iron fences and the white buildings, the dormant, leafless trees, and a concluding, calm statement narrating his final walk to the gates of the Israeli Embassy[19]:

> [...] my name is Aaron Bushnell. I am an active duty member of the United States Air Force and *I will no longer be complicit in genocide*. I am about to engage in an extreme act of protest; but, compared to what people have been experiencing in Palestine at the hands of their colonizers, it's not extreme at all. This is what our ruling class has decided will be normal.

Bushnell's consummate act of protest suggests a qualitative shift in anti-war and anti-imperialist protest in the imperial core, heralding, seemingly, a new era in which tactics have become more extreme—the stakes even higher. But in the face of stronger and more well-organized tactics,

---

climate crisis lead to an increasingly militarized response by our ruling classes" (Guevara, Che. 1967. *Message to the Tricontinental*. Accessed on March 14, 2024, online at https://www.marxists.org/archive/guevara/1967/04/16.htm).

18   Gustavo Petro, the president of Colombia, who has been more forthright in words and action than many of his Global South contemporaries clearly articulated this when he said "[w]hy have large carbon-consuming countries allowed the systematic murder of thousands of children in Gaza? Because Hitler has already entered their homes and they are getting ready to defend their high levels of carbon consumption and reject the exodus it causes." (Fadul L. G. 2023. "What We See in Gaza is the Rehearsal of the Future," Colombian President at UN Climate Summit. Anadolu Ajansi).

19   Our usage of the name of the State of Israel is in no way an acknowledgment of the legitimacy of the settler-colonial project in Palestine; see footnote 3.

so too grows the repressive power of the state. State apparatuses engaged in social circumscription, surveillance, and in the quelling of dissent have become aware of this shift and have adjusted their tactics accordingly. In the face of a systematic genocide which appears to know no end, an increase in the repressive capacities of the state, and the increasing professionalization of state and nongovernmental counter-protest and reactionary elements, the necessity for progressive humanitarian activists and organizers in core geographies to *professionalize* their work, strategies, and organizations has never been greater.

SEVERAL IMPLICATIONS OF THE PALESTINIAN STRUGGLE FOR CRITICAL ORGANIZATIONAL STUDIES

In the social and organizational histories of liberation movements, few have been so scrutinized, debated, and challenged as the Palestinian struggle for self-determination. Ongoing attempts at erasure and sustained, blatant acts of aggression carried out upon Palestinian civilian populations by the Israeli Occupation Forces bring the legitimacy of Palestinian statehood once again into the public eye, with regional conflicts currently underway in Gaza and the surrounding areas catalyzing other regional struggles, uniting progressive forces around the world against the Zionist entity and its financial sponsors in the United States—and, further, igniting the potential for larger-scale, symmetrical, global wars.

It is no small underestimation to say that revolutionary peace-building movements are needed now more than ever. Yet these movements face challenges both in public and academic spaces. Consider this lengthy quote from Edward Said:

> Nothing in my view is more reprehensible than those habits of mind in the intellectual that induce avoidance, that characteristic turning away from a difficult and principled position, which you know to be the right one, but which you decide not to take. You do not want to appear too political; you are afraid of seeming controversial; you want to keep a reputation for being balanced, objective, moderate; your hope is to be asked back, to consult, to be on a board or prestigious committee, and so to remain within the responsible mainstream; someday you hope to get an honorary degree, a big prize, perhaps even an ambassadorship. For an intellectual these habits of mind are corrupting par excellence. If anything can denature, neutralize, and finally kill a passionate intellectual life it is the internalization of such habits. Personally I have encountered them in one of the toughest of all contemporary issues, Palestine, where fear of speaking out about one of the greatest injustices in modern history has hobbled, blinkered, muzzled many who know the truth and are in a position to serve it. For despite the abuse and vilification that any outspoken

supporter of Palestinian rights and self-determination earns for him or herself, the truth deserves to be spoken, represented by an unafraid and compassionate intellectual.[20]

Western academic consensus is largely biased against the Palestinian perspective, and has, for the most part, bought wholesale into the carefully-crafted political narratives of Zionism; yet this bias provides an opportunity for progressive, revolutionary elements inside of academe to counter these narratives.

As Seyed Borhani pointed out, "[t]he West's support for Israel constitutes a central controversy in the Middle Eastern Studies; knowledge production about the question of Israel/Palestine in Western academia, where a pro-Israeli is the dominant one, is one significant extension of that controversy."[21] In light of this, a growing body of work exists within the fields of Palestine Studies, and organizational studies more generally, to extract organizational theory from the Palestinian context.[22] Following Raja Khalidi, critical scholars can be "increasingly encouraged that there is indeed a new movement in Palestinian development scholarship already correcting the historical record that was distorted by two decades of intellectual collusion with the political imperatives of the peace process and 'state-building' agenda, instead of scholarship engaging with the real challenges of national and societal liberation."[23]

The present volume—and, by extension, the series in which it is situated—exist to contribute to this growing body of work with the explicit purpose of not only cataloging primary sources for present and future studies, but for professional organizers and activists in the anglosphere to *apply* Palestinian organizational theory to the activist project in the Global North. The collection of documents presented in this volume offer an important glimpse into the inner workings of the PLO and its constituent organizations—a grouping at the heart of the Palestinian struggle. These documents—bracketed with an insightful preface from

20 Said, Edward. 1996. *Representations of the Intellectual: The 1993 Reith Lectures*, Vintage Books, p. 100.

21 Borhani, Seyed H. 2015. "Palestine Studies in Western Academia: Shifting a Paradigm?." *Iranian Review of Foreign Affairs*, vol. 5, no. 4, p. 119.

22 See, generally, Gawerc, Michelle I. 2013. "Organizational Adaptation and Survival in a Hostile and Unfavorable Environment: Peacebuilding Organizations in Israel and Palestine," in *Research in Social Movements, Conflicts and Change*, Emerald Group Publishing Limited, pp. 167-202.

23 Khalidi, Raja. 2016. "Twenty-First Century Palestinian Development Studies." *Journal of Palestine Studies*, vol. 45, no. 4, pp. 7-15.

our comrades, colleagues, and collaborators from Guerrilla History, as well as an afterword by the brilliant Paweł Wargan from the Progressive International—span organizational rules, ideological treatises, and operational strategies, and provide a rich, thorough collection for both organizers and scholars to better understand the evolution of the struggle for Palestinian statehood, as well as the political ideas and the development of the Palestinian national liberation movement.

Lessons from the PLO

Contemporary labor organizers and activists willing to study the primary source documents included in the present volume will find not only a wealth of organizational theory, but—for those willing to read a little deeper and through a lens of application and *praxis*—a blueprint for action that is both revolutionary in spirit and pragmatic in its application. The PLO's struggle, captured and cataloged in these documents, offers both a theory and a narrative of resilience, adaptability, and unwavering commitment to collective, national liberation. Taken together, these documents comprise a story—one which resonates with labor organizers and activists confronting the challenges of mobilizing workers, navigating complex political landscapes, and achieving tangible social change under circumstances of increasing and direct political and military hostility. Thus does the PLO's experience serve as a guide, offering lessons on building real world collaborative solidarity under fire by fostering direct democratic participation, while enacting the core organizational principles of practice required for the maintenance of organizational integrity.

The PLO's journey, from its inception in 1964 to its current status as the officially recognized national authority of the Palestinian people, headquartered in the city of Al-Bireh in the West Bank, has been marked by a relentless pursuit of legitimacy, professionalization, practical and purposeful organization, liberation, justice, and national self-determination. Membership in the PLO has not been only a matter of affiliation but of a deep commitment to the cause of liberation and statehood, evidenced by the rigorous qualifications required and by solemn oaths that members are often urged to take.[24] This dedication is further reflected

---

24 "By Allah, the almighty and by my honor and beliefs I swear to remain faithful to Palestine, and to spare no effort to liberate it; I swear not to disclose any of the Movement's (*Fateh*) secrets and affairs; this is a free oath, to which God bears witness" (See this volume, "Constitution of the Palestinian National Liberation Movement [Fateh], p. 119")

in organizational principles that govern the movement itself, including commitment, discipline, centrality, and democracy. Operational strategy within the PLO is characterized by meticulous planning, accountability, and a culture of public and self-criticism. These practices are not only integral to the movement's tactical and political success, but also to its applied moral and ethical frameworks, which includes a commitment to gender equality and the eradication of social ills.[25]

In taking together the writings included in this volume, an action plan derived from the PLO's so-called "best practices" might best be summed up in the following points. We provide these points as a reading guide for organizers and readers looking to navigate the core actionable points of the included, foundational political writings of the PLO:

1. The organization must first establish and clarify a clear vision with realizable goals. For the liberation-focused organization to be successful in its endeavors, it must engage in a "continuous process of clarification of the policy of the revolution in its broadest aspect," with the knowledge that "[s]uch a clarification will provide the revolution with people who believe in it, and will help to discover the elements who are qualified to join the revolution."[26] The establishment of a practical organizational vision can be brought about in at least two ways: firstly, by defining the overarching vision for the organization, and ensuring it aligns with the most progressive and realistic needs and demands of the organization's stakeholders; and, secondly, this organization must set specific, measurable, achievable, relevant, and time-bound goals.[27]

2. The PLO emphasizes the necessity of mass, direct, public participation in the struggle, highlighting that the public should not merely be observers but active participants in the struggle. "Thus Palestinian resistance is neither regional nor isolationist. It demands that the [...] people with the totality of their capacities should adopt it."[28] In this regard, the organization must build inclusive and adapt-

---

25   Ibid., "State of Palestine: Declaration of Independence," p. 185.

26   Ibid., "The Political Struggle," p. 34.

27   Bjerke, May Britt, and Ralph Renger. 2017. "Being Smart About Writing SMART objectives." *Evaluation and Program Planning*, no. 61, pp. 125-127.

28   This book, "The Resistance: How Does it Think and Act? How Does it Face the Present? How does it See the Future? A Dialogue between Al-Fateh and Al-Talfah," p. 99. Original source: *Basic Political Documents of the Armed Palestinian Struggle*, translated and edited by Leila S. Kadi, 1969, Palestine Liberation Organization Re-

able internal structures, creating platforms and opportunities that cater to diverse, multi-ethnic, and multicultural groups within the working class, allowing for various levels of engagement and political awareness.[29] The organization must also develop a flexible, dynamic organizational structure that can adapt to changing circumstances and scales of operation.[30]

3. The liberation-focused organization will face, and must overcome, challenges in balancing the need for further training with the imperative to act quickly due to political, military, and security considerations; that is, social and political exigency will always drive the organization to act before it feels ready. The organization must take this into account and train proactively but with the understanding that it must operate on incomplete knowledge and the demands of a rapidly changing, dynamic climate. Further, the organization must design and implement its own education programs for the purposes of training, skill-sharing, and to raise awareness among members about their roles and duties within the organization.[31]

4. The training of organizational membership must be in line with larger ethical and political goals, operating prefiguratively to train membership in theories of collectivism, actively working to "reject individualism and egoism, adhere to the group, [to] get used to the most difficult work pertaining to the struggle, and other sacrifices in difficult circumstances."[32] Furthermore, emphasis on cadre[33] and member development is paramount. The revolutionary organizations of the cadres are, for the PLO, the "backbone of the revolution," and highlight the necessity for organizers to invest in the training and development of dedicated members who can carry forward the movement's objectives with conviction and with revolutionary discipline.

---

search Center.

29   This volume, "The Political Struggle," p. 40.

30   Ibid., "The Resistance," p. 39.

31   Ibid., "The Political Struggle," p. 21.

32   Ibid., "The Resistance," p. 89.

33   Ibid., "The Political Struggle," p. 29: "These are the backbone of the revolution, its security and moving force. The weakness of the cadres or their absence will cause the disintegration of the relationship between the will of the revolutionary leadership and the masses, thus depriving political struggle of one of its most important links."

5. The PLO recognizes the importance of not only admitting but actively correcting mistakes within its ranks, encouraging constructive criticism from other organizations and public observers. As Abu Eyad observed, "[t]here is a truth which should be admitted by our brothers in the different guerrilla organizations. Such an admission should be preceded by an admission on the part of Al-Fateh to the effect that it is not an ideal and infallible organization. Since in Al-Fateh there are wrong things, it is the duty of the other guerrilla organizations and honest critical outside observers to point out the mistakes to the members of Al-Fateh who cannot discern them in order to get rid of the mistakes which any national liberation movement commits."[34] The PLO's commitment to self-criticism and continual improvement is a critical takeaway for organizers and organizational planners. The practice of public and self-criticism, along with active participation in organizational sessions, ensures that the movement remains dynamic, responsive, and accountable to its constituents.

6. The legitimacy and strength of both the organizations and the movement are derived from its popular support and the effectiveness of its actions on the ground.[35] The organization that does not effectively respond to real social and political needs will not thrive in an atmosphere of increasing hostility. Furthermore, the organization must be successful in its endeavors. When cultural existence is at stake—when national liberation and liberation of the oppressed class are at stake—public support does not and will not follow ineffective and failing organizational efforts; it must follow those organizations which are capable of most successfully and practically responding to the crises of their time. An organization must be able to mobilize public, economic, and political support for its endeavors if it is to succeed and to continue to derive the popular support critical for its survival.

7. Social justice and progressive public welfare are crucial aspects of the liberation-focused organization. The PLO for example has established internal social institutions as part of its commitment to social justice and taking responsibility for the welfare of the Palestinian people. The question of social justice is, for the PLO, and contrary to the chauvinist trend exemplified by many reactionary elements, a

---

34 Ibid., "The Resistance," p. 90.
35 Ibid., p. 54.

"backbone of the revolution,"[36] co-equal with the political education of the cadres and of the general membership. Social justice, inclusive of progressive stances on LGBTQ+ justice, disability justice, the deconstruction of environmental racisms, and Indigenous liberation must be woven deeply within the fabric of the liberation-centered organization.

8. In the context of escalating fascist violence and reactionary extremisms, general PLO organizational theory calls for intensified action at all levels to confront the fascist threat. The global resurgence of far-right ideologies necessitates a vigilant and proactive stance from organizers and organizations engaged in liberation struggles. The cynical weaponization of terms like *antisemitism* to silence legitimate criticisms of state actions must be combated with a nuanced understanding of the issues at hand, ensuring that the fight against *genuine* antisemitism is not undermined. Furthermore, the PLO's appreciation expressed for the various "Israeli forces for peace" also serves as a reminder that alliances with sympathetic forces—even within opposing structures—can be a strategic asset. On this, organizers must be clear in their communication with the masses about the nature of their actions to avoid confusion and ensure effective mobilization.

9. The organization must be aware of the psychological impact of direct repression, military operations, and the need to prepare both membership and the organization's stakeholders for various forms of warfare—from both the repressive and ideological apparatuses of the state. While the organization's primary mission is in the seeking of peace, security, and independence for the organization's stakeholders, it must face the reality that under circumstances of direct colonization, imperialism, and the fascist, genocidal tactics of occupation and manifest destiny, it is, ultimately, a revolutionary organization set against the hegemony of the status quo. As noted in this volume, in "Address to the Security Council of the United Nations on the Situation in the Occupied Palestinian Territories" by Yasser Arafat, "[o]ur people are determined to attain their political, national and human rights like all other peoples in the world. We are determined to do so because we are an indivisible part of the community of nations and of human society, with which we have participated in carrying the torch of culture, for it was in our land that the three

---

36 Ibid., "Abu Lutf Answers Questions," p. 44.

heavenly religions were formed, flourished and lived side by side in harmony."[37]

10. The struggle against imperialism as the primary contradiction; the primary struggle. The PLO also argues that, on broader global issues such as ecological crises and the looming threat of nuclear war, the organizational struggles of liberation must be framed within the context of robust global resistances to imperialism. As noted in Paweł Wargan's afterword to the present volume, "[s]ince 1960, the old colonial powers of the Global North have drained $152 trillion from the Global South through structures of unequal exchange."[38] Herein lies the most crucial target of struggle for the liberation-centered organization; the great linking together of all struggles as one comes under the guise of the great global resistance of all subaltern and oppressed peoples against European and American-led colonialism; organizers and organizations in the Global North and in anglosphere locales must recognize this struggle as primary, and must take every effort to subvert the project of imperialism at home first; abroad second.

11. With a final re-commitment and reaffirmation to peace and the right to self-determination, the organization must, upon application of these principles of practice, develop a plan in which core values are developed and codified, and where all future challenges and struggles are approached from a lens of these values—inclusive of the organization's driving mission.

Taken together as a longitudinal narrative of organizational resistance-based practice, the PLO documents provided in this book exemplify—if we read closely enough and, often, between the lines—a loose plan of action that can be envisioned across the previous series of steps.

CORE TAKEAWAYS FROM THE BOOK FOR CRITICAL ORGANIZATIONAL THEORISTS

The PLO's foundational principles of commitment, discipline, centrality, and democracy[39] offer an organizational blueprint for understanding how revolutionary organizations under active, direct repression can

---

37   Ibid., "Address to the Security Council of the United Nations on the Situation in the Occupied Palestinian Territories," p. 197.

38   Ibid., "Disarming Empire," p. 201

39   Ibid., "Constitution of Fateh," p. 115.

maintain coherence and direction amidst the tumult of social change and push-back. For the PLO, internal emphasis on public and self-criticism[40] as a mechanism for continuous improvement is particularly instructive for organizations seeking to remain dynamic and responsive to their constituents. Further, we find coherent examples in the writings within this book of the following core takeaways most pertinent for critical organizational studies from the Marxist lens.

The Role of Political Education. The PLO's approach to political education underscores the importance of enlightening the masses about the aims of the revolution without necessarily prescribing a definite political ideology. Its approach is thus prosaic and practical, acknowledging that a revolutionary sector of society will by nature contain many differing trends in thinking. This reflects a rather nuanced understanding of the need to develop political consciousness while allowing for ideological fluidity as the landmarks of the revolution become clearer.

Organizational Structure and Membership. The PLO's organizational structure, with its emphasis on collective leadership and adherence to majority decisions,[41] provides insights into how revolutionary organizations can balance the need for decisive action with democratic participation. The criteria for membership and leadership[42] highlight the importance of personal commitment and revolutionary conduct, which are essential for sustaining the movement's legitimacy and influence.

Strategic Adaptability. The PLO's ability to operate within both lawful and revolutionary frameworks[43] demonstrates the strategic adaptability necessary for organizations to navigate complex, and rapidly shifting, political landscapes. This dual approach allows for the recruitment and mobilization of a broad base of support while advancing the revolutionary aims.

Class Struggle and Mass Mobilization. The PLO's focus on establishing popular organizations[44] and recruiting politically aware cadres[45] aligns with the Marxist principle of mass mobilization as a driving force for social change. The documents in this book further provide detailed,

---

40 Ibid..

41 Ibid., "The Political Struggle," p. 29

42 Ibid., "Constitution of Fateh," p. 120.

43 Ibid., "The Political Struggle," p. 33, p. 41.

44 Ibid., p. 28.

45 Ibid., p. 23.

practical examples of how class consciousness can be fostered and channeled into revolutionary action.

Dialectical Development of Political Ideas. As suggested by Adnan Husain in the foreword below,[46] an examination of the historical evolution of the PLO's political ideas and tactics offers a case study in applied dialectics and historical materialism, illustrating how revolutionary organizations best develop their strategies in response to changing and hostile historical circumstances. This dialectical approach is central to Marxist organizational science, emphasizing the importance of learning from practice and adapting to new realities and circumstances.

Intersectionality and Justice. The PLO's commitment to addressing social ills and discrimination, particularly gender discrimination,[47] reflects a deeply intersectional approach to social justice. This commitment to liberating individuals from all forms of oppression is a key aspect of the revolutionary project more generally, and is adhered to by the membership, cadre, and leadership of the PLO.

Geopolitical Context and International Solidarity. The PLO's understanding of its struggle as located within broader historical and geopolitical contexts, as well as its efforts to gain international support,[48] underscore the importance of international solidarity and deep collaborative efforts for any organization engaged in liberation work. The organization's ability to navigate and influence international relations is a testament not only to the interconnectedness of local and global struggles, but to the necessity that all struggles under capitalism are linked.

Conclusion

The documents contained in this book offer a wealth of knowledge for organizational theorists and researchers interested in Palestinian studies, but, most importantly, for contemporary labor organizers and activists. By adopting many of the PLO's core strategies of popular organization, political education, democratic participation, and international solidarity, labor and peace movements in the anglosphere can strengthen their capacity to mobilize workers, to create robust and collaborative networks, and better achieve their organizational objectives. This book thus,

---

46 Ibid., "A Guerrilla History of the PLO," p. xxxiii.
47 Ibid., "Constitution of Fateh," p. 110.
48 Ibid.

implicitly, serves as a road map for labor organizers and peace activists, providing the requisite theoretical materials and frameworks necessary for the building up of resilient and effective organizations that can effectively navigate the challenges of the modern protest landscape and contribute to the broader struggles for justice and liberation.

This book also provides a detailed primary source account when, taken in totality, demonstrates a narrative of the PLO's organizational approach, its commitment to active (armed) struggle and political action, and the challenges it, and organizations like it—operating under threat of *direct* repression and military action—face. It also underscores the importance of deep, collaborative solidarity, and the building of intra-movement networks, both locally and internationally, as well as the need for the organization to adapt and respond to changing circumstances. The PLO's dedication to the Palestinian cause of liberation is clear, as is its determination to achieve its goals through a combination of military and political means, while also addressing the social needs of the Palestinian people.

In the face of an increasingly fascist and hostile atmosphere, organizers in the core anglosphere and core-adjacent locales should lean into and draw upon the lessons of resilience and strategic adaptability exemplified by the PLO. The documents within this volume provide a practical blueprint for confronting such challenges, emphasizing the critical necessity for organizers to engage in ideological clarity, practical action, and high-level implementations of professionalism, and critical organizational theory.

Organizers and organizational theorists must take these lessons to heart, and continue to be inspired by the courage and wisdom of the Palestinian organizations and fighters, and organize our communities to serve the goal of Palestinian liberation, and wider progressive struggles. As Ghassan Kanafani reminds us in his quote, from which the title of this introduction was taken: "The Palestinian cause is not a cause for Palestinians only, but a cause for every revolutionary, wherever he is, as a cause of the exploited and oppressed masses in our era."[49]

---

49   Kanafani, Ghassan. 1972. *The 1936-39 Revolt in Palestine*, Committee for a Democratic Palestine, New York, p. 67.

A Guerrilla History of the PLO

Henry Hakamäki, Adnan Husain, and Breht O'Shea

The Guerrilla History Podcast dedicated an episode to discussing *Historical Documents of the PLO: A Collection for Critical Organizational Study* and introducing its documents for the political education and the historical consciousness of its audience.[1] Below is an edited transcript reworked to serve as a preface reflecting on the value of these documents from the Palestine liberation movement for guerrilla historians, those who want to use history as a tool of liberation and in support of the struggle for justice, everywhere. We have preserved the conversational format among ourselves, the three co-hosts (Henry Hakamäki, Breht O'Shea, and Adnan Husain),[2] as an example of the dialectical value of political and historical discussion based on these invaluable records. We hope that readers will themselves engage in such dialogues, discussions, and analyses with colleagues and comrades.

Henry Hakamäki: In presenting this collected edition of historic documents from the Palestinian Liberation movement, we're setting out on a journey that not only sheds light on the struggles of resilient and courageous people, but also reinforces our commitment to standing in

---

1 https://guerrillahistory.libsyn.com. The episode was originally published on 25th November 2023 for Guerrilla History subscribers, and will be opened for general release to coincide with the publication of this volume.

2 Henry Hakamäki is an educator and activist, host of Guerrilla History, and Editorial Board member of Iskra Books. Professor Adnan Husain is a historian, and Director of the School of Religion at Queens University and is also a co-host, as well as hosting *The Majlis* podcast. Breht O'Shea is an organizer and co-host, also hosting *Revolutionary Left Radio* and *Red Menace* podcasts.

unwavering solidarity with their cause. It's critical to believe in the innate and inalienable rights of all oppressed peoples and recognize the imperative of understanding history to build a brighter future. It's within this context that we invite readers to delve into the rich tapestry of documents that have shaped and amplified the Palestinian struggle, appreciating their value as essential tools for education, activism, and mobilization. In order to fully understand the Palestinian issue, we must turn to the primary sources that have been curated in this collection

These documents chronicle a long and arduous journey, marked by a relentless desire for freedom, justice, and self-determination—from the displacement and dispossession of the Nakba in 1948 to the ongoing occupation, blockade, and annexation still occurring today, these documents bear witness to the systematic and enduring oppression faced by the Palestinian people. The importance of studying historical primary documents cannot be overstated. These sources provide an unfiltered lens through which we can examine the complex historical, political, and social dynamics that have shaped the Palestinian struggle. They offer firsthand accounts of the experiences, aspirations, and grievances of those on the front lines of resistance. By engaging with these documents we break free from the stifling narratives that have sought to marginalize and distort the Palestinian cause.

BREHT O'SHEA: First and foremost, I think it's crucial to understand this conflict—this ongoing genocidal attack on Palestinians—in its full breadth, its full scope, its full historical totality. We cannot start a discussion of the current conflict on October 7, 2023; we can't start it in 1973 or 1967, and we can't even start it in 1948, even though the formal material process of dispossession and occupation began around that time. It goes back much further. It goes back to Jewish experiences in Europe. It goes back to pogroms and the Holocaust. It goes back to the early Zionist movement and the nationalist movements in Europe more broadly—all of which need to be wrestled with. If we're going to understand this conflict, our goal should be to understand the current conflict in its full totality, its full historicity, its full global dynamics, and its relational and ever-evolving nature. With that in mind, the first thing that I would say is that the existence of Israel *is* the existence of occupation.

It is the existence of a settler-colonial apartheid state, and with its more recent hard right-wing turn, it is internally, I think, rising to the status of a fascist state. This is the concrete, actually existing reality of Zionism, despite the utopian and idealist conceptions on offer from liberal Zionists. Additionally, when you don't understand this conflict in its totality, you'll hear things or you'll begin to say things like "Israel has a right to exist" and "Israel has a right to defend itself." Well, let's break those claims down briefly. Does any state have an inherent right to exist? Does a state that is premised on occupation, on the oppression and brutalization of other human beings, really have a right to exist? Or, rather, do *people* have a right to exist? Certainly, Jewish people have an absolute right to exist. Muslim people, Christian people, secular people, all have a right to exist, but no state in and of itself has an inherent right to exist, and certainly no state that is premised on the oppression of another people has a right to exist, as its existence is synonymous with the unfreedom of those its brutalizes and suppresses.

Therefore, when we talk about this topic, we have to understand it in its full historical totality, and we have to begin to question some of the keystone talking points of those who wish to obscure that history and who wish to present Israel as a regular country so as to mystify the actual basis of its existence, which is, of course, the violent occupation and oppression of another people; the Palestinian people.

ADNAN HUSAIN: I think it's absolutely crucial to bring together primary source documents in particular, to appreciate exactly the kind of history that leads to understanding and effective political action. We don't get a good sense of history just from the view of outsiders. What original documents produced by the Palestinian National Movement—including official documents of the Palestinian Legislative Council, the Palestine Liberation Organization and its sub-groupings—allow us to do is to have the voices of participants, those who were most concerned with freedom for Palestinians, and to understand how they envisioned it. It presents to our historical consciousness internal perspectives so that we have more than just an outsider's viewpoint on the historical unfolding of this liberation struggle. It is vital to appreciate how Palestinian political actors wanted to represent themselves to the world.

These documents gathered into this helpful edited volume serve as a wonderful venue for seeing how political ideas and political organizations develop in history, something absolutely crucial for any liberation cause that would like to learn from history, to appreciate how the struggle developed, how it related both to local as well as geopolitical conditions on a larger scale. This interaction between local forces and the wider geopolitical context can be appreciated even in the early foundational documents of the PLO. For example, note how at the outset in 1964, the PLO wanted to define who the Palestinians were, how they fit within the larger sphere of Arab nations and Arab nationalism, how Palestinians should understand the historic injustice and wrong done to them, and how and against whom precisely they needed to struggle. It is so interesting what the documents reveal. You notice right away that there is a very inclusive, secular political vision of what it means to be a Palestinian and yet simultaneously an articulation of its particular cultural and religious contexts. I noticed resonances with a contemporary anti-colonial liberation struggle, that of the *Front de Liberation Nationale* in Algeria against French settler-colonialism. There are natural connections in language and ideology at that shared historical moment. The FLN likewise drew on a sense of the spiritual and cultural resources the people would have to draw upon in their national struggle. Examining primary source documents allows us to appreciate the particular and shared features of anticolonial movements of that era.

Another valuable example is the PLO's charter from 1967, which reveals how there has been development geopolitically in relation to institutions like the non-aligned movement. The PLO was connecting its struggle to the demands of the non-aligned bloc in the Global South and this language and consciousness suffuse the charter. Without reading primary source documents, these connections aren't so visible. So, what a collection like this allows guerrilla historians to do is to appreciate the evolving, ideological and political struggle in history, how different political ideas are being sharpened and clarified dialectically, the tactics that likewise develop in relation to historical circumstances. The documents reveal this unfolding history when analyzed dialectically. How did Palestinians themselves come to national consciousness and what did that involve? Those are the questions that studying the words and expressions of Palestinian actors and organizations help answer.

BOS: I think Adnan makes a really good point. The thread that I would like to pick up from what he said is this point about settler-colonialism. I think the essential analytical lens through which we can come to a concrete understanding of this entire situation is the lens of settler-colonialism. When one abandons that analytical lens—and many people invested in Israel's continued existence go to great lengths to obscure or denounce this approach—you will become more susceptible to various forms of Zionist mystification. You'll get presented with framings and premises that are hostile to Palestinian liberation and Palestinian humanity. For example, you'll be told that the Palestinian resistance are terrorists, you'll be browbeaten to accept a decisive split between "innocent" Palestinians whose humanity we can recognize, if only peripherally, and those Palestinians who are fighting back, who we are not allowed to see as fully human or to express any sentiments of affection or understanding toward. Once you've accepted something like this, you've already ceded bedrock elements of the ideological battle to the Zionists.

In contradistinction to such mystification, the settler-colonialism analysis allows us to see clearly that the armed resistance of the Palestinians is not terrorism, but rather a just national liberation struggle. Moreover, we are able to apprehend the dialectic of violence, and see clearly that the whole cycle of violence that has plagued the Levant for over 75 years is a direct product of the existence of Israel and its brutal colonial occupation of Palestine. If we want to end such cyclical violence, then, we have to address the problem at its root. The settler-colonial framing allows us to understand that this is not some thousand-year-old religious dispute between Jews and Muslims, nor is it some super-complicated geo-political Rubik's cube; rather it is a struggle between the colonizer and the colonized, and thus the real solution lies in addressing that inaugural injustice.

Imagine one democratic, multi-ethnic, multi-religious state of Palestine which codifies and protects the civil, constitutional, and human rights of Jews, Muslims, Christians, and the secular alike, embracing them all as fully equal citizens and honoring the diversity of peoples that have called Palestine home for centuries and millennia. This would, of course, require full decolonization as a necessary prerequisite to the formation of such a state, but it would actually solve the underlying problem in a way that Israel's continued existence, and even the idea of a two-state solution, will never be able to.

The fact that Israel would rather drop a nuclear bomb on the region than accept such an arrangement speaks to the pathological rot at the core of the Zionist project. But it's worth noting that we have seen such obstinance to the idea of basic equality before among the white colonial populations within the Jim Crow American South, in apartheid South Africa, in French-occupied Algeria, and in the former Rhodesia, among others. This fact adds yet more weight to the analysis I have been offering, by highlighting the shared origin of Israel and these other projects of occupation: European settler-colonialism.

HH: Understanding Israel as a settler-colonial project, and the Palestinian liberation movement as a national liberation struggle is crucial when analyzing the historical and ongoing dynamics in the region. From a Marxist/socialist/communist perspective, it's essential to defend decolonial movements and support the struggle for national liberation, self-determination, and justice. The establishment of Israel as a settler-colonial state involved the displacement, dispossession, and marginalization of the indigenous Palestinian population with this process unfolding through systematic policies of colonization, including the expulsion of Palestinians, the destruction of their homes and villages, and the establishment of Jewish settlements on Palestinian land.

Recognizing Israel as a settler-colonial project helps expose the underlying power dynamics, structural violence, and the ongoing oppression faced by the Palestinian people. Conversely, framing the Palestinian Liberation Movement as a national liberation struggle acknowledges the legitimate aspirations of the Palestinian people to reclaim their land, secure their rights, and determine their own political, economic, and social future. It recognizes their right to resist and struggle against their oppressors, who are backed by a dominant global order that upholds and perpetuates colonial and imperialist systems, or rather structures.

Defending decolonial movements means standing in solidarity with those fighting against oppressive structures and seeking to dismantle systems of domination and exploitation. It involves supporting the self-determination of peoples who have been colonized, affirming their rights to their land, culture, and identity, and advocating for the restoration of justice and equality. This solidarity is rooted in the understanding that the struggle for liberation extends beyond a single nation or region. It is a global endeavor against the underlying capitalist, imperialist, and colonial systems that perpetuate oppression and inequality. We must align ourselves with movements and struggles that challenge the status quo, offering support to those who fight against settler-colonial projects, and demand justice for historically oppressed peoples.

Turning our eye to the role of "Israel" for a moment, it's important to also see "Israel" as an extension of Western imperialist domination. Various thinkers have stated that "Israel" is essentially akin to a landed aircraft carrier, operating as an extension of the imperialist order of the West as a forward operating base within the Middle East. It acts in pursuit of the Western imperialist ambitions within the region and beyond. We can look at how Israel has related militarily to its closest Arab States, as well as how Israel has upheld the imperialist structures more globally, including, but not limited to supporting apartheid South Africa monetarily and militarily, even after the Western imperialist nations themselves no longer were able to explicitly defend the apartheid project themselves. Understanding the role of Israel in these ways as a settler-colonial project and as an extension of Western Imperialist domination is not unique to us, nor is it a particularly new school of thought. This is a school of thought that was seen even in the historic documents that are presented within this text, and, as we see, Palestinians who have been operating on the front lines of the struggle have been seeing this very struggle through this lens since the inception of the national liberation struggle against the Zio-imperialist entity that is the "State of Israel."

AH: Historically, it has to be observed that Zionist began a very late settler-colonial project, which accounts for some particular or unique conditions. More than just identifying Israel as a settler-colonial state that structures the characteristics of Palestinian national liberation struggle against it, decolonization now and over the last several decades responds dialectically to the position that Israel inhabits in the imperialist, capitalist global order. It is more than just an outpost of Western colonialism but a forward base of empire, a front-line state in a key oil producing and transit region vital to the global capitalist economy and imperial hegemony.

In fact, its significance, and therefore the importance of the Palestinian struggle, is the model of global apartheid sustained through militarism, surveillance, hi-tech security apparatus and algorithms of repression and exclusion. It is the crucible and testing ground for the industrial complex of control in the future of inequality, of climate fascism to protect the global elite. This is why I think the Palestinian struggle is so important as a world historical struggle. Studying its history informs us of the prospects for liberation and resistance against a broader form of global oppression ahead. Israeli society, surrounded by and separated from its environs and the Palestinian people through an apartheid wall, represents in miniature a broader, developing global order developing of the one per cent.

A Fortress Europe that uses the Mediterranean as its kind of boundary wall to separate itself from the peoples of the Global South, a U.S. militarized border wall with Mexico to keep refugees of its wars and climate disaster out. Israel has attempted to create a zone of security in which the settler-colonists can live as Europeans in this land, in the Middle East, and wall themselves off from the conditions of the rest of the region. What was demonstrated most recently on October 7—but it has been historically demonstrated over and over again—is that this is an unsustainable model. It's an unjust model that will always engender resistance.

And that's what the documents of this collection portray: at every stage in different periods of history, Palestinian resistance takes on new forms and above all endures. These documents reveal a history of resistance. Despite 75 years of dispossession, ethnic cleansing, genocidal killing, military occupation, and imprisonment, Palestinians have refused to surrender. They have simply refused to surrender while facing the hi-tech, advanced militarized techniques of repression costing billions and supplied by the West. That's of world historical significance.

Like the documents show, during the 1960's the struggle for Palestinian liberation, equality and justice was connected to anti-colonial resistance and national liberation struggles across the Global South and in the 1980's with the anti-apartheid struggle in South Africa. So too, today, the struggle to free Palestine strikes a chord with the oppressed and with those who struggle for justice globally. Even in the imperial core, whether it is for indigenous rights/Land Back/decolonization or Black Lives Matter/anti-racism and police brutality struggles, activists can identify with the Palestinian people who are fighting the Empire and are bearing the brunt of its diverse forms of violent control, exclusion, and suppression. So that's why solidarity with Palestine and studying how the struggle for its liberation has developed and unfolded over time through Palestinians' own expressions of their political consciousness is so valuable for guerrilla historians.

BOS: There is something fundamentally human about resisting oppression, it's as natural to us as taking flight is for birds or as swimming is for fish. And this urge for freedom cannot be beaten or humiliated out of people, though every empire in human history has tried its best to do just that. The Palestinian struggle is, in a fundamental respect, humanity's struggle against oppression and domination. I think that's one of the major reasons why it resonates so strongly across the world and why their resistance is such an inspiration to people fighting for their own humanity and freedom in other contexts of oppression. It's a universal struggle and it's in our nature as human beings not only to resist oppression, but to see ourselves in the brave resistance of others, and to connect with that on a deep, visceral level. That is why we see these beautiful acts of solidarity and these long-standing bonds of solidarity between the Black Liberation struggle in the United States and the Palestinian resistance movement. You also see it in the Irish resistance against English imperialism and domination. You certainly see it in indigenous movements for self-determination across the entire world, including throughout Turtle Island. Such solidarity with the Palestinians is, of course, reciprocated in full by the Palestinians. So there's this really beautiful dynamic happening here where we can all see our own humanity in the other, and thus generate a universal, egalitarian vision of what humanity *could become*.

We can ask ourselves: what would a human civilization free from occupation, free from oppression, free from domination look like? What would it mean for human beings to live as true equals under the sun and to cooperate in order to create a world finally worthy of the claim that it is inhabited by an intelligent species? Pardon me for waxing poetic here, but sometimes I think about the future of humanity and the possibility of taking our explorations into space; into the cosmos. At the moment, despite all of our self-congratulatory rhetoric about how far we've come, I do not believe we're mature enough as a species to do that in a dignified and authentic way. As long as there are human beings here on earth consigned to various forms of wretchedness, we simply don't deserve a seat at the cosmic table; we don't deserve a seat at the table of Intelligent Species, if such a thing exists, while we allow this brutality and this oppression to continue to exist down here on Earth. So, the aspirations and the inherent dignity of humanity is not only encapsulated in the Palestinian struggle, but it points towards a possible human future in which we grow up as a species, and overcome what Albert Einstein called "this predatory era of human history," by which he meant all forms of class society and the intrinsic injustice that they require. I truly think that a universalist vision of our common humanity is important.

HH: As stated previously, "Israel" does serve as a sort of model to modern settler-colonial states as well as ethno-religious movements. In recent years there's been a rise in fascist movements around the world with two prominent examples being the settler-colonial state of "Israel" and Hindutva in India. These movements share troubling similarities in their policies of ethnic cleansing, discrimination and the suppression of dissent. Undermining the settler-colonial state of "Israel" is critical to undermining similar fascist movements like Hindutva in India for several reasons.

Firstly, both movements are built on the foundations of exclusivity, where one ethno-religious group claims superiority over others. By challenging the legitimacy of "Israel's" settler-colonial state, we can expose the inherently discriminatory nature of such ideologies. Secondly, these fascistic movements rely on the support and legitimization they receive from other countries. "Israel" in particular benefits from extensive military and economic aid from global powers, which allows it to continue its oppressive policies. By withdrawing support and actively opposing, and hopefully dismantling, the settler-colonial state of "Israel," we can send a strong message to other countries that enabling such fascist movements will not be tolerated. Furthermore, undermining the settler-colonial state of "Israel" can serve as a powerful example for those fighting against Hindutva in India. Directly it can demonstrate that resistance is possible, and inspire others to challenge oppressive systems and ideologies. Lastly, both Israel and Hindutva pose a threat to regional stability and peace, with their policies of occupation, land grabbing and religious discrimination fueling tensions and conflict, not only within their own borders, but also in neighboring regions. By undermining the settler-colonial state of "Israel," we can contribute to the broader goal of peace and justice in the region.

BOS: As an American, I would also be remiss if I did not point out emphatically the US's complicity in the Israeli occupation and brutalization of Palestinian people. Since virtually day one, the baton was handed off by the British Colonial Empire, but the US, ever since then has really been the main nation state, the main ally, the main enabler of Israeli aggression and crimes against the Palestinian people. As an American sitting here, I might not be able to influence Israeli politics or Palestinian politics or Middle Eastern politics, but I do have a moral and political responsibility and obligation to call out my own government, to do whatever I can to hold my own government accountable, and to support any and all movements here in the United States aimed at disrupting the continued brutalization of the Palestinian people through American complicity. America has a unique power in the world to put an end to this. It has the leverage over Israel that no other country has ever had, and its refusal to use that leverage to bring about peace makes the U.S. just as complicit as Israel in these crimes, and I think the entire world, maybe outside of the American borders in some parts of Western Europe, see that extremely clearly. I think, as this current iteration of the brutality continues, the reputation of both Israel and the U.S. around the world will continue to decline, and will have massive implications for politics in the latter half of the 21st century.

I would like to make another point, as well: when you're saying any of the stuff that we've been saying thus far and when you begin to talk about settler-colonialism, and when you publicly recognize the humanity of the Palestinian people and their resistance, the first thing you'll hear from those invested in the status quo, or those invested in Zionism, will be accusations of antisemitism, and I think it's worth saying that we cannot be silenced by these bad faith accusations of bigotry. Accusations that, to be sure, are simply meant to shut down conversation, because Israel and its supporters around the world know on some level that if open and honest discourse were to take place around the world in regards to this conflict, Israel would come out looking very bad. So one of the main tactics they've used over many decades of propaganda is to label their critics as antisemitic.

I have two quick points that I think are worth saying. First and foremost, I would argue that Zionism in itself is antisemitic, insofar as it attempts to tie all Jewish people, by virtue of them being Jewish, to the many crimes of the Israeli State, and secondly, I find the over-application of accusations of antisemitism to aid antisemitism insofar as such clearly cynical accusations water down and dilute that very serious allegation. There is a far right global resurgence that we're living through in the 21st century that employs genuine antisemitism as a matter of course which desperately needs to be combated. But when you over-apply that label to anybody criticizing Israel (or even its newest iteration, the notion that criticizing or protesting American-based weapons manufacturers like Elbit who sell weapons to Israel as antisemitic) you're actually being incredibly antisemitic by watering down that accusation, cynically weaponizing it, and thus rendering it less meaningful when it's actually needed.

Ultimately, we want a world that is safe for Jewish people, for Muslim people, and for everyone else on Earth. That's the world that we want to create. Our criticisms of Israel are in service to the construction of such a world; a world that is safe for all people to live in dignity as equals. We must refuse to be browbeaten into accepting oppression via the cynical employment of such accusations; the cynical employment of progressive rhetoric for abjectly regressive ends.

HH: One other note that could have gone earlier in the conversation is that the genocidal actions of the settler-colony of the state of "Israel" are often combated with claims that if they didn't genocide the Palestinian people that the Palestinian people would genocide the Jewish population. This is often put out into popular consciousness alongside the idea that various groups associated with the Palestinian Liberation movement, have explicitly stated their desire to eliminate, in whole or in part, the Jewish people from the area of historic Palestine, rather than simply aiming to dismantle the settler-colonial state of "Israel." By providing historic documents from these groups themselves within this text, readers will be able to combat these bad faith accusations with direct evidence provided by the groups in question that show that their aims are not genocidal in the least, but simply relate to the national liberation of their people and the creation of a just, multi-ethnic, multi-religious society.

Section I
The Palestine Liberation Organization

Proclamation of the Establishment of the Palestine Liberation Organization[1]
[1964]
STATEMENT OF PROCLAMATION
OF THE ORGANIZATION

Jerusalem
May 28, 1964

Believing in the right of the Palestinian Arab people to its sacred homeland Palestine and affirming the inevitability of the battle to liberate the usurped part from it, and its determination to bring out its effective revolutionary entity and the mobilization of the capabilities and potentialities and its material, military and spiritual forces;

And in realization of the will and determination of our people to wage the battle of liberating its homeland forcefully as the effective and fighting vanguard of the sacred march;

And in realization of a genuine aspiration of the Arab nation embodied in the resolutions of the League of Arab States and the First Arab Summit Conference;

And depending upon God Almighty and in the name of the First Arab Palestinian Congress held in the city of Jerusalem this day on the 16th of Muharram of the year 1384, corresponding to 28 May 1964,

I do hereby proclaim the establishment of the Palestine Liberation Organization as a mobilizing leadership of the forces of the Palestinian Arab people to wage the battle of liberation, as a shield for the rights and aspirations of the people of Palestine and as a road to victory.

AHMAD SHUKAIRY
Chairman of the First Palestinian Conference

---

1   Source: Permanent Observer Mission of Palestine to the United Nations (Accessed on January 25, 2024, online at: https://web.archive.org/web/20111211172543/http://www.un.int/wcm/content/site/palestine/pid/12355).

PALESTINIAN NATIONAL CHARTER[1]
[1964]
ADOPTED IN 1964 BY THE FIRST PALESTINIAN CONFERENCE

We, the Palestinian Arab people, who waged fierce and continuous battles to safeguard our homeland, to defend its dignity and honor, and who offered all through the years continuous caravans of immortal martyrs, and who wrote the noblest pages of sacrifice, offering and giving.

We, the Palestinian Arab people, who faced the forces of evil, injustice and aggression, against whom the forces of international Zionism and colonialism conspire and worked to displace it, dispossess it from its homeland and property, abused what is holy in it and who in spite of all this refused to weaken or submit.

We, the Palestinian Arab people, who believe in its Arabism and in its right to regain its homeland, to realize its freedom and dignity, and who have determined to amass its forces and mobilize its efforts and capabilities in order to continue its struggle and to move forward on the path of holy war (*al-jihad*) until complete and final victory has been attained.

We, the Palestinian Arab people, based on our right of self-defense and the complete restoration of our lost homeland—a right that has been recognized by international covenants and common practices including the Charter of the United Nations—and in implementation of the principles of human rights, and comprehending the international political relations, with its various ramifications and dimensions, and considering the past experiences in all that pertains to the causes of the catastrophe, and the means to face it.

---

1 Source: Permanent Observer Mission of Palestine to the United Nations (accessed on January 25, 2024, online at: https://web.archive.org/web/20071212010343/http://www.un.int/palestine/PLO/PNA2.html).

And embarking from the Palestinian Arab reality, and for the sake of the honor of the Palestinian individual and his right to free and dignified life.

And realizing the national grave responsibility placed upon our shoulders, for the sake of all this.

We, the Palestinian Arab people, dictate and declare this Palestinian National Charter and swear to realize it.

ARTICLE 1: Palestine is an Arab homeland bound by strong Arab national ties to the rest of the Arab Countries and which together form the great Arab homeland.

ARTICLE 2: Palestine, with its boundaries at the time of the British Mandate, is an indivisible territorial unit.

ARTICLE 3: The Palestinian Arab people has the legitimate right to its homeland and is an inseparable part of the Arab Nation. It shares the sufferings and aspirations of the Arab Nation and its struggle for freedom, sovereignty, progress and unity.

ARTICLE 4: The people of Palestine determine its destiny when it completes the liberation of its homeland in accordance with its own wishes and free will and choice.

ARTICLE 5: The Palestinian personality is a permanent and genuine characteristic that does not disappear. It is transferred from fathers to sons.

ARTICLE 6: The Palestinians are those Arab citizens who were living normally in Palestine up to 1947, whether they remained or were expelled. Every child who was born to a Palestinian Arab father after this date, whether in Palestine or outside, is a Palestinian.

ARTICLE 7: Jews of Palestinian origin are considered Palestinians if they are willing to live peacefully and loyally in Palestine.

ARTICLE 8: Bringing up Palestinian youth in an Arab and nationalist manner is a fundamental national duty. All means of guidance, education and enlightenment should be utilized to introduce the youth to its homeland in a deep spiritual way that will constantly and firmly bind them together.

ARTICLE 9: Ideological doctrines, whether political, social, or economic, shall not distract the people of Palestine from the primary duty of liberating their homeland. All Palestinian constitute one national front and work with all their feelings and material potentialities to free their homeland.

ARTICLE 10: Palestinians have three mottos: National Unity, National Mobilization, and Liberation. Once liberation is completed, the people of Palestine shall choose for its public life whatever political, economic, or social system they want.

ARTICLE 11: The Palestinian people firmly believe in Arab unity, and in order to play its role in realizing this goal, it must, at this stage of its struggle, preserve its Palestinian personality and all its constituents. It must strengthen the consciousness of its existence and stance and stand against any attempt or plan that may weaken or disintegrate its personality.

ARTICLE 12: Arab unity and the liberation of Palestine are two complementary goals; each prepares for the attainment of the other. Arab unity leads to the liberation of Palestine, and the liberation of Palestine leads to Arab unity. Working for both must go side by side.

ARTICLE 13: The destiny of the Arab Nation and even the essence of Arab existence are firmly tied to the destiny of the Palestine question. From this firm bond stems the effort and struggle of the Arab Nation to liberate Palestine. The people of Palestine assume a vanguard role in achieving this sacred national goal.

ARTICLE 14: The liberation of Palestine, from an Arab viewpoint, is a national duty. Its responsibilities fall upon the entire Arab nation, governments and peoples, the Palestinian peoples being in the forefront. For this purpose, the Arab nation must mobilize its military, spiritual and material potentialities; specifically, it must give to the Palestinian Arab people all possible support and backing and place at its disposal all opportunities and means to enable them to perform their role in liberating their homeland.

ARTICLE 15: The liberation of Palestine, from a spiritual viewpoint, prepares for the Holy Land an atmosphere of tranquility and peace, in which all the Holy Places will be safeguarded, and the freedom to worship and to visit will be guaranteed for all, without any discrimination of race, color, language, or religion. For all this, the Palestinian people look forward to the support of all the spiritual forces in the world.

ARTICLE 16: The liberation of Palestine, from an international viewpoint, is a defensive act necessitated by the demands of self-defense as stated in the Charter of the United Nations. For that, the people of Palestine, desiring to befriend all nations which love freedom, justice, and peace, look forward to their support in restoring the legitimate situation to Palestine, establishing peace and security in its territory, and enabling its people to exercise national sovereignty and freedom.

ARTICLE 17: The partitioning of Palestine, which took place in 1947, and the establishment of Israel are illegal and null and void, regardless of the loss of time, because they were contrary to the will of the Palestinian people and its natural right to its homeland, and were in violation of the basic principles embodied in the Charter of the United Nations, foremost among which is the right to self-determination.

ARTICLE 18: The Balfour Declaration, the Palestine Mandate System, and all that has been based on them are considered null and void. The claims of historic and spiritual ties between Jews and Palestine are not in agreement with the facts of history or with the true basis of sound statehood. Judaism, because it is a divine religion, is not a nationality with independent existence. Furthermore, the Jews are not one people with an independent personality because they are citizens to their states.

ARTICLE 19: Zionism is a colonialist movement in its inception, aggressive and expansionist in its goal, racist in its configurations, and fascist in its means and aims. Israel, in its capacity as the spearhead of this destructive movement and as the pillar of colonialism, is a permanent source of tension and turmoil in the Middle East, in particular, and to the international community in general. Because of this, the people of Palestine are worthy of the support and sustenance of the community of nations.

ARTICLE 20: The causes of peace and security and the requirements of right and justice demand from all nations, in order to safeguard true relationships among peoples and to maintain the loyalty of citizens to their homeland, that they consider Zionism an illegal movement and outlaw its presence and activities.

ARTICLE 21: The Palestinian people believe in the principles of justice, freedom, sovereignty, self-determination, human dignity, and the right of peoples to practice these principles. It also supports all international efforts to bring about peace on the basis of justice and free international cooperation.

ARTICLE 22: The Palestinian people believe in peaceful co-existence on the basis of legal existence, for there can be no coexistence with aggression, nor can there be peace with occupation and colonialism.

ARTICLE 23: In realizing the goals and principles of this Convent, the Palestine Liberation Organization carries out its full role to liberate Palestine in accordance with the basic law of this Organization.

ARTICLE 24: This Organization does not exercise any territorial sovereignty over the West Bank in the Hashemite Kingdom of Jordan, on the Gaza Strip or in the Himmah Area. Its activities will be on the national popular level in the liberational, organizational, political and financial fields.

ARTICLE 25: This Organization is in charge of the movement of the Palestinian people in its struggle to liberate its homeland in all liberational, organizational, and financial matters, and in all other needs of the Palestine Question in the Arab and international spheres.

ARTICLE 26: The Liberation Organization cooperates with all Arab governments, each according to its ability, and does not interfere in the internal affairs of any Arab states.

ARTICLE 27: This Organization shall have its flag, oath and a national anthem. All this shall be resolved in accordance with special regulations.

ARTICLE 28: The basic law for the Palestine Liberation Organization is attached to this Charter. This law defines the manner of establishing the Organization, its organs, institutions, the specialties of each one of them, and all the needed duties thrust upon it in accordance with this Charter.

ARTICLE 29: This Charter cannot be amended except by two-thirds majority of the members of the National Council of the Palestine Liberation Organization in a special session called for this purpose.

Palestinian National Charter[1]
[1968]
Adopted in 1968 by the 4th Palestinian National Council

Palestinian National Charter

Article 1: Palestine is the homeland of the Arab Palestinian people; it is an indivisible part of the greater Arab homeland, and the Palestinian people are an integral part of the Arab nation.

Article 2: Palestine, with the boundaries it had during the British Mandate, is an indivisible territorial unit.

Article 3: The Palestinian Arab people possess the legal right to their homeland and to self-determination after the completion of the liberation of their country in accordance with their wishes and entirely of their own accord and will.

Article 4: The Palestinian identity is a genuine, essential, and inherent characteristic; it is transmitted from fathers to children. The Zionist occupation and the dispersal of the Palestinian Arab people, through the disasters which befell them, do not make them lose their Palestinian identity and their membership in the Palestinian community, nor do they negate them.

Article 5: The Palestinians are those Arab nationals who, until 1947, normally resided in Palestine regardless of whether they were evicted from it or stayed there. Anyone born, after that date, of a Palestinian father- whether in Palestine or outside it—is also a Palestinian.

Article 6: The Jews who had normally resided in Palestine until the beginning of the Zionist invasion are considered Palestinians.

Article 7: There is a Palestinian community and that it has material, spiritual, and historical connection with Palestine are indisputable facts.

---

[1] Source: Palestine Affairs Council (accessed on January 25, 2024, online at: https://www.pac-usa.org/the_palestinian_charter.htm).

It is a national duty to bring up individual Palestinians in an Arab revolutionary manner. All means of information and education must be adopted in order to acquaint the Palestinian with his country in the most profound manner, both spiritual and material, that is possible. He must be prepared for the armed struggle and ready to sacrifice his wealth and his life in order to win back his homeland and bring about its liberation.

ARTICLE 8: The phase in their history, through which the Palestinian people are now living, is that of national (*watani*) struggle for the liberation of Palestine. Thus the conflicts among the Palestinian national forces are secondary, and should be ended for the sake of the basic conflict that exists between the forces of Zionism and of colonialism on the one hand, and the Palestinian Arab people on the other. On this basis the Palestinian masses, regardless of whether they are residing in the national homeland or in Diaspora (*mahajir*) constitute—both their organizations and the individuals—one national front working for the retrieval of Palestine and its liberation through armed struggle.

ARTICLE 9: Armed struggle is the only way to liberate Palestine. This is the overall strategy, not merely a tactical phase. The Palestinian Arab people assert their absolute determination and firm resolution to continue their armed struggle and to work for an armed popular revolution for the liberation of their country and their return to it. They also assert their right to normal life in Palestine and to exercise their right to self-determination and sovereignty over it.

ARTICLE 10: Commando (*Feday'ee*) action constitutes the nucleus of the Palestinian popular liberation war. This requires its escalation, comprehensiveness, and the mobilization of all the Palestinian popular and educational efforts and their organization and involvement in the armed Palestinian revolution. It also requires the achieving of unity for the national (*watani*) struggle among the different groupings of the Palestinian people, and between the Palestinian people and the Arab masses, so as to secure the continuation of the revolution, its escalation, and victory.

ARTICLE 11: Palestinians have three mottoes: national unity, national (*al-qawmiyya*) mobilization, and liberation.

ARTICLE 12: The Palestinian Arab people believe in Arab unity. In order to contribute their share toward the attainment of that objective, however, they must, at the present stage of their struggle, safeguard their Palestinian identity and develop their consciousness of that identity, oppose any plan that may dissolve or impair it.

ARTICLE 13: Arab unity and the liberation of Palestine are two complementary goals, the attainment of either of which facilitates the attainment of the other. Thus, Arab unity leads to the liberation of Palestine, the liberation of Palestine leads to Arab unity; and the work toward the realization of one objective proceeds side by side with work toward the realization of the other.

ARTICLE 14: The destiny of the Arab Nation, and indeed Arab existence itself, depend upon the destiny of the Palestinian cause. From this interdependence springs the Arab nation's pursuit of, and striving for, the liberation of Palestine. The people of Palestine play the role of the vanguard in the realization of this sacred (*qawmi*) goal.

ARTICLE 15: The liberation of Palestine, from an Arab viewpoint, is a national (*qawmi*) duty and it attempts to repel the Zionist and imperialist aggression against the Arab homeland, and aims at the elimination of Zionism in Palestine. Absolute responsibility for this falls upon the Arab nation- peoples and governments-with the Arab people of Palestine in the vanguard. Accordingly, the Arab nation must mobilize all its military, human, moral, and spiritual capabilities to participate actively with the Palestinian people in the liberation of Palestine. It must, particularly, in the phase of the armed Palestinian revolution, offer and furnish the Palestinian people with all possible help, and material and human support, and make available to them the means and opportunities that will enable them to continue to carry out their leading role in the armed revolution, until they liberate their homeland.

ARTICLE 16: The liberation of Palestine, from a spiritual viewpoint, will provide the Holy Land with an atmosphere of safety and tranquility, which in turn will safeguard the country's religious sanctuaries and guarantee freedom of worship and of visit to all, without discrimination of race, color, language, or religion. Accordingly, the Palestinian people look to all spiritual forces in the world for support.

ARTICLE 17: The liberation of Palestine, from a human point of view, will restore to the Palestinian individual his dignity, pride, and freedom. Accordingly, the Palestinian Arab people look forward to the support of all those who believe in the dignity of man and his freedom in the world.

ARTICLE 18: The liberation of Palestine, from an international point of view, is a defensive action necessitated by the demands of self-defense. Accordingly, the Palestinian people, desirous as they are of the friendship of all people, look to freedom-loving and peace-loving states for support in order to restore their legitimate rights in Palestine, to re-establish peace and security in the country, and to enable its people to exercise national sovereignty and freedom.

ARTICLE 19: The partition of Palestine in 1947, and the establishment of the state of Israel are entirely illegal, regardless of the passage of time, because they were contrary to the will of the Palestinian people and its natural right in their homeland, and were inconsistent with the principles embodied in the Charter of the United Nations, particularly the right to self-determination.

ARTICLE 20: The Balfour Declaration, the Palestine Mandate, and everything that has been based on them, are deemed null and void. Claims of historical or religious ties of Jews with Palestine are incompatible with the facts of history and the conception of what constitutes statehood. Judaism, being a religion, is not an independent nationality. Nor do Jews constitute a single nation with an identity of their own; they are citizens of the states to which they belong.

ARTICLE 21: The Arab Palestinian people, expressing themselves by armed Palestinian revolution, reject all solutions which are substitutes for the total liberation of Palestine and reject all proposals aimed at the liquidation of the Palestinian cause, or at its internationalization.

ARTICLE 22: Zionism is a political movement organically associated with international imperialism and antagonistic to all action for liberation and to progressive movements in the world. It is racist and fanatic in its nature, aggressive, expansionist and colonial in its aims, and fascist in its methods. Israel is the instrument of the Zionist movement, and the geographical base for world imperialism placed strategically in the midst of the Arab homeland to combat the hopes of the Arab nation for liberation, unity, and progress. Israel is a constant source of threat *vis-à-vis* peace in the Middle East and the whole world. The liberation of Palestine will destroy the Zionist and imperialist presence and will contribute to the establishment of peace in the Middle East. That is why the Palestinian people look to the progressive and peaceful forces and urge them all, irrespective of their affiliations and beliefs, to offer the Palestinian people all aid and support in their just struggle for the liberation of their homeland.

ARTICLE 23: The demand of security and peace, as well as the demand of right and justice, require all states to consider Zionism an illegitimate movement, to outlaw its existence, and to ban its operations, in order that friendly relations among peoples may be preserved, and the loyalty of citizens to their respective homelands safeguarded.

ARTICLE 24: The Palestinian people believe in the principles of justice, freedom, sovereignty, self-determination, human dignity, and the right of peoples to exercise them.

ARTICLE 25: For the realization of the goals of this Charter and its principles, the Palestine Liberation Organization will perform its role in the liberation of Palestine.

ARTICLE 26: The Palestine Liberation Organization, the representative of the Palestinian revolutionary forces, is responsible for the Palestinian Arab peoples movement in its struggle—to retrieve its homeland, liberate and return to it and exercise the right to self-determination in it—in all military, political, and financial fields and also for whatever may be required by the Palestinian cause on the inter-Arab and international levels.

ARTICLE 27: The Palestine Liberation Organization shall cooperate with all Arab states, each according to its potentialities; and will adopt a neutral policy among them in light of the requirements of the battle of liberation; and on this basis does not interfere in the internal affairs of any Arab state.

ARTICLE 28: The Palestinian Arab people assert the genuineness and independence of their national revolution and reject all forms of intervention, trusteeship, and subordination.

ARTICLE 29: The Palestinian people possess the fundamental and genuine legal right to liberate and retrieve their homeland. The Palestinian people determine their attitude toward all states and forces on the basis of the stands they adopt *vis-à-vis* the Palestinian revolution to fulfill the aims of the Palestinian people.

ARTICLE 30: Fighters and carriers of arms in the war of liberation are the nucleus of the popular army which will be the protective force for the gains of the Palestinian Arab people.

ARTICLE 31: This Organization shall have a flag, an oath of allegiance, and an anthem. All this shall be decided upon in accordance with a special law.

ARTICLE 32: A law, known as the Basic Statute of the Palestine Liberation Organization, shall be annexed to this Covenant. It will lay down the manner in which the Organization, and its organs and institutions, shall be constituted; the respective competence of each; and the requirements of its obligation under the Charter.

ARTICLE 33: This Charter shall not be amended save by [vote of] a majority of two-thirds of the total membership of the National Council of the Palestine Liberation Organization [taken] at a special session convened for that purpose.

10-Point Program of the PLO[1]

[1974]

Political Program Adopted at the 12th Session of the
Palestine National Council Cairo

June 8, 1974

The Palestine National Council,

On the basis of the Palestine National Charter and the Political Program drawn up at the eleventh session, held from 6-12 January 1973;[2] and from its belief that it is impossible for a permanent and just peace to be established in the area unless our Palestinian people recover from all their national rights and, first and foremost, their rights to return and to self-determination on the whole of the soil of their homeland; and in the light of a study of the new political circumstances that have come into existence in the period between the Council's last and present sessions, resolves the following:

1. To reaffirm the Palestine Liberation Organization's previous attitude to Resolution 242, which obliterates the national right of our people and deals with the cause of our people as a problem of refugees. The Council therefore refuses to have anything to do with this resolution at any level, Arab or international, including the Geneva Conference.

2. The Palestine Liberation Organization will employ all means, and first and foremost armed struggle, to liberate Palestinian territory and to establish the independent combatant national authority for the people over every part of Palestinian territory that is liberated.

---

    1   Adopted at the 12th Session of the Palestine National Council, Cairo, 8 June 1974. Source: Permanent Observer Mission of Palestine to the United Nations (accessed on January 25, 2024, online at: https://web.archive.org/web/20071225085723/http://www.un.int/palestine/PLO/docone.html).

    2   **Ed. Note:** The website used as the source states here "6-12 January 1997," but the 11th session of the Palestine National Council actually took place in 1973.

This will require further changes being effected in the balance of power in favor of our people and their struggle.

3. The Liberation Organization will struggle against any proposal for a Palestinian entity the price of which is recognition, peace, secure frontiers, renunciation of national rights, and the deprival of our people of their right to return and their right to self-determination on the soil of their homeland.

4. Any step taken towards liberation is a step towards the realization of the Liberation Organization's strategy of establishing the democratic Palestinian State specified in the resolutions of the previous Palestinian National Councils.

5. Struggle along with the Jordanian national forces to establish a Jordanian-Palestinian national front whose aim will be to set up in Jordan a democratic national authority in close contact with the Palestinian entity that is established through the struggle.

6. The Liberation Organization will struggle to establish unity in struggle between the two peoples and between all the forces of the Arab liberation movement that are in agreement on this program.

7. In the light of this program, the Liberation Organization will struggle to strengthen national unity and to raise it to the level where it will be able to perform its national duties and tasks.

8. Once it is established, the Palestinian national authority will strive to achieve a union of the confrontation countries, with the aim of completing the liberation of all Palestinian territory, and as a step along the road to comprehensive Arab unity.

9. The Liberation Organization will strive to strengthen its solidarity with the socialist countries, and with the forces of liberation and progress throughout the world, with the aim of frustrating all the schemes of Zionism, reaction and imperialism.

10. In light of this program, the leadership of the revolution will determine the tactics which will serve and make possible the realization of these objectives.

The Executive Committee of the Palestine Liberation Organization will make every effort to implement this program, and should a situation arise affecting the destiny and the future of the Palestinian people, the National Assembly will be convened in extraordinary session.

Section II
Fateh

THE POLITICAL STRUGGLE[1]
[1969]

Since the establishment of the state of Israel in May 1948, the Palestinian and Arab people have hoped that the Arab regimes and their regular armies would liberate Palestine. As the attitudes of the individual Arab states towards the adoption of the Palestine question have varied greatly, the hopes for liberation, at different times, have been concentrated on different Arab states to lead the rest in the war of liberation. Following the establishment of the state of Israel there were a number of *coups d'état* in Arab states. These coups were an expression of the Arab peoples' resentment of their governments. At the same time they were an assertion of their belief in a regular war for the liberation of Palestine. In the different Arab countries the Palestinian people have taken leading roles in bringing about these changes. Thus the Palestinians have focused their attentions on the internal problems of the Arab states in order to establish regimes which would build up strong armies, equipped with modem heavy armaments and capable of defeating the enemy's army.
In the light of this analysis two facts should be pointed out:

1. The war of liberation against the Zionist conquest is a war against great forces in alliance with Zionism and capable, in every circumstance, of maintaining the military superiority of Israel. The Arab nation, including the Palestinian people, cannot wage a successful regular war against Israel and its allies. The Arab nation is composed of a great number of underdeveloped states. These are, by themselves, incapable, at least in the near future, of industrialization and unifying their forces to be able to wage a regular war against the enemy. Imperialism and the forces which are in alliance with it are able to hamper the desired change in Arab society until Israel can consolidate its existence and attain its objectives. Past experience has proved

---

1 *Al-Fateh*, a special weekly bulletin published by the Central Information Bureau of the Palestine National Liberation Movement (Al-Fateh), Nos. 12 (July 7, 1969), 13, 14, 13, 16, 17, and 18.

to the Arab nation that it should be aware of the role of all of the enemy forces, and at the same time it should distinguish, isolate and fight the enemies most harmful to its development in order to be able to concentrate on the principal enemy. Thus in the war of liberation it is necessary to use weapons which the enemy is unable to defeat. Furthermore, it is necessary to eliminate the enemies one after the other.

2. The Zionist enemy in its struggle to attain its objectives in our homeland was able to mobilize material and human forces to a far greater extent than it was able to mobilize regular armies. The Zionists were able to mobilize global Jewish populations to fight a war by diverse methods. The role of the regular army was the spearhead for the attainment of the enemy's objectives. Thus it has become not only difficult for the Arab forces to attain victory by a simple preparation of superior armies which are capable of inflicting a military defeat but, due to reasons already mentioned, it is impossible.

These two facts, in addition to other less important facts, caused the Arab struggle for the liberation of Palestine to reach a dead end. The Arab nation should have been aware of its experience and should have devised a method which would fit the reality of the Palestinian and Arab people. At the same time these methods should have been an expression of the will of the people with regard to total liberation.

This is the revolutionary way which expresses historical necessities as exemplified in the reality of the Arab nation. Their will has been the historical justification for the creation of Al-Fateh with its actions and methods that express its belief in the people as the main force capable of attaining victory, and call for the people's participation in a revolutionary war in order to attain their objectives.

The revolutionary war, which Al-Fateh calls for, aims at liberating the people of Palestine, giving them back their country, and establishing a legal political power emanating from the will of the Palestinian people and serving their interests. The method is that of waging a popular war of liberation in which the people will participate on a large scale. This war of liberation will be exemplified by political struggle and armed struggle which go hand in hand and in which the people participate. Thus it should be made clear that both the political and the armed struggles are inherent means for attaining the aims of the revolutionary war. Whereas, differentiating between political struggle and armed struggle, or being satisfied with only one of them, will deprive the popular war of its ability to attain victory.

If we only adopt armed struggle and undertake to mobilize the people in armed units, and if we consider that this alone will serve our purpose, then we will condemn ourselves to failure. The military forces which we can mobilize will not be able, in every circumstance, to face a regular military force. At the same time if the military forces are separate from the people, one cannot evaluate them except from the point of view of their number, equipment and technical capabilities. Such revolutionary forces cannot face the existing challenge.

On the other hand if we only understand political struggle to mean the mobilization of the people, their education, organization and leadership, then such a struggle is going to run against a self-evident reality, namely that the enemy will not desist from following his policy of aggression unless his military forces are crushed. The unarmed organized people cannot fulfill this role. The enemy will maintain his positions by force of arms and he is capable of striking against the people without the latter being able to hit back or even defend themselves.

Thus political struggle without armed struggle *cannot achieve the aims of the revolution.*

In the light of the above-mentioned, the method of armed struggle and that of political struggle are complementary. Adopting one method at the expense of the other will lead the revolution to failure. The attempt to differentiate between the two methods in this study has been done to explain the method of political struggle and it is not considered as the sole method necessary to accomplish the tasks of our struggle.

The first question to be answered is: Why is political struggle a necessity?

Political struggle is one of the important methods of our revolutionary war for the following reasons:

1. The revolutionary war that we are waging is not based on the belief that regular war alone can achieve the aims of the revolution. Revolutionary war is based on the rejection of the traditional concept which considers parity with the enemy in military strength a basic condition for victory. Our understanding of the revolutionary war is that it should be waged by the people's armed forces and the ordinary people who believe in the aims of such a war. The participation of the people on the side of their armed forces will hamper the effec-

tiveness of a great number of the enemy's armaments; it will make it lose its ability to use the methods of modem warfare and will force the enemy to face different weapons, some of which are modem and others primitive. This will prohibit the enemy from setting up stationary front lines at which it can assemble and mobilize its military forces in a manner that best serves its interests.

2. The ability of political struggle to enlighten, educate and organize the masses will guarantee the revolutionary program and ensure that the military struggle will not deviate from its aim. Furthermore it will create the forces necessary to direct the armed struggle in a way that accords with the tactics and strategy of armed revolution and avoids falling into the logic of regular warfare which the enemy is always trying to draw us into.

3. The effectiveness of armed struggle among the people will make them capable of supplying the armed forces with the required fighters who are aware of the aims of the struggle and capable of bearing all the difficulties which they will encounter in it. If the elements who join the straggle have revolutionary awareness and experience their solidarity and ability to resist become greater.

The mobilized people will offer the armed forces their experience and capabilities and will provide them with the necessary armaments and other material aid. The masses have proved, through a great number of revolutions which have taken place in different parts of the world, that they are capable of discovering and inventing effective methods, for encountering the enemy and inflicting heavy losses on it, despite their apparent primitiveness.

4. The revolutionary war which we are waging spreads over a wide area which our military forces cannot defend. The enemy is capable of striking in different places, thus we cannot consider that we have front lines. Moreover, the enemy occupies a large area inhabited by a great number of our people. These, through their struggle, can prevent the enemy from setting up front lines which it can protect. As far as the enemy is concerned, the absence of front lines is a very important matter, since it paralyzes its ability to carry out its military operations in a manner which suits the structure of its army and the training of its soldiers.

5. Our enemy, in addition to its military campaigns, has been waging a political campaign for a long time. It has solid political bas-

es all over the world, including the Arab homeland. It is capable of moving these political bases in a coordinated and effective manner to support its military aggression. We cannot confront the political bases, which the enemy has established, with military weapons. We must carry out an arduous political struggle to isolate and paralyze the political bases of the enemy and hinder their ability to support the aggression against us.

The second question to be answered is: What are the aims of political struggle?

The aims of political struggle are numerous, but the most important are the following:

1. Political struggle will mobilize the people for the purpose of their participation in the struggle. Such a mobilization should pass through different stages. Moreover, one should take into account that there are differences in people's readiness and ability to participate in the revolution. The phases of the mobilization of the masses are as follows:

> a. To enlighten the people about the aims of the revolution, its basic program and its political and social outlook. This enlightenment does not necessarily imply the adoption of a definite political ideology, nor is it subject to development as the landmarks of the revolution become clearer. The people should get acquainted with the new society which the revolution is planning to establish. They should also understand, to a great extent, the compelling reasons for carrying out the revolution and the necessities for which the people have to sacrifice.

> b. To educate the masses politically by defining the stand of the revolution and the role of the different external and internal forces. There are a great number of forces in the world which are natural allies of the enemy and ate ready to participate in its aggression, protect it and defend it At the same time there are other forces and nations which are ready to stand by the revolution, participate in it to varying degrees, and support the people's struggle; knowing the role of the international forces of liberation is a basic factor in evaluating the future of the revolution. It is necessary that the people should know their allies and their enemy. Palestinian society and Arab society ate tom by internal factions and are made of different classes. In every

society there are revolutionary forces which are capable of carrying arms and of sacrifice. However, there are also other forces whose readiness is less than the above-mentioned, and still others who do not feel the necessity of making any sacrifices. While in complete contrast, there are yet other forces who are against the revolution. Some of them have expressed their antagonism from the very beginning of the revolution and others have kept it hidden for as long as they can. The people should be educated in all these matters in order to know their true course and in order to be able to act in a manner which serves the interest of the revolution. In addition to that, the people should be educated in all the activities of any section in order not to follow a course which does not serve the interest of the revolution. At present there are a number of proposals and solutions which are accompanied by attempts to terrorize or persuade people into accepting them. The people, who are politically educated, ate in a position to choose the appropriate position. They are also capable of uncovering the plots aiming at the destruction of the revolution, and thus at all our hopes of liberation.

c. The people should be organized to enable them, through their different organizations, to move at the appropriate time and in the right direction. The organized people are the only ones who are capable of offering sacrifices and of acting in harmony with the program of the revolution. Otherwise, the people's affection for the revolution will be lost. We, at the moment, enjoy wide support and we are proud of it. But, if this support does not stem from organized people, we cannot consider it as a constant force on the side of the revolution on which we can depend in every circumstance.

d. The people's organizations cannot be led through a pyramid-style system. They need cadres which are politically aware at all levels. Such cadres require training and experience in order to provide the effective link between the people and the leaders of the revolution.

2. The second aim of political struggle is the establishment of a unified command. This will lead the people and the armed struggle by ensuring complete coordination between the different forces in such a manner that will best serve the interest of the revolution. This lead-

ership, which bears the main responsibility, has to transfer its determination and will to the armed forces and the people.

3. The third aim of political struggle is to carry out continuous uprisings which aim at:

a. Enlightening the people and increasing their adherence to the revolution. Through these uprisings the people's sense of responsibility and enthusiasm will be sharpened. The people will become gradually aware of the slogans and aims of the revolution.

b. Mass uprisings constitute a determining factor in protecting the armed forces. The people, more than once, were able to protect armed action from destruction and from plots planned and carried out by certain Arab regimes. The experiences of the revolution in Jordan and Lebanon are a clear manifestation of the people's physical ability to protect the revolution more successfully than weapons. This is especially so since we are living in an Arab land, and any armed confrontation with the Arab armies will cause great difficulties for the development of the revolution. As for the people who are residing in the occupied territories, they are capable of protecting armed action and paralyzing the enemy's ability to strike such action and to ensure its lines of communication and supply routes. There is no doubt that the people will be able to provide armed action with assistance and protection at the time when they become highly mobilized.

c. In addition to maintaining legal rights, mass uprisings aim at achieving new benefits. However minute these benefits may be, they increase the link of the masses to the revolution and their conviction of the necessity of supporting it. The revolution cannot achieve all of its aims at one time. The people, through these uprisings, should take by force their rights, one after the other, so as to be able to take up a position from which they will be more capable of action.

4. The people will be in a stronger position to exploit the conflicts within the enemy when they are mobilized through political struggle. Our enemy's affiliations differ, thus the methods of exploiting the conflicts among its members differ. The army of the enemy is composed of members of the Jewish sect who do not belong to one nationality and who are not directed by the same motives. The mass-

es, by interacting with the forces of the enemy, will be in a position to recognize and feed these conflicts, and even win over certain elements to work for our interest. Moreover, there are non-Jewish forces in the enemy's army, some of whom are Arabs, and it is not difficult to handle them. These forces, whether they agree, or not, cannot forget about their origin and relatives, one hopes to revive the spirit of nationalism among them. As for the Arab armies, which in their entirety are composed of national elements, the mobilized people can easily establish relations with members and officers of these armies to form a protective shield for the revolution whatever the plans and intentions of the Arab regimes may be with regard to it.

5. Political struggle aims, through the mobilization of the people, at choosing the effective elements for the formation of the people's militia. This militia will be responsible for protecting the people from oppressive acts directed against them by the enemies of the revolution. The ability of the people to resist will be affected, to a great extent, by their ability to protect themselves and prohibit the acts of annihilation carried out by the forces of counter-revolution. The militia is a defensive organization whose task is to defend the people. Thus it is not a part of the armed forces but of the people who undertake political struggle.

6. Political struggle through mobilizing the people aims at crushing the arguments of the psychological warfare waged by the enemy. Psychological warfare is a great force which the enemy has skillfully used. This kind of warfare has left the marks of its handiwork on our struggle. It has led to the disruption of the unity of the Palestinian forces and the weakening of their morale. In addition, the mobilized people will be able, through their resistance, to wage a counter-psychological war and accomplish the goals which such a war is supposed to achieve.

7. The people who actively participate in political struggle will be able to defeat the espionage plans, uncover the agents, and prohibit the acts of sabotage which the enemy carries out among their ranks. At the same time they will be able to protect the lines of supply and the armed bases and prevent the enemy from inflicting any harm on them. Moreover, the people will be able to communicate to the armed forces and the revolutionary leadership, information about the enemy forces, movements and military equipment so that the revolution will be in a better position to confront the enemy. Fur-

thermore, the people will become the eye of the armed forces in order not to fall into the traps and ambushes of the enemy.

8. Political struggle ensures the ability of the revolution to continue the struggle. Our revolution depends on the participation of the people through their contributions. We cannot depend on such a situation for a long time, because such overt contributions might be discontinued when any political changes occur. The revolution needs a great amount of money, arms and supplies. Its dependence on contributions which are threatened with disruption endangers the destiny of the revolution. The aim of political struggle is to mobilize the organized people and to make them the pillar of revolutionary resistance in every way possible. If the people are aware of their responsibilities, they can provide the revolution with its requirements and thus enable it to resist all pressures exerted on it and plots planned by certain Arab governments to curtail it. The people should distribute the responsibilities among themselves, so that while the peasant is in his field, the worker in his factory, and every other producer in his proper place, they will still be in a position to participate in supporting the revolution through production, in addition to supporting it by struggle. The people's participation in securing the material needs of the revolution will increase its solidarity and the people's adherence to it.

9. Political struggle will ensure the support and participation of the Arab forces and progressive forces of the world. The political struggle of the Palestinian people residing in the Arab states should be directed towards the Arab people to increase their solidarity with the revolution. The Arab people are involved in the war of liberation and capable of participating in it. The Palestinian people who are involved in the political struggle should focus their attention on the Arab people to make them participate in the battle and play their role in protecting the revolution against the plots of certain Arab governments. The world progressive forces, led by the countries of the socialist camp, and the rest of the nations who support justice, love and peace could play a role in supporting and protecting the revolution. This requires an organized political struggle to be carried out by the Palestinian people to contact the mentioned forces and win over their support for the revolution. Our view of the war of liberation should not be limited to the Palestinian level, recruiting supporters requires political struggle on the international and Arab levels. Different forces outside the Palestinian arena are capable of

giving military and financial aid and experience. In addition they can support and exert pressure on their government or other governments to prevent them from joining the enemy camp and secure their support for the revolution.

10. Political struggle makes the people feel the necessity of self-dependence. The principle of self-dependence is basic to securing the right direction of the revolution and its victory. All the forces of the world can play a role in supporting the revolution, yet the Palestinian people are the ones who have suffered from the aggression. Consequently they should always be in the first line in fighting the enemy. We cannot depend on external support because it is always threatened with disruption as a result of political changes. There is no doubt that such support inflames the revolution and increases its effectiveness. In spite of all that, the Palestinian people should be able, always and under all circumstances, to keep the revolution going. This is a basic safety factor for the revolution. In its first phases the revolution expressed its belief in the principle of self- dependence. After the expansion of revolutionary action it has become necessary to translate this principle into a reality which the Palestinian people will live everywhere. The present interference of certain Arab regimes in the affairs of the revolution could be traced back to the fact that the Palestinian people have not been self-dependent. They have limited their activities with regard to the revolution to contribution campaigns and contacting money holders in a disorganized manner. Thus the revenues of the revolution have become unstable.

11. Political struggle increases the attachment of the people to the homeland through reviving its heritage, culture, local habits, and historical struggle, so that the people will be totally linked to the homeland. Such an act will revive among the people the need to go back to their homeland, in addition to their feeling of pride and dignity.

The Arab regimes, during the past years, have put into effect the international plot to cancel the identity of the Palestinian people, and allow the factor of time the opportunity to weaken the will of the Palestinian people and their attachment to the homeland. Reviving the national heritage will unite the people and make them feel the irreplaceable loss. National heritage cannot be separated from national feelings and love of the homeland.

12. The ability and qualifications of the people to use all means to defend the homeland will be increased by political struggle. The

mobilized masses have played an important role in the progressive world revolutions through the application of the methods of primitive warfare. The people can set up traps and ambushes and exploit all natural means such as irrigation and tillage in fighting. Furthermore, they can, through their long experience, exploit animals for their purposes. The people, in their struggle, can find a role for bees, camels, doves and other animals.

Following this presentation of the necessity for political struggle and its aims, we should answer the third question which gives these aims their factual picture and points out the means for their achievement. Political struggle is a practical stand which requires the people to participate in the revolution. Keeping political struggle within its theoretical framework makes it lose its basic value and gives armed struggle the opportunity to be the only practical expression of the revolution with the resultant dangers that would involve. A detailed study concerning the method of undertaking political struggle does not aim at putting forward definite formulas for it inasmuch as it puts forward means which do not necessarily imply that they are the sole possible means available. Our knowledge of the aims of political struggle will suffice to put us in a position in which we can apply different means to enable our people to express their ability to invent new means. In this way our people's experience will participate in enriching the revolutions of other people.

Yet we must base our political struggle on the rich revolutionary experience fought by different people. Our revolution is a humane one which often resembles the revolutions of other people from the point of view of aims. Thus it was necessary for us to adopt the following methods which they have applied:

1. Establishment of popular organizations. This is the basis of political struggle. Generally speaking the masses' political awareness and readiness to bear the burdens of the struggle differ. Thus it is necessary to take into consideration these differences and establish popular organizations on different levels. It can be summarized as follows:

   a. Broadly-based popular organizations which may act lawfully, such as the worker, student, peasant and merchant federations; religious, sports, social, and women's organizations; and any other kind of organizations whether they be based on a trade or anything else.

The distinguishing feature of such organizations is their ability to encompass all the elements of the people irrespective of their readiness to be committed to the program of the revolution. Thus the revolution can work through these organizations and influence their members. Moreover, through these organizations, the revolution can get in touch with the leadership and direct them on an individual basis in order to induce them to enlighten the people with regard to the aims of the revolution. Furthermore, these organizations are capable of transforming the masses from being diversified, ineffective and helpless, even with regard to matters which concern their interests, into pressure groups capable of taking by force their rights and taking up attitudes that accord with their will. These organizations open the door for organized revolutionary action. Yet this does not imply that the above-mentioned organizations are capable of undertaking effective actions unless the revolution completes its work in this field. This is especially so since the enemies of the people's cause have established vague popular organizations whose aim is to distract the people from their revolutionary program and prevent them from practicing their role.

b. Establishment of groupings and organizations with political affiliations. These differ from the above-mentioned popular organizations since they represent a phase of action which is more developed. These organizations have different forms, but, generally speaking, they can be limited to two:

    i. The groupings which are created by the revolution within the popular organizations. For example, the revolution, through its action among members of the workers' federations, can recruit workers who believe in the aims and slogans of the revolution and attempt to gather the largest possible number of workers in one grouping which represents the revolutionary workers. Through this grouping, which calls for the implementation of the aims of the revolution, the revolutionary workers can get in touch with and recruit different elements of the workers. In addition they will recruit an avant-garde of politically aware workers to strengthen their commitment through revolutionary organizations. The distinguishing feature of these groupings is their ability to operate lawfully, and, at the same time, work among organizations with the largest membership. Moreover, through their struggle, these groupings can achieve social and economic benefits for the workers. Thus, these groupings improve the workers' conditions and increase their ability to resist, and, at the same time, they recruit the mass of workers for the revolution.

ii. Organizations with definite political aims. These organizations are not based on popular organizations but encompass elements recruited from different organizations who agree to pursue an objective which is in harmony with the aims of the revolution. There are many such organizations; for example, youth organizations whose aim is grouping different elements of the youth for the support of the revolution and who undertake exploration and light training. Moreover, one can set up organizations to resist Zionist occupation. These will be responsible for holding discussions and rallies, undertaking financial projects and publishing pamphlets, etc.

Committees for the support of the revolution can be established with the aim of contacting the Arab peoples to make them aware of and participate in the revolution in one way or another. Moreover, committees of solidarity with friendly people can be established such as the Afro-Asian committees of solidarity. Furthermore, organizations for combating anti-Semitism, or organizations of friendship between the Arab people and the non-Zionist Jews can be established. Along these lines the following organizations can be cited: The Committee for Reviving the Camp, Friends of Jerusalem Society, The National Enlightenment Society Against the Dangers of Zionism, The Fighter's Sweater Committee, The Committee for the Care of the Martyrs' Families, The Fifth of June Society, etc. These different organizations should be organized in such a way that they direct their efforts according to a revolutionary orientation.

c. The revolutionary organizations of the cadres. These are the backbone of the revolution, its security and moving force. The weakness of the cadres or their absence will cause the disintegration of the relationship between the will of the revolutionary leadership and the masses, thus depriving political struggle of one of its most important links. As a result, the subject of the cadres should be given great attention and effort. The cadres are the connecting link between the revolution and the masses, and they constitute the true leadership of the people. In the absence of the cadres the revolution will be exposed to a profound split between itself and the people. The building of the cadres will be achieved naturally through the application of (a) and (b). Through the struggle of the organizations which have political affiliations, the revolution becomes better acquainted with the avant-garde elements among the people and can recruit the leading elements who are in harmony with the revolution's political program. The cadres should be disciplined, politically aware, able to move easily and ready to sacrifice. When the revolution is equipped with such cadres, it becomes capable of leading all kinds of popular organizations, thus any popular movement becomes complementary to the political struggle of the revolution. The revolution cannot afford to commit many errors in building up its cadres because these will be directly reflected in its ability and destiny.

2. Using legal methods to carry out political action which aims at protecting and acquiring the legal rights of the people. Every regime which is against the people is bound to allow certain legal forms of mass agitation, and has to give the people some of their rights, however few these may be. As far as our people under Zionist occupation are concerned, the Zionist regime, despite its arbitrary and terrorist measures, cannot deprive them of the right of movement in every circumstance. For example, our people in the occupied territories can gather in mosques and churches, can visit the tombs of the dead, and can pay family visits. In addition, the Arabs in the territories occupied prior to 3 June participated in one or other of the political aspects of the political life of the country. They had the right to vote and belong to political parties. Moreover, there are social, religious, sports and charity organizations and establishments. Through these rights, despite their paucity, the revolution can carry out different activities such as making people politically aware, developing organizations and getting to know different elements who have never been organized or contacted.

As for the Palestinian masses in the Arab countries their situation, although it differs from one state to the other, is, generally speaking, very different from those in the occupied territories. They have legal rights which we are not going to enumerate here.

The revolution must benefit from these rights to the fullest extent, because, as it is able to work through legality, it is easier for the revolution to contact the people for the purpose of enlightenment and participation. As a general rule, the masses, before undertaking serious political struggle, will not be ready to carry responsibility or offer sacrifices. A great number will only participate in legal activities which are permitted by the official authorities, in order to avoid any acts of revenge on the part of the authorities. The absence of contact between the people and the revolution makes the former weak and incapable of resistance. Thus it is necessary that revolutionary action should reach the hearts and minds of the people through lawful activity, after which the relationship will develop.

The development we are talking about in the relationship between the masses and the revolution should happen in stages. At first the revolution should push the masses to struggle to get more lawful rights. Thus, the revolution will make the masses feel that it aspires to acquire more benefits for them, and at the same time it will create more favorable conditions to increase the people's ability to struggle. In April 1968, when the crisis broke out in Lebanon, there was a great disparity between the level of armed struggle in establishing bases on Lebanese territory and the Palestinian people who had been deprived for more than 20 years. This disparity disabled the masses from protecting armed action in a serious and definite manner.

The masses who possess more rights will be more capable of supporting, protecting and escalating armed action. The relationship between armed action and the lawful rights of the Palestinians will become stronger as long as the revolution is aware of its importance.

3. Political struggle and armed struggle should go hand in hand. Our revolution, at present, suffers from the disparity between the level of political action and that of armed action. Such a disparity poses a threat since it proposes the adoption of armed struggle as the only method of struggle. Thus it was necessary to depend on armed struggle to protect and develop political struggle, at a time when the latter was preparing itself to become the nucleus of revolutionary action. Political struggle, at present, can carry out activities to support armed struggle as a means of developing itself. In this context political action must accomplish the following:

> a. To create the necessary atmosphere for armed action by adopting it, calling for its support and expressing the desire of

the people to strengthen it. The slogan calling for the support of armed struggle is an easy one to work through and the revolution can mobilize the people to carry it out. The enemies of the revolution will find that it is difficult to fight the idea of armed action and its implications, since it represents readiness to die, sacrifice, altruism, heroism, and idealism. Those elements who do not hide that they ate against the content of the revolution, do not dare to attack or severely criticize armed action. One of the methods of undertaking political struggle was adherence to armed struggle: not to use it and be protected by it, but to give political action a dimension equivalent to that of armed struggle as far as heroism, idealism, commitment to the revolution and the resulting sacrifices are concerned.

b. To choose the right elements to participate in armed action. Our masses, as a result of their eagerness to struggle, and their long endured deprivation, are ready to participate in armed struggle to retrieve their lost pride and dignity. Political struggle, if it aims at achieving closer association between the revolution and the masses, should be the road to secure contact between the right elements and the armed struggle. When the people feel that their political organization is the only link between them and armed struggle; and when they are assured that participation in political struggle will open the road for armed struggle and martyrdom, they will respond more to that struggle.

c. To build the political groups as a center for armed bases. The people, especially in the first stages of their political awareness, feel that their political struggle aims at transforming the places where they are grouped into bases in which to live and protect the members of the armed forces. Political struggle must respond to this aim so that places of mass groupings will become a primary source for armed bases. This matter is obvious with regard to the Arabs in the occupied territories and the people residing in places near the armed bases.

d. To create a popular militia. The creation of the militia in the political bases and places of mass groupings achieves, in addition to defending the people, a suitable atmosphere for political struggle.

Political struggle, in which broad sections of the masses participate, needs to offer them a degree of self-confidence. For example, the presence of the militia in the camps is, no doubt, an incentive to participate in the political struggle, and, at the same time, it is a factor which will protect the people against being crushed.

4. Establishment of a wide national front from among the different national forces. The revolution struggles to recover the homeland and liberate it and its people.

This slogan answers the needs and wishes of many of the groups and national forces.

Every nation which is passing through the phase of national struggle needs to find a common formula to unify its efforts. Thus the creation of a national front is a fundamental determining factor in preparing the basic conditions for the continuation of the revolution, and its victory. The fragmentation of our society through the dispersion of our people has contributed to their weakness *vis-à-vis* their enemies. There are many forces and groups who are loyal to our nation, but because of their political beliefs and social status cannot join the revolutionary organizations. There are other forces and groups who can, at one stage, participate, in one form or other, alongside the revolution. Thus the revolution, in its different phases, should establish a national front which will fulfill the aims of each phase. The structure of the national front is not meant to be a permanent one which organizes relations among the national forces and groups. On the contrary, it is a temporary framework which develops in accordance with the changes that occur in each phase. The revolution, as it progresses, attempts to group all the forces which serve a certain phase. In case the revolution is faced with difficulties which require it to retreat to less developed positions, it should establish relations with different forces and groups to be in a better position to protect itself while preparing for a counter-attack. The national front's slogans and aims will differ at every phase. In the first stages of its development, the front's aim will be fighting Zionism, later fighting Zionism and its allies, etc.

In its first stages the national front can include all the popular groupings, but in its more developed stages the front becomes clearer and more revolutionary so that it expresses all the political aims of the revolution. A large number of the allies of yesterday become the enemies of today, many of the allies of today will become the enemies of tomorrow, and many of the allies of tomorrow will abandon the revolution all together. We cannot build the national front on the basis of achieving all the aims of the revolution. However, under no circumstances, should this imply that we should avoid knowing our temporary and permanent political aims during the process of establishing the national front. These aims should be always remembered so that the national front will be a step forward instead of being a step backward which would result in diluting the revolution and blurring its aims.

5. A continuous process of clarification of the policy of the revolution in its broadest aspect. Such a clarification will provide the revolution with people who believe in it, and will help to discover the elements who are qualified to join the revolution. If the political program of the revolution is clear, the atmosphere of political struggle becomes dear and attractive. The revolution does not struggle for the sake of revenge, or to inflict harm on the Jews, or to bring to an end economic competition between our people and the aggressors. The revolution struggles to recover the homeland for its people and for the sake of the coming generations of our people who must live on their land, practice their rights, enjoy their freedom and the fruits of their land. It is a revolution against all forms of exploitation. It is a revolution which believes in the right to self-determination for all peoples. It is a revolution which is linked with all the progressive forces of the world. It fulfills its humane role of enriching the experience of the people struggling for liberation. It also endeavors to place our people in their natural place so that they may carry out their obligations and commitments towards humanity. The Palestinian people cannot join the revolution unless it is positive and aims at building before demolishing. In terms of the revolution, the acts of demolishing is a step in the direction of the creation of reliable individuals. This clarity in the policy of the revolution is a basic factor in strengthening the political struggle and clarifying its details. The means of such clarification are numerous, but the most effective is the direct verbal explanation at both the individual and collective levels, in addition to other educational means, such as books, pamphlets, newspapers, broadcasting, post, communiqués, etc.

6. Political education of the people. The aims of such education are: to point out to the people who are the enemies and who are the allies of the revolution; and to acquaint them with the political situation of the revolution in order to increase their ability to react favorably to its slogan, and know the true program for which

we are struggling. The enemies of the revolution are numerous, but we have to know the main enemy, to isolate it and destroy it. Then the revolution will choose the second enemy to concentrate on and confront. Thus political struggle, by educating the people, can lead them in the direction which serves the policy of the revolution, and will not allow temporary commotions against secondary enemies to create pockets which will distract the revolution from its basic program. There can be no doubt that political education, which aims at making the people know their enemies and capable of evaluating them, will help to clarify and strengthen political struggle. Political struggle which does not educate the people along these lines will find itself hesitating before different courses; this will be reflected by the people and will weaken the struggle. Knowledge of the enemies of the revolution and the ability to evaluate them are basic factors in the political struggle; yet there is another, and no less important factor, and that is knowing the friends of the revolution. The friends of the revolution vary. There are temporary friends who may become enemies in the future. There are other long term friends who may lag behind the revolution in its development. There are also permanent friends who will be able to support the revolution under all circumstances. A discussion concerning the friends of the revolution should be based on a political and sociological study which is not the subject of this paper. Yet educating the people along these lines is very important; because, in this way, the revolution will maintain its leadership of the people, and will prevent the people, in the future, from adopting stands which will put them under a non-revolutionary leadership and make their ability to side with the revolution temporary.

7. Leading the people gradually according to the way in which they have been prepared—from a lower to a higher level of struggle. The people who have never struggled and home hardships and dangers are usually in no position to participate in the highest level of revolutionary struggle. Thus one of the obligations of political struggle is to undertake such preparation of the people. Raising the standards of the people with regard to struggle requires their gradual participation in it. We can encourage individuals to voice their support of the revolution verbally, or to support certain primary demands pertaining to the revolution. Then we proceed to allow the people to sign petitions, form delegations to contact those who are responsible, and submit demands however simple. After that we can call for closed

or open meetings in houses and dubs, and then proceed to call for licensed rallies to celebrate a memory, an occasion, or in support of a demand of the people. Following that we can call on the people to participate in licensed demonstrations, then unlicensed ones which usually lead to a confrontation with the authorities.

Such a confrontation will require the people to strengthen their ability to defend themselves and carry arms. These steps give only an idea of the methods that should be followed in advancing the mobilization of the people to the point at which they will be able to participate in the revolution. The experiences of each particular camp or state will help to give a clearer guideline on the methods of helping people participate in the political struggle. At times we can exchange one of these methods and use another, and at others we can dispense with certain steps if the people prove their readiness to surpass them. The danger of pushing the people to a high level of struggle without preparation will lead to the revolution's separation from the people and a discontinuation of the sacrifices that they give. The above-mentioned steps cannot all be applied at once, but should be applied gradually to different groups so that the experience of one group will be more advanced than another.

8. To exchange services. Political struggle aims at recruiting the masses to participate in revolutionary action. Yet the people do not have the same degree of political awareness, and many of them have personal problems concerning education, work, health, residence, production, etc. The revolution cannot mobilize the people and put them in their proper place without offering them something in return. Interaction between the revolution and the people requires continuous exchange in services. The masses offer sacrifices for the revolution in addition to assistance and support; the revolution offers the masses what it can achieve in the form of benefits and protection with regard to the requirements of daily life.

This sort of exchange in services increases the masses' adherence to and belief in the revolution. Our revolution has attempted many times to achieve this. There is no doubt that it has not yet been able to offer the required assurances which express its belief in the necessity of exchanging services. What the revolution offers at present in the fields of medical and educational services does not suffice the needs of the people. But the revolution, in addition to the services it does offer, can revive among the people the spirit of cooperation so that they can serve each other and lighten the burdens of others. The revolution should assist all those whose houses are blown up by the enemy authorities so that they will not be exposed to emigration. The sons of the locality in which a house is blown up can cooperate to rebuild it in a short period in order to give confidence to every citizen that the loss of his house will not be final. Another example is that many people suffer from arbitrary dismissal by their employers. The revolution can, through different means at its disposal, strive for the re-employment of the dismissed worker or provide him with another job. In this way people will feel that the revolution gives as much as it takes, and that they should give it as much as they can. This cooperative spirit among the people themselves and between them and the revolution must truly exemplify itself in the cadres. Members of the cadres should set an example by being the first ones to offer their services.

9. To purge the ranks of the revolution from the bad elements. In order to undertake political struggle we should give the masses a good image of the elements participating in the revolution. In the eyes of the masses revolutionary elements should set an example in morality, discipline, good behavior, altruism, and humility. Thus the revolution has to purge its ranks of all the bad elements in order to preserve its translucence *vis-à-vis* the masses who do not accept being led by elements whom they do not trust or admire.

10. To destroy agents. Political struggle needs an atmosphere of mutual trust among the people so that the individual will not feel that he is surrounded by agents who will report him to the official authorities. In many incidents people have desisted from continuing their resistance for fear of being reported tty agents. An atmosphere of confidence among the people will protect their movement, and at the same time will increase their self-confidence and belief in their ability to participate in the revolution. Our revolution has carried out some of these activities and threatened a number of agents in the occupied territories and executed others. In spite of this there are many agents who are still safe from the power of the revolution. As for the agents operating outside the occupied territories, their role in aborting the revolutionary trend is known, and using different means to nullify the harm they inflict on the people will be another of the factors which will prompt political struggle among the people.

11. To raise slogans and honor heroes and martyrs. The masses are not expected to be aware at one stroke of all the means that will lead to their participation in the political struggle. The revolution must raise different slogans to help in enlightening and educating the people, prompting them to work in different fields that, in the final analysis, will serve the trend of the revolution. General slogans can be raised among the masses which express our political aims and methods, such as, "Guns... all guns against the enemy." This slogan is an emotional call for the creation of the national front and the rejection of internal struggles. Another slogan is, "Let us carry the hammer and plow in one hand and the gun in the other." This slogan urges the people to pay attention to production and at the same time to prepare themselves for sacrifice so that the worker will not be in a position to choose between productive work and revolutionary work. Other slogans can be raised, such as, "The land for those who liberate it," expressing the belief of the revolution in the masses and its determination to prohibit exploitation. In this context we can mention slogans calling for the improvement of health and a strengthening of the economic situation thus manifesting the ability to confront the enemy at any place or time. Moreover there can be slogans directed to students, teachers, women, youth, or any other group.

As for the martyrs, fighters, heroes, by announcing their heroism and reminding the people of their sacrifices, the people will, no doubt, be led to sense the high spirit of the revolution, and to increase their adherence to it. A readiness and desire to act in a similar way may be awakened in them.

These are the means for carrying out political struggle. They are general guidelines which portray forces that show that political struggle is a difficult and long term work, but that, at the same time, it deserves every effort and sacrifice. The means of political struggle are numerous. The revolution can fill each day with struggle and make the masses participate in every step it takes without separating the daily reality of the masses from their inevitable role in the war of liberation.

As has been pointed out in this study, political struggle is the sound base for revolutionary action. The movement of armed struggle should pass through an act of continuous escalation of political struggle. The reality of the present situation forces us to exert every effort in order to fill the vacuum created by the emergence of armed struggle before the natural development of political struggle. The circumstances which forced the revolution to undertake armed struggle make it our duty not to leave this struggle without its basic pillar, which is, political struggle.

Abu Lutf Answers Questions[1]
[1969]

Question: What do we mean if we say that Al-Fateh is a movement?
Answer: Al-Fateh is a movement. It is not a party or a front. A party has a constant social ideology. A front is composed of revolutionary organizations based on a specific work program. Al-Fateh is a movement because it believes in the necessity of subjecting its thought to practice and experience. It is dynamic. Through practice and experience it can enrich the necessary contents of its thought. It does not believe in the logic of static theory. It is a movement which has specific aims and acts in accordance with basic principles. It has incontestable principles, yet the contents of Al-Fateh's thought cannot be determined except through actual practice because a theory is the result of experience, and practice is the test of thought and attitudes. In this sense Al-Fateh is a movement which is continuously subjecting the totality of its concepts and policies to practice. It continues to change these concepts and policies in order to build the final thought of the movement Thus as long as Al-Fateh is a movement it rejects the logic of static theory and cannot define the man of the future, because in doing so it will be following a metaphysical line of thinking which determines the form of man. This is an ideal understanding which cannot be applied to reality.

Al-Fateh and the Left

Leftism as defined by many of leftist ideologues is, in short, "the will to abolish the exploitation of man by man." The leftist movement always speaks in the negative form. The left resists so and so, revolts against so and so and fights so and so. The left does not have a positive content except when exemplified in the form of a party or movement, and then this

---

1   **Ed. Note:** Faruq al-Qaddumi, also known by the *kunya*/teknonym Abu al-Lutf, was Secretary-General of Fateh until 2009 and Chairman of Fateh's central committee and the Palestine Liberation Organization's political department, operating from Tunisia, in 2004-2009. This interview is dated from July 12, 1969.

content becomes the tool for continuous change. The element of time in the leftist movement is not continuous. When we fight against a specific society because it is corrupt, and we are able to change it radically, then, with the passage of time, all the changes attained become positive connotations. These, in their turn, are rejected because the movement of history is in a continuous state of revolution and rejection. The given society, after a period of time, becomes rightist, and the creation of a leftist movement is inevitable in order to reject this society.

AL-FATEH AND THE BOURGEOISIE

Many people claim that the classes of peasants and workers are the classes on which the Palestinian revolution depends. This statement is contrary to reality because the new class of refugees, which has not been taken into consideration by many thinkers, is the class on which the Palestinian revolution depends. Workers, especially in the underdeveloped countries, form a simple and ineffective class which cannot be easily relied on. Palestinians were evacuated from their homes, the implication being that a class of refugees has been formed and not one of workers and peasants. If the Palestinian revolution represented by Al-Fateh is said to be bourgeois, this implies that there should be factories, capitalists and workers, in other words specific classes. We cannot say that there is a bourgeois class if there is no working class. What is this class? Because of the evacuation of the Palestinians, Al-Fateh represents the refugees. It is the only revolutionary movement which has transcended the Arab movements, Arab parties and the Palestinian regional movements, and it has done this because it has depended on the refugee class. The bourgeois concept, on the other hand, is one of attributes. For example there have been socialist thinkers who have come from the bourgeoisie, yet they have lived under the same material conditions as those of the toiling people and have become truly revolutionary and not bourgeois. "Bourgeois" is a material condition under which a human being lives and which makes him tend towards bourgeois intellectualism. Then where are the bourgeois tendencies in Al-Fateh?

Yet there is an infantile leftism among those who propagate socialist thought by applying the experiences of others. On this basis such movements can be described as idealistic and infantile, because any movement must study the given reality. These movements have not studied the given reality but described it according to descriptions of other societies. As a result their understanding and description is abstract. Our description is nearer to reality Thus Al-Fateh is the only actual revolutionary movement in the Palestinian field.

Social Ideology

The act of being committed to a specific social ideology implies a commitment to a specific social principle. As long as the revolution is fighting against the present situation, it rejects the leftist connotation of general rejection. For we have made our intellectual revolution against the existing situation, rejected it and undertaken armed resistance. In other words, we have undertaken, in a practical way, to change the existing situation. The thought and action of the left is directed towards the rejection of the existing situation and actually changing it This is the leftist trend. Evidently, then, Al-Fateh movement, if it is given the proper name, is further to the left than any movement in the Arab world.

The Arab parties wanted to find a historical justification for their existence, so they created guerrilla organizations to prove that they should exist. These organizations, which are affiliated to parties, are a justification for the parties' historical existence. Their task is not easy. For every movement that has lost its dynamic ability to awaken the masses through its political organizations has, by implication, lost its historical values. But, through the existence of guerrilla branches, it wanted to create an historical justification. This is a temporary thing which is bound to come to an end. However, the historical revolutionary movement in the Arab world, which has quite different political, military and theoretical dimensions, is Al-Fateh. It is mote of a leftist movement because, intellectually and practically, it is committed to the act of changing the existing situation in which the Palestinian people are living. All those who say that Al-Fateh is a bourgeois movement are using an abstract terminology because they want to apply theories that have resulted from the experience of specific people and do not fit our present experience.

Why Has Al-Fateh Not Put Forward a Specific Social Ideology?

It is not easy to put forward a specific social ideology at a time when the struggle is against the occupying power. In the present phase, the struggle should be a national one. This means that all the classes which are against Zionism and imperialism should form an alliance to destroy the Zionist imperialist occupation of Palestine. Thus, to put forward a social concept would have a direct effect on the alliance by sowing dissension among its members. Since, within the alliance, there are secondary conflicts, these should be frozen for the sake of the main conflict which is that of our existence or the Zionists. Calling for any social concept in this phase implies the adoption of a specific error, namely, the destruction of the popular alliance, or the forces of the Palestinian people. This is the phase of national struggle. If one studies the history of the Chinese people, one finds that Mao [Zedong] formed an alliance with [Chiang Kai-shek], who was extremely reactionary, because it was a phase of national struggle.

REMARK FROM THE AUDIENCE

Question: Can we say that Zionism and imperialism in Palestine represent the Japanese colonialism of China and the Chinese bourgeoisie, and that we are fighting Zionism and after solving the question of Zionist colonialism we start to solve the secondary conflicts?

Answer: It does not matter whether the forces against us are imperialism, the bourgeoisie or capitalism. It will be inevitable that new conflicts will emerge during the act of development of struggle between the people and the enemy, and at the phase of liberation. For example, a conflict with the bureaucrats in the revolution may appear. A bureaucratic class in the revolution may emerge which should be resisted. There may develop differences in the ideas of the revolution because we aim at social justice and abolishing the exploitation of man by man.

REMARK FROM THE AUDIENCE

Question: Then we are leftists?

Answer: Leftism does not mean that. A leftist is the one who rejects a specific reality and works to change this reality. Leftism has many trends. The communist movement in Jordan is a reactionary movement because it lags behind the national movement which has carried arms and started to change the reality. The Jordanian communist movement wants to maintain this reality while it raises the slogan of national rule and we want to blow up the basis of this reality. Thus as far as we are concerned it is a rightist movement.

As for the social content, any such content requires certain bases before it can be realized.

1. There must be land—a regional unity.

2. There must be people living on this land—a social unity—and not a divided people like ours.

3. There must be a political unity, namely a state, in order to achieve the social content.

We have not yet built these bases. We must have land on which our people will be grouped, and a state in order to put forward the social content.

REMARK FROM THE AUDIENCE

Question: If we compare the Palestinian revolution with the Algerian revolution, we find that the latter did not put forward any social content. It started as a national liberation movement struggling against French colonialism. After the liberation it became a national bourgeois movement because it did not have any social content. Thus, when the revolution was on the verge of attaining victory, the contradictions within the movement exploded into the open.

Answer: Firstly, in the Arab homeland there has not actually been any experiment with social content that has proved itself a guiding experience. Secondly, world socialist experiments differ from one country to the other, such as Yugoslavia, Poland, the Soviet Union, and China. In the Soviet Union the concept of state capitalism has emerged which the Chinese call socialist imperialism. If we believe that evolution is inevitable, then, as long as there are differences in the social content of the different experiences of the socialist revolutions, it will be difficult to judge the future in the light of a specific social content. We should, however, adopt the following general principles:

1. The abolition of the exploitation of man by man.

2. The question of social justice.

These general goals are the backbone of the Palestinian revolution. We have started to apply the question of social justice by establishing social institutes such as: The School of the Martyrs' Sons, the Martyrs' Institute, the Cubs' Institute.

The idea behind the establishment of such institutes is that we should become responsible for all our people. This experiment will inevitably mature and become enriched, achieving the social content we desire. It is not permissible to put forward a specific social content Whoever does that works in the abstract and is an infantile leftist. There are many infantile leftists in the Palestinian and Arab fields. They are called, if this expression is correct, revolutionary missionaries.

REMARK FROM THE AUDIENCE

Question: We always say that the peak of ideology is armed struggle. What does this mean?

Answer: To say that the highest form of struggle is armed struggle is more leftist than any other ideology; for it is an intellectual rejection followed by a practical rejection.

Question: What is Al-Fateh's attitude towards the progressive parties in Israel?

Answer: Progressiveness and progressive parties should have concepts of right, justice and the non-exploitation of man by man. However, the trends found in Israel are part and parcel of the Zionist existence. They believe in the existence and the consecration of this racist state, and their struggle is merely against the governing group. Consequently they are part of that aggressive entity which is contrary to any teal progressive trend. There will be no progressive trends and parties in Israel as long as arms are not carried against the Israeli racist entity and an armed struggle is not embarked upon for its elimination as a state, society, Zionist movement, and military establishment. If the members of these parties start fighting the Zionist presence or the Israeli political presence with arms to destroy the so-called Israeli state, if they fight and struggle against the Israeli army to eliminate the existence of this fascist military establishment, if they fight against class discrimination between Eastern and Western Jews, Arabs and Zionists, if they struggle against Zionist ideas for the establishment of the Israeli state, then these parties become progressive. In reality these parties accept the political, military, intellectual and social situation, but they claim that the men in authority ate deviationists. Thus these parties are part and parcel of the Israeli fascist aggressive entity and they are not progressive.

REMARK FROM THE AUDIENCE

Question: The Israeli Communist Party's Secretary General, Meir Vilner, has drawn a plan recognizing the right of the Palestinians to return and to be compensated for their land. The problem, according to Vilner, does not pertain to the existence or non-existence of the state of Israel, or to an Israeli and a Palestinian; but it is a problem of struggle between reactionary and progressive forces. The party considers Israel to be reactionary because it supports imperialism and it is a base for the US, and it claims that it is against the Zionist movement which is militarily controlling Israel. But if Israel is ruled by a progressive party, it will recognize the right of the Palestinians, for as long as Palestine can take in seven million Jews "according to Ben Gurion," it can take in the Palestinian refugees who do not exceed two millions. The Palestinians will return but within the framework of the Israeli state. Vilner claims that carrying arms against Israel strengthens the presence of Zionism and the military Zionist movement in Israel, because the man in the street fears arms being carried against him, and the only persons who can give him a feeling of security are the military Zionists. Israel is a reality and carrying arms against it will never solve the problem, on the contrary it will complicate it even more.

Answer: Actually this opinion is one of the contradictions found in Israel which may develop into struggle. Carrying arms is the way of the Palestinian armed struggle against this entity. The Israeli entity is an artificial one contrary to the logic of evolution. The existence of any state in the Arab area of Palestine which is not an Arab Palestinian state is contrary to the logic of history and evolution. If a non-Arab Palestinian state was created, it would face the same problems, but from a different angle, that the Israeli state is facing.

The international existence of Israel is what we are objecting to, and it is contrary to the nature of Arab existence in this area. Israel, as a state, contradicts the logic of evolution, for a state must have its civilization, economic, political, and historical roots in the area in which it exists. This means that the people who live there and want to form a state should be in harmony, with regard to civilization, with the peoples of the Arab area. On the other hand if they want to secede and form a new civilization or way of life, the logic of history will inevitably condemn them to death. What we are objecting to is the existence of the state of Israel because we cannot separate its substance from its form. If you strike at the substance, you also strike the form. The claim of the Israeli Communist Party contradicts the facts and is an attempt on the part of these deviationist forces in the Zionist entity to paralyze progressive forces in their work by making them adopt ideas which are far from reality.[2] For these reasons the

---

2 **Ed. Note:** The Israeli Communist Party (ICP) in the 1960s was in constant conflict in regards to the question of Palestine, with one side nearing Zionist policies and the other following the Soviet line. The party following the Zionist line retained

existence of Israel contradicts the logic and evolution of history, and it also contradicts the way of life of the peoples in the Middle East, namely the Arab people. Any state created, whether Israel or any other that was not civilizationally, politically and linguistically harmonious with the peoples of this area, would inevitably wither away. Thus the Zionist or Israeli entity is what is objected to, the termination of this entity will put an end to all these contradictions.

REMARK FROM THE AUDIENCE

Question: Some people say that if we allow the Jews to remain, the problem will be solved. For the Jewish state will be founded on the basis of a Jewish nation which will result in the establishment of a socialist society.

Answer: A progressive socialist society cannot be established in Israel because there are basic principles for building such a society. Moreover in the Arab world, the establishment of socialism cannot be achieved if each state attempts it separately. This experiment in socialism has failed in Egypt, Syria, and Iraq. A basic requirement for creating a socialist state is regional unity. Israel, as a state, does not have the natural and social forces to enable it to be a progressive state. The reason is that this artificial state urgently and continuously needs foreign aid and support. This support is given by capitalism and world imperialism. Thus Israel will depend on colonial forces as long as it remains a state. It will also remain a tool in the hands of world imperialism to hinder the Arab progressive movement in the Arab East and West. Thus the Israeli state cannot become a progressive state, nor be a basis of socialism. Israel does not possess the natural resources to enable it to survive as a progressive state. It will remain a colonial state via which technical aid is passed to the Arab, Asian and African states. Moreover, the economy of Israel cannot help in establishing a socialist or progressive state. There will always remain in Israel the class of middlemen, or the comprador class, which monopolizes foreign capital and then sends it to other areas in the form of technical aid. Israel is a means of hindering the Arab progressive movement. It must be ter-

---

the name of the ICP, also known as *Maki* in Hebrew, while the Soviet-aligned grouping were renamed the New Communist List, or *Rakah*. For more on the history of the Israeli communist parties, see, more generally, "The Palestinians and the Israeli Communist Party: 1948-Present," *Interactive Encyclopedia of the Palestinian Question*, accessed on March 14, 2024, online at: https://www.palquest.org/en/highlight/23915/palestinians-and-israeli-communist-party.

minated as a state in order to put an end to these contradictions and have peace in the Arab Middle Eastern area.

REMARK FROM THE AUDIENCE

Question: Some people say that Israel is the only socialist state in the Middle East. The example given is the Kibbutz.

Answer: Israel is not a socialist state. The evidence is found in its class structure. There is discrimination between Eastern and Western Jews which means that there is a class struggle. If that statement means that Israel is nearer in time to socialism because it has readied the stage of capitalism, whereas the Arab states are still at the stage of feudalism according to Marxist interpretation, this is correct. Israel is coming close to the peak of the conflict which can result in a struggle between the poor classes and the exploiting classes. Moreover, the nature of Israeli society is artificial. It has not evolved through long historical interaction; it is 20 years old. The act of social homogeneity cannot be created in such a short period; man's struggle needs a long time. The leftist societies are hundreds or thousands of years old. How could these people who came from the west, others from the east, north, and the south, who spoke different languages and had different habits and nationalities, form a homogeneous society in such a short period? Such a society needs a long time for there to be an interaction between it and its objective economic and material conditions. Moreover, the Israelis are living under circumstances of continuous struggle with the Arab people, whose land they have stolen. Thus the question of being more progressive and nearer to socialism is a great deception, and those who propagate it are deceived by Zionist propaganda.

REMARK FROM THE AUDIENCE

Question: Don't you think that Al-Fateh's aim of having Muslims, Jews and Christians live together with equal rights in Palestine, after a struggle has taken place between them is utopian and idealistic?

Answer: No, our aim is neither utopian nor idealistic. On the contrary it is realistic because past experience has proved that the Arabs do not have any anti- Semitic tendencies since they are Semites. The Arabs' civilizational structure is such that, if we admit that the Islamic civilization has created a tolerant mentality toward other religions, the Jews can live in peace with the Arabs. Judaism in our view is a religion and not a nationality. There are Arabs whose religion was Judaism, thus there are Arab Jews. There are also non-Arab Jews such as French Jews, etc.

We do not view Judaism as a nationality but as a religion. We can live peacefully with the Jews and we were doing so until foreign colonial and imperial forces and the Zionist movement, the offspring of colonialism and its ally, filled Jewish society with such poisonous views and made them move in another direction. Nazism produced the same alienation from human society in the Germans. When Nazism was finished, the Germans started to live peacefully with the peoples of the world.

REMARK FROM THE AUDIENCE

Question: After attaining victory what will be the attitude of Al-Fateh to the Jews who wish to remain in Palestine, taking into consideration that numerically they may be greater than the Palestinians?

Answer: If the revolution attains victory it will apply its humane and practical principles. It is not a question of numbers and a defeat (1967). It is not a numerical but a potential, practical and revolutionary question. The victory of the revolution implies the implementation of the humanitarian principles of the Palestinian revolution. The fate of the Jewish group will be decided according to the principles of the revolution, which are humanitarian.

The Resistance[1]
How Does it Think and Act?
How Does it Face the Present?
How Does it See the Future?
[1969]

A Dialogue between Al-Fateh and Al-Talfah[2]

LUTFI AL-KHOULI: I think that it would be beneficial to start the discussion from the present state of the battle with the enemy. Can we find out something of Al-Fateh's attitude about this? Perhaps you agree with me that to know this we have to know the enemy's and our own strong and weak points. I mean in particular by "our," Palestinian, and, in more general terms, Arab.

ABU EYAD: Naturally, any scientific analysis must include both what is weak and what is strong, *i.e.*, the positive and negative. If we start the discussion with the Palestinian attitude, in Al-Fateh's opinion there are a number of positive things which have been achieved, but at the same time we do come across negative approaches.

Among the positive factors has been the coming together in guerrilla action of large effective groups. This has found expression in the Armed Struggle Command following the reorganization of the PLO. If this is able to function in an atmosphere devoid of the earlier emotionalism, it will have a great effect in unifying guerrilla action.

The Armed Struggle Command has taken the place of the Military Bureau of Coordination and the guerrilla organizations inasmuch as it is

---

1   Source: Kadi, Leila S. 1969. *Basic Political Documents of the Armed Palestinian Struggle,* Palestine Liberation Organization Research Center.

2   A dialogue between Abu Eyad, member of Al-Fateh's Central Committee; and Lutfi al-Khouli, editor-in-chief of the Egyptian monthly magazine *al-Tali'ah* in its June 1969 issue, concerning the Arab-Israeli struggle and the Palestinian resistance movement.

the real unified leadership of four large groups of the guerrilla movement, the Popular Liberation Forces, al-Sa'iqah, al-Asifah and PDFLP; if the forces of PLA are added, in accordance with the last decision of the Executive Committee of PLO, this means that 90 percent of the fighters are under the command's leadership. This is a clear indication of the participation of the revolutionary fighting groups in a national front within the framework of the PLO. In reality these positive developments have deprived the enemies of Palestinian action of the justifications with which they used to point out the strife among the Palestinian factions. But this position is still opposed—and here I want to make it clear that I am not referring to the Popular Front for the Liberation of Palestine (PFLP). For we judge that it will ultimately agree to the new formula, if it understands the reality of the situation. Since the question is not that of Al-Fateh or others dominating the leadership.

KHOULI: Would you explain what you mean by "understanding the reality of the situation?"

ABU EYAD: It's well known that PFLP's refusal to join the command is based on the principle of percentage of representation. Of course, there are some trying to exploit this to maintain the status quo and keep PFLP out of the command. Therefore they are putting forward an illusory argument that Al-Fateh and others want to monopolize the leadership and organization. Here I want to make it clear that the question is not one of monopolization but, to be exact, it is one of conformity to Palestine and Arab public opinion. Our aim is to group the largest possible number within the framework of a national front and a unified command.

KHOULI: Don't you think that it has become absolutely necessary to demand and insist on unity of action at least, if not complete unity on tactics, strategy and aims?

ABU EYAD: Exactly, we must understand that the outward differences, with regard both to the enemy and to calculations of profit and loss in building up the national front of the Palestinian people, will be ultimately eliminated if our brothers in PFLP understand the real attitude they should adopt towards the organization and the Armed Struggle Command. On the whole building up the national front through the organization, and also the unified military command for action are the essence of positivism in the present phase.

KHOULI: What about the negative aspects?

ABU EYAD: In our opinion the negative aspects are confined to the stands adopted every now and then by the small organizations, in attempts to destroy the principal forces of Palestinian action. What can I say? I think this is enough.

KHOULI: I don't think it is enough. What you are saying is very important. In my opinion the Arab people have the right to know all about this matter so that they can view from a position of awareness. It's not enough to talk in general and abstract terms because this would mean that this accusation would be without any substantiation and would not indicate who was responsible. The war of liberation cannot endure such things and we should avoid them. What have you to say?

ABU EYAD: Yes, it really is important. For example there are a few groups, such as Fateh al-Islam, who have mobilized reactionary elements under leaders who have been rejected by the Palestinian people. The aim behind Fateh al-Islam or similar organizations is the destruction of guerrilla action. They have no allegiance with the resistance movement and they were formed to support certain regimes.

KHOULI: How do you meet this situation?

ABU EYAD: If we complete the building of the front and the Armed Struggle Command and if these two occupy their true places in Palestinian action, we are sure that this abnormality will be destroyed by the convictions of the people concerned. If we don't succeed, then we will have to use other methods.

There are other negative factors connected with aid which is distributed at times, and at other times heavy conditions are put on it. In addition certain quarters attempt to link Palestinian action with the official Arab position. This entails many dangers: first, imposing a mandate by limiting financial aid unless those receiving the aid adopt the official Arab position, and at the same time isolating guerrilla action and the Palestinian revolution from the Arab masses. It is not necessary to have a tax collector who collects money from the people. But it is necessary and important that the Arab citizen should feel that he is participating in the revolution by personal contacts with the active guerrilla forces. In addition there are certain Arab regimes which are waging a psychological war concentrated against the guerrillas, and I mean Al-Fateh in particular. Believe me, and I am not saying this with any conceit or narcissism, but as a result of actual facts, they think that if they can destroy Al-Fateh, they can destroy all guerrilla action. This is because of Al-Fateh's size and popularity. The strange thing is that this campaign has grown more intense following Al-Fateh's entry into the PLO. Al-Fateh was called upon to achieve national unity as it was the basic force in Palestinian action hindering unity. Al-Fateh's duty—and this is true—was to achieve unity. This unity could have been achieved in different ways.

A national front could have been formed in which PLO could have been one of its members and not the framework of the national front as its National Charter stipulates. Al-Fateh could have overlooked this stipulation and considered PLO like any other organization such as PFLP, and then Al-Fateh would have entered the national front on the basis of full equality with PLO. Al-Fateh did not oppose this tendency, on the contrary we were ready to go along with it till the very end. However, there was a different way of viewing the question of the PLO—an objective way which took into account the interests of the Palestinian people before those of Al-Fateh. Thus, the PLO, for the first time, is considered as the representative of the official Arab commitment to the Palestinian people. Considering the PLO as a special force implies weakening it and breaking the commitment. The PLO could become the general framework of the national front, especially so because since its establishment the PLO has not had any political organization but it has had a military force—the Palestine Liberation Army, and basically the Forces of Popular Liberation.

If we had insisted on joining the PLO on the basis of the principle of equality, although such an attitude might be unrealistic, it would have paralyzed the PLO. Paralyzing the PLO implies that the equal forces should unanimously agree to enable the PLO to move or take a decision. If a unanimous agreement is not reached this implies that any small organization can veto any decision and we will be going in a vicious circle. The opinion agreed upon was that the PLO should have a steering committee, or what others call a leading force. This does not at all imply that the other organizations will lose their identity in the PLO or the national front. This is the case because what determines the taking of decisions is not the fact that the PLO has four members and Al-Fateh five members, but the size of the latter in the Palestinian field and its effects on the front.

The voice of the representative of any organization will be influenced by its actual size in the field of action. In other words if we decide to carry out a big operation, the one who decides and whose voice will have more weight is the one whose material size is effective in what it offers the operation. Thus the question put forward is not one of voting or imposing an opinion, but it is a question of what the organization in question offers and what its actual size in the field is. I believe, if good intentions, objectively and subjectively, prevail in the relations of a sound front, then it is possible for the organization whose representatives ate a minimum, in the event of their putting forward a good proposal which can be executed, to have their way adopted irrespective of other considerations.

This is the case with regard to the Palestinian position. We can summarize this by saying that there are strong positions; guerrilla action has become more popular; Palestinians are joining it in a manner which supersedes the present ability of their organizations; the size, quantity and quality of the operations are developing. I believe that the future will enable the Armed Struggle Command to adopt more positive positions and thus impose itself.

The present program which, I think, is linked with the solutions put forward for the area, is the question of the small organizations, and this is a new danger facing guerrilla action.

KHOULI: I notice that in your discussion of the negative aspects you concentrate on the phenomenon of the establishment of new resistance organizations. No doubt this is not a healthy sign and causes continuous restlessness among the Arab people who are looking forward to both the military and political unity of the Palestinian people. It is noticeable that this phenomenon comes at a time when efforts are made to establish the national front of the Palestinian people and their commando forces. These efforts have given positive results. There must be a quick and final solution to this phenomenon. Here it does not suffice to say that these organizations exist but their causes, roots and aims must be known. Would you clarify for me how Al-Fateh explains this phenomenon? How does Al-Fateh evaluate it and what is its solution?

ABU EYAD: Of course it is an unhealthy sign, and we think that it is linked, in different forms, to the internal situation of guerrilla action in order to destroy it. The method of destruction is not overt and direct, but covert and indirect. The small organizations are well-known for their intelligence. Each organization carries special slogans, as if it attempts to convince the masses that these slogans are not found among the other Palestinian groups. For example, the organization of Fateh al-Islam carries the slogan of Islam for a special and particular aim, and it attempts to point out to the masses that Al-Fateh is not Muslim or that it does not stem from Islam. Thus Fateh al-Islam appears as if it complements this missing part in the Palestinian action in accordance with its claims which are ill-founded. There are also other organizations. I referred to Fateh al-Islam because it uses the particular name Fateh. However, there are other small organizations which are founded on the basis that Al-Fateh, and other real guerrilla organizations, have a regional or unclear view of matters, and still others outbid each other in leftist claims lacking any reality.

KHOULI: To determine the size of this phenomenon, how many new organizations have been formed during *1969?*

ABU EYAD: Three organizations have been formed, one on the basis of religion, another regionalism, and the third on a leftism which makes gross claims. If we analyze this phenomenon, we notice that our people do not believe in force as a principle and basic method; especially since Palestinian action has not yet taken final form. As a result we have followed, and we are still following, the method of persuasion and direct dialogue. In our opinion the cadres of these organizations are honest but the deviation comes from the leaders. Thus it is necessary to go over the heads of the leadership and contact directly the cadres and make them understand the harm that these small organizations can inflict upon the Palestinian movement. We should not get tired of discussing with these cadres until we negate all justifications put forward by their leaders for the establishment and existence of such organizations.

KHOULI: How do you carry out this discussion?

ABU EYAD: It can be carried out through information or direct contact. It is our conviction that the revolutionary struggling youth, when they know the truth, will come back and join one of the real branches of Palestinian action which have proved their real existence in the struggle against the enemy.

KHOULI: Have you achieved any positive results in this way?

ABU EYAD: Some positive results have been achieved and more will be achieved as a result of increasing the contact and deepening it.

KHOULI: The method which you have adopted to solve the phenomenon of small organizations in the Palestinian field leads us to the following question: Why do you not use the same method with the PFLP since you consider it to be a real guerrilla organization, in order to overcome the obstacles hindering it from joining the PLO, or the national front, or the Armed Struggle Command? I believe I am right when I say that it is

Al-Fateh's responsibility to achieve this since it is the biggest organization in the Palestinian field of action?

ABU EYAD: As far as the PFLP is concerned we have always carried on a dialogue with it, and we will never disrupt it. We started the dialogue before PFLP was divided into three different groups. The first division resulted in secession of the National Liberation Front which is known as Ahmad Jibril's group. This was followed by ideological differences within the PFLP which resulted in its division into two groups. One of these groups proclaimed that it was Marxist-Leninist and was led by *al-Hurriya*[3] group and Nayef Hawatemah. It called itself the Popular Democratic Front for the Liberation of Palestine (PDFLP). The other, which also proclaims Marxism but differs in its method of application, is led by Dr. George Habash. These circumstances—the internal divisions of the PFLP—continuously—hindered the dialogue. Instead of carrying on a dialogue with PFLP with regard to its participation within the framework of Palestinian unity of action, the dialogue pertained to the resumption of talks among the two splinter groups. Frankly speaking this was a matter of great importance and took a long time.

When events took the shape of a struggle between the two groups, great effort was required from us to put an end to the resort to arms by the quarreling fighters in the streets of Amman and other places. We had to exert every effort to prohibit armed struggle among the different splinter groups of PFLP. Thus the dialogue was continuous; but it could not bring about the unity of PFLP with Al-Fateh, or PFLP's joining the Armed Struggle Command, unless the principal problem among the members of PFLP was solved. As a result, discussing the unity of PFLP took long days and nights. It is true we succeeded in hindering armed struggle; differentiating between PDFLP, PFLP which basically represents the Arab Nationalist Movement (ANM), and the Ahmad Jibril group which distinguished itself by the name of General Command.

In the first phase which took almost three months of discussion, we succeeded in differentiating between the three groups by giving them different names. Actually when the question of the last National Congress of the PLO came up, none of the PFLP members was in a position to discuss this question. Some groups in the PFLP requested the postponement of the date of the congress, others, such as Ahmad Jibril's group, requested increasing their percentage of representation, the third group,

---

3   *Al-Hurriyah* is a Beirut weekly which used to be the organ of the Arab Nationalist Movement.

namely PDFLP, rejected the principle of considering the PLO as a meeting ground for the different Palestinian organizations. Later PDFLP withdrew from its position and joined the Armed Struggle Command.

As you can see the dialogue with PFLP has never been discontinued, but has been related to questions of primary importance pertaining to the PFLP itself. In spite of all this, after matters had been settled in the PFLP and after the convening of the National Congress and the election of the new Executive Committee we undertook to contact the three branches of PFLP. PDFLP asked to join the Armed Struggle Command. The condition put forward by the Executive Committee was that PDFLP must recognize, in writing, the National Charter of the PLO. PDFLP complied with this condition and declared that it adheres to the contents of the National Charter "as a minimum program" to govern the internal relations of the Armed Struggle Command.

As far as Ahmad Jibril's group is concerned, negotiations center around an important subject of a special nature which must not be discussed now. It includes a definite attitude which needs clarification after which we decide to continue negotiations or not. As for the ANM group, the PFLP, we have contacted them through the PLO Executive Committee. All the reservations of PFLP regarding the PLO were put forward. As I understood there were no differences on the question of PFLP joining the PLO except with regard to general unspecific matters. It was agreed to prepare for another meeting to discuss specifically all these matters. Another meeting between Al-Fateh and PFLP was held to convince the latter to join, as a first step, the Armed Struggle Command, since it does not have any conditions or aspects which involve sensitive issues. The Command's field of activity is that of unified military action which is not directly linked to the PLO in its present form.

Our brothers in the PFLP declared that the nature of the composition of the National Congress must be reviewed to enable them to join the Armed Struggle Command. The implication being, as we have said before, that the meeting inside the National Congress will be granting PFLP an equal percentage along with the other organizations. As the discussion progressed to the subject of the small organizations and the method of their representation, PFLP put forward a condition that all the small organizations should have an equal percentage of representation in the congress. This brings back anew the question of the national front and its formation. On the whole the dialogue is still going on and will continue.

KHOULI: This is what we want, and we hope that you will achieve positive results through such a dialogue, the minimum of which—in my opinion—is unity of action. There are other points pertaining to the Armed Struggle Command which I would like to tackle. As I see it, this Command came after what was known as the Military Coordination Bureau. The first question is the following: Is the Armed Struggle Command, as its name implies, a more developed formula, with regard to the unity of resistance action, than the Coordination Bureau? The second question is: If the Armed Struggle Command is more advanced than the Coordination Bureau, what are the more advanced features? The third question: Is the Armed Struggle Command—in the opinion of Al-Fateh—the final step on the road to unity of action of the resistance or are there other steps, and what are they in the light of what can be published and announced?

ABU EYAD: The Armed Struggle Command is an important step on the road to the unity of guerrilla action. It is also—without any doubt—more advanced than the Coordination Bureau.

The Coordination Bureau was a committee composed of representatives from the different organizations. Also I frankly tell you, we believe that we must discuss our problems frankly, the bureau's activities were limited to coordinating relations among the guerrilla organizations and attempting to solve the problems that might arise among them. The bureau did not discuss, in any of its meetings, a military operation or plan, or a common act to be planned and executed under one leadership. Yet the different organizations, independently, carried out common operations on the battlefield in the face of the enemy's challenges.

It is true that the Coordination Bureau was a first step on the right road, yet—I believe and scientific experience has proved—it was not enough, unsatisfactory, and the wrong way to achieve a general command for armed struggle for the Palestinian people. When the new Executive Committee of the PLO was elected, it was interested in drawing up a new basis for establishing strong relations among the organizations participating in the National Congress and the leadership of the PLO. Care was taken to ensure that the leadership would not only be on paper or nominal with a flashing name, nor would it only inherit the Coordination Bureau. It must be a real leadership in action for all the participating groups in the leadership.

As we know any action must be studied in detail and objectively: firstly, the reality and the potentialities; secondly, a plan should be drawn up on the basis of this reality and these potentialities; and thirdly, the actual execution of this plan. It can be said that we have almost completed the first two steps and we are embarking on the third.

KHOULI: Can we understand from the above-mentioned that we are on the verge of carrying out common resistance actions in which all the forces of the organizations who have joined the PLO participate under the unified leadership of the Armed Struggle Command?

ABU EYAD: Yes. There will be common training in the operations under a unified leadership in which side by side the fighters of al-'Asifah, PLA, al-Sa'iqah and PDFLP will participate. All the fighters will carry out common operations according to a unified system of allocation, ability, sufficiency, and work conditions. This means that at times—and within the framework of the plan—a group, from *e.g.*, al-'Asifah, would be chosen to carry out a definite operation, or a group from al-Sa'iqah and al-'Asifah, or al-'Asifah and the Popular Liberation Forces, etc. In other words operations would be carried out according to what the leadership sees fit from the point of view of training, sufficiency, experience with the land, etc.

I am not telling a secret when I say that the Armed Struggle Command will start its activities at an important level in the near future.

And I do not tell a secret when I say that the latest "Himmah" operation was carried out according to plans drawn up by the Armed Struggle Command, in spite of the fact that al-'Asifah forces carried it out alone, yet the planning for the operation resulted from a new way of thinking among the members of the Armed Struggle Command.

KHOULI: I notice that you have used the expression "new way of thinking" with regard to the planning of the "Himmah" operation. Does it imply that this operation represents—in your opinion—a new development in resistance action?

ABU EYAD: There is no doubt that the Himmah operation represents a point of departure and a new development in guerrilla action.

KHOULI: How?

ABU EYAD: As you know, our commando action remained limited to the general classical theory of guerrilla warfare "hit and run." In spite of the necessity of adhering to this general theory, especially in the early stages of guerrilla action, we have actually carried out a kind of limited confrontation with the enemy in certain phases which were not dominated by the theory of "hit and run." An example of such a confrontation, on a wide scale proportionally speaking, is the Israeli aggression on al-Karameh in March 1968. After al-Karameh we carried out other operations of the nature of limited confrontation such as that of Wadi al-Qilt and others.

These limited confrontations were an introduction to the Himmah operation. What does the latter operation mean? It means the occupation of a post under the control of the enemy for a limited period to clear it of the enemy forces and their capabilities. Thus with the Himmah operation we are embarking on a new phase of guerrilla warfare, namely, occupying certain positions and completely clearing them of enemy forces. Of course, we choose these posts very carefully and according to very complicated considerations in order to inflict the heaviest losses on the enemy in addition to the political, military, economic, and psychological effects that will result in the enemy front.

In turn this phase is a preparation for the next one, namely, the permanent occupation of the enemy posts. Such a phase will start after we complete the movement of our bases into the occupied territories, when the act of organic link becomes total, deep, and moves effectively among all the forces inside the occupied territories.

KHOULI: Does it mean control of "liberated areas" as known in guerrilla warfare?

ABU EYAD: Exactly.

KHOULI: There is no doubt that if the resistance was capable of taking "liberated areas" from the enemy by force then it would enter the phase of total liberation. But allow me, since we have agreed to face our problems frankly, to ask a question. The question takes into consideration what has been reiterated by observers, foreign correspondents and Israeli sources that Israel has been successful in combating the resistance movement's operations as a result of its use of electronic devices and electric wire in certain occupied areas. Moreover, Israel has discovered many cells of the resistance movement inside the occupied territories. I am sure that this news is exaggerated for psychological reasons, yet it is true that electronic devices and electric wires have been set up and that a number of cells have been discovered by the enemy. Thus the question is to what extent has this actually affected commando operations and the required development toward the phase of liberated areas that we have talked about? Naturally, historical experiments have proved to us that the progressive resistance movements have been confronted with these difficulties and finally have been able to overcome them.

ABU EYAD: Naturally, not everything the enemy or foreign observers say is true. Exaggerations are made on purpose for psychological effects.

Yet honesty and responsibility require us to say that some of what is said is true. We do not deny or hide this fact; on the contrary we face it and try to overcome it. We cannot compare our human, technical and military capabilities when we embarked upon the armed struggle before the June 1967 war with our present state of readiness. What I want to point out is that we are aware of the enemy's strength and capabilities, especially since the experience of imperialism in the area is put at its disposal. The enemy benefits from Nazism and the American experience in Vietnam. We all know that Dayan[4] stayed with the American army in Vietnam to benefit from its experience there in confronting the Vietnamese Liberation Army and guerrilla warfare. In addition the enemy acquires new weapons all the time, and benefits from the colonialist experts in combating popular armed resistance all over the world. As a result we are facing an enemy which has well-developed education, technique, and experience. Thus, we are aware that the resistance movement must have these three basic conditions.

I would like to raise the complicated question of Arab support of the resistance movement. The latter now depends solely on itself, in the sense that the Arab mentality, education and experience are far from actually and effectively participating in solving the problems that they face. They are now called upon to participate in Palestinian resistance. For example, the electronic line and the fortifications which Israel has set up along the borders, the narrowness of our land, the regulations pertaining to the occupied territories such as dividing Palestine into security zones. The first thing that Israel has done in the West Bank and the other occupied territories is to open roads to make it easier for its security units to move quickly to any area where a clash or a guerrilla operation takes place. This is the reason behind the quick movement of Israelis and not the result of the strength of its intelligence services. I can affirm here, from experience and with total responsibility, that the rumors about the strength of the Israeli intelligence services is a myth. Israel is not particularly advanced in its intelligence as such. But this is not to deny the fact that it benefits from the simple information it gets and immediately diffuses it among its

---

4   Ed. Note: Moshe Dayan (1915-1981), minister of defense of "Israel" from 1967-1974. Prior to this he had been in Vietnam observing U.S. tactics and operations.

units to get the full benefit from it.

The truth that we must stress here is that the resistance movement is in need of Arab support on the level of education and technical experience in order to confront and defeat the well-advanced Israeli education and experience.

KHOULI: Naturally this is the duty of all the educational establishments and technical experts in the Arab world. In this connection the resistance movement could have its technical experience bureau composed of Arab volunteer scientists and experts. But you have not answered my definite question pertaining to the effect of the electronic devices and electric wires on guerrilla action. What is the extent of their effect? And does it greatly prohibit the entry to the occupied territories?

ABU EYAD: No it does not. Naturally it has affected the entry, and thus we changed our tactics. We still enter the occupied territories, the proof is the daily operations of our forces inside the occupied territories.

Here I would like to point out a fact which you have always referred to in your articles, namely, the exaggerations in the resistance movement's communiqués with regard to its operations. What is the source and reality of the exaggeration? Actually exaggeration is absent in the communiqué issued by Al-Fateh or the Armed Struggle Command when they carry out an operation. But exaggeration results from the totality of communiqués issued by the big and small organizations together.

I shall give you a live example. In the Jordan Valley every week five or six tanks are actually blown up by the principal organizations. Yet every small organization claims these operations for itself. If the minimum number of these organizations is six or seven, the total number of tanks blown up according to the communiqués will be at least 24. This is the basis of the regrettable exaggeration. You as an Arab citizen sense the general exaggeration in the military communiqués of the principal organizations. Yet these communiqués tell the truth without exaggeration or falsification.

KHOULI: How do you calculate the losses of the enemy resulting from the operations you carry out? I recall that during a discussion with Ché Guevara in 1965, he declared that calculating the real losses of the enemy is one of the most difficult problems of any armed resistance movement or guerrilla warfare.

ABU EYAD: This is true. That is why in Al-Fateh—and maybe you noticed it—we decided not to specify the total number of the losses of the enemy in al-'Asifah communiqués prior to its joining the Armed Struggle Command. That is, we said a number of men were killed and wounded. In spite of the fact that it is a standard expression, its effect on the Arab citizen is lighter than saying we have killed 10 or 20 and wounded 30 or 40. It was also agreed in the Armed Struggle Command not to specify the number of the killed and wounded although we are often sure of the real numbers. This does not hinder us from evaluating the actual losses of the enemy in every operation we carry out, and that is based on the reports of the fighters who have participated in it. Each fighter submits to his command a detailed report on the operation and the losses; an average then is calculated from the reports. These precautions are taken to avoid exaggeration. We know that our people are sensitive with regard to this point.

KHOULI: Now permit me to shift the discussion to another point which, in my opinion, is very important. How does Al-Fateh conceive of the relationship between military and political action? In other words how does it conceive of the military and political leadership, and which directs the other? Who takes the decisions? Who has the final say when differences arise *vis-à-vis* main issues? Perhaps you are aware of the accusations directed against Al-Fateh that its activities are limited to the military field without linking them to definite political viewpoints of definite programs and organized popular mobilization of the Palestinian people. Such a criticism—in my opinion—is very important and we need to know your opinion of it, especially as Al-Fateh was the first organization to embark upon armed struggle in the Palestinian field.

I hope that in answering this question you will clarify the following points: Firstly, how was Al-Fateh organized, or what are the objective conditions which resulted in the adoption of the line of armed struggle? Secondly, does Al-Fateh believe that armed struggle is an end in itself, a strategic aim, or one method among others in its struggle? If it is one method how does it relate to the others? Thirdly...

ABU EYAD: One by one.

KHOULI: Don't you think that it is better to give you a comprehensive idea about the subject?

ABU EYAD: It is so. But the second point of your question pertaining to armed struggle as an end in itself or a method needs clarification.

KHOULI: I mean, does Al-Fateh in viewing the methods of struggle against Zionism and its Israeli entity end with armed struggle alone, or does it consider that other methods alongside armed struggle are necessary and vital for its direction? Thus what leads Al-Fateh: military thinking or comprehensive political thinking equipped with different kinds of experience among which is military experience?

ABU EYAD: Understood. Actually Al-Fateh is a reaction to a totality of Arab circumstances, error of Arab politics and Arab parties. This had led a great number of the Palestinian youth to realize that partisanship, dissipation, and fragmentation are not the road that will lead to the solution of their problem. This was a strange phenomenon in the fifties. In those days you rarely found a Palestinian who was not affiliated to a party or a political movement, and those who were not were considered a burden on society and were not respected. The affiliations of the Palestinian youth tanged from the extreme right to the extreme left. Some of them thought that religious affiliation could solve their problem. Others thought that communism could achieve this end. A third group adopted a nationalist line, namely, the nationalist parties represented in the Ba'th Party and later in the Arab Nationalist Movement (ANM), the movement which erupted on the basis of revenge, blood, iron, and fire. A group of this youth who have joined the above-mentioned parties and movements, and were unable to discover the road to liberate their homeland, actually withdrew as a result of the awareness they acquired from their membership in these parties and movements. It might not be correct to claim that the withdrawal pertained to the thought but it was from partisan affiliations which, in their view, could not achieve any positive results. The world is suffering from the experiences that are tearing the left to pieces.

We hear of the left of the left, and a third left might erupt. These were the objective conditions. Actually they are the conditions of the Arab homeland which is boiling with restlessness. In the early stages this feeling of restlessness was expressed by the Palestinian people through the formation of a great number of secret organizations. It can be said that the victory of the Algerian revolution played a great role in this thinking when the Palestinian youth felt that they were as capable as their Algerian brothers; that they, too, were capable of raising the slogan of armed struggle and putting it into effect. Yet the totality of the Arab circumstances was against this slogan and its application. Thus the Palestinian youth had no choice but to take refuge in secret action. There was a conviction that the aim behind the establishment of the PLO was to absorb the faith which began to spread among the Palestinian people and express the feeling of true restlessness and belief in building up a Palestinian national revolutionary movement. In short the attempt to establish the PLO at the beginning was to abort the true feeling of revolutionary restlessness. This was the reason behind our objection to the PLO at the beginning. It was imposed from above and represented a super-structure. The people did not create it. Under these circumstances we began to think of secret Palestinian action. Of course secrecy has its shortcomings and its advantages. If we analyze a great number of these organizations we find that they are part of a plan to strike at the true revolutionary movements. A number of Arab embassies established such organizations. Palestinian personalities whose historical role had ended at a certain stage also established organizations. At the same time a number of Arab parties attempted to establish secret organizations in order not to be outdone by the true revolutionary organizations. Al-Fateh's thought realized that words are of no use and serious and practical struggle must be carried out even with meager resources. This is how we started.

KHOULI: At this starting point what was Al-Fateh, and who was Al-Fateh?

ABU EYAD: At that time Al-Fateh represented a group of Palestinian youth who had revolted against existing conditions as exemplified by the divisions among the Arab states, especially after Syria's secession from the UAR,[5] and by the failure of the Arab parties to take up any struggle. The youth, who have lived through this experience, established Al-Fateh.

KHOULI: What is the social background of these youth who have organized Al-Fateh and led it? I think that they are basically middle class educated Palestinians.

ABU EYAD: Of course they are basically educated Palestinians who wanted to open up the road and change these conditions. In order to accomplish such a change they had to carry out armed struggle, which depended on meager resources.

I will not be telling a secret if I say that at that time there were two viewpoints. One believed that it was impossible to embark on armed struggle until Al-Fateh's popular and military roots had become stronger so that its strength and continuity could be ensured. The other believed that armed struggle must begin even with the minimum resources, as these, through action, would develop, become stronger and deep rooted. The latter viewpoint was the one that was adopted.

Like any other true revolutionary action, in its early stages Al-Fateh was strongly attacked. The nature of the attack depended on the circum-

---

5   **Ed. Note:** United Arab Republic—Syria seceded in 1958.

stances of each of the Arab states. The Arab progressive circles considered Al-Fateh as a reactionary movement. The Arab reactionary circles accused Al-Fateh of being communist and Marxist.

KHOULI: In reality it was...?

ABU EYAD: This is a secret which only God knows. On the whole a decision was taken to start the armed struggle in spite of the limited resources.

Actually prior to the start of military action, we published a simple magazine, [*Our Palestine*]. It used to express the view of the members without bluntly mentioning Al-Fateh or al-'Asifah. When this magazine declared that the Palestinian people must have an independent entity with a will and a personality of its own, we were faced with another accusation—that we were regionalists. This accusation came from the national parties. Of course they began to review their stand with regard to this question. We were also accused of Nazism and Fascism. We realized the necessity of proving ourselves to the Palestinian and Arab people by undertaking a national progressive armed action that would lead them to liberation. As I have already said, the viewpoint favoring the start of military operations won in spite of limited resources, and this coincided with the establishment of the PLO.

KHOULI: Before we move to another subject, would you permit me to inquire about the financial sources of Al-Fateh in this early stage that enabled it to embark on its military operations. There is no doubt, however limited were the resources, that the question of financing is relevant.

ABU EYAD: Al-Fateh was financed by its Palestinian members. In reality, and because of our desire for secrecy, we decided not to take one penny except from members of Al-Fateh. We can now declare—and it is no longer a secret—we aspired to technical work and activity in rich Arab oil areas such as the Arab Gulf. This might have also resulted in surrounding Al-Fateh with a special atmosphere. This did not frighten us because our aim was to secure total self-dependence for the revolutionary movement especially so with regard to financing. The members used to deprive themselves of the simple things which one can buy in the Gulf area, in order to save as much as they could from their salaries for the movement; a minimum of half the salary or more than that.

Before embarking on military action—now we can announce this secret—we levied a heavy tax on all our members which they paid to a special fund. Those who did not have the required sum had to borrow it. The reason behind this step was to secure for the families of those who die in the military operations financial assistance in case the movement fails. We deposited this fund with certain trustworthy Palestinian personalities to be responsible for the distribution of the money.

KHOULI: Al-Fateh started the armed struggle in January 1963. Is this true?

ABU EYAD: Yes, on 1 January 1963.

KHOULI: Can we know something about the first military operation of Al-Fateh? Precisely what was its aim militarily and politically speaking?

ABU EYAD: The first operation was a confrontation with an Israeli armed patrol. Actually the second operation of Al-Fateh was of value. Its aim was to attack the installations set up to divert the Jordan River. As you know, the basic issue in 1963 was the diversion of the Jordan River and for this purpose the Arab summit conferences were convened. We held the view that through the diversion issue we could erupt the beginnings of the Palestinian revolution. A revolution which can continue and leave its effective landmarks on the Zionist, racist, imperialist presence in our homeland; and thus develop the partial issue, namely that of diversion, into a whole—that of liberation—by blowing up the Israeli diversion operations with our limited potentialities. We carried out this operation in which the first fighter of al-'Asifah, Mahmoud Hijazi, was captured. He was tortured and imprisoned. He was captured because his gun was rusty and was of no use to him.

Also in this operation our first martyr, Ahmad Musa, was killed not by the enemy bullets, but by those of an Arab upon his return after the operation was carried out. The groups which entered the occupied territories were given orders not to shoot the Arab soldiers under any circumstances, even if the latter fired on them. The aims behind this were that a commando must not kill an Arab even if he were defending himself, and that guerrilla action must express the tragedy of the Palestinian people.

KHOULI: What were the reactions to your first operation?

ABU EYAD: The truth is that we felt that the Palestinian and Arab people reacted positively to our action, with the exception of a few groups and individuals. Some of these attacked us directly, such as certain Arab news papers which accused the commandos of being agents of CENTO[6] in

---

6   **Ed. Note:** The Central Treaty Organization (CENTO) was a Cold War military alliance. Originally named the Middle East Treaty Organization (METO) and also recognized as the Baghdad Pact, it was established in 1955, by Iran, Iraq, Pakistan, Turkey, and the United Kingdom, CENTO dissolved on March 16, 1979.

the area.

Others directly admitted that such action is good and beneficial but reprimanded it for not having coordinated its activities with the progressive Arab states before embarking on it. Yet others requested the implementation of a common plan between the commandos and the Arab states at that time. A third group said that the timing was wrong. And a fourth said that these are one or two adventurous operations and such action has no future. Yet the operations continued and the communiqués too. Those who carried the attack against guerrilla action were silenced and the people began to reciprocate on a larger scale. Yet at the same time obstacles in the face of Al-Fateh and its movement began to increase. In addition to limited arms the national organized forces did not support the armed struggle of Al-Fateh, contrary to expectations.

The majority of the Arab governments were against Al-Fateh. This hostility was expressed in several ways. The Unified Arab Command, for example, recommended and gave orders, which we now possess, requesting the Arab governments to discourage the commandos and not to broadcast or publish any military operation of al-'Asifah forces.

KHOULI: What do you think was the aim behind that?

ABU EYAD: I believe that the aim was not to link the masses with the armed struggle by knowing about it, so that they would take it as their own and assist it. To be fair you should mention that certain Arab newspapers tried to publish the Israeli communiqués about our operations when they were incapable of publishing the military communiqués of Al-Fateh.

Of course we did not keep quiet in face of this wall of silence. We tried to penetrate it by issuing secret publications which were distributed all over the Arab world. In spite of the great number of pamphlets that were distributed, as regards the Arab homeland, it was still limited.

KHOULI: In your estimation when was the wall of silence removed, before or after the June 1967 defeat?

ABU EYAD: It was removed in 1966 at the time of the Israeli aggression against al-Samu' village. The Jordanian people strongly expressed their support of guerrilla action and called for freedom for such action. The country witnessed large and spontaneous demonstrations which expressed the consciousness of the people. The national and progressive forces could not understand these demonstrations and did not have a unified program to reap their advantages. That was the reason behind the failure of the demonstrations, and guerrilla action was subjected to more severe persecution and counter-propaganda through press conferences and broadcasting services pointing out that the subject of commandos does not pertain solely to Jordan but to a general Arab attitude in accordance with the decisions of the Arab Unified Command. Of course this command was exploited in an organized manner because it included, in addition to Jordan, certain Arab progressive regimes at the time.

The most important result was that the wall of silence surrounding guerrilla action was broken. The number of people who were arrested in Jordan was great. They were not all from Al-Fateh, but included every nationalist who was accused of being a member of Al-Fateh, or a guerrilla, or a supporter of guerrilla action.

KHOULI: What happened after the June defeat?

ABU EYAD: The defeat has resulted in a feeling of bewilderment among the Arab masses who have refused, at the same time, to surrender. The six-day war did not end with the Israeli victory on 10 June, because on the second day al-'Asifah men attacked the occupied territories for the first time after the defeat. The value of carrying out military action on 11 June was to overcome the feeling of despair and bewilderment, and manifest the determination of the Arab people in general and the Palestinian people in particular not to surrender and to carry on the war against the enemy.

Following that, our fighting patrols increased their visits into Palestine. I will not be telling a secret if I disclose that the great majority of Al-Fateh leaders entered the occupied territories, in addition to those who were there already, to organize the popular Palestinian resistance movement. Such an operation was not easy at the beginning and we met many difficulties. For example, it was difficult to train fighters under occupation in spite of absolute secrecy. The enemy's ability to move its intelligence services was quick at a time when our intelligence services had not yet been trained actively to confront that of the enemy as is the case now. As a result the enemy was able to discover, every now and then, some of our training cells in the mountains. The enemy used to attack these cells fiercely, and the commandos, at that time, were not yet able to hit back effectively because they had primitive weapons. Consequently a number of them were killed during training.

KHOULI: Without interfering with military secrets how did you then face the problem of modern arms?

ABU EYAD: The set-back, in spite of its bitterness, has helped us in solving the problem of armament. After the defeat we sent special patrols to the battlefields of the occupied territories with one aim, namely, to collect the largest amount possible of the arms left behind by the Arab armies. We can bluntly say that Al-Fateh took amounts of arms from the occupied Arab territories after the defeat which superseded, qualitatively and quantitatively, the arms it possessed throughout the earlier period of its struggle, even after the Arab states' recognition of Palestinian resistance and its struggle. This was our main source of armament.

KHOULI: But the need for arms is continually increasing in proportion to the growth of the resistance movement's operations. Naturally other sources must be found. Yet, in accordance with the historical experiments of the resistance movements, an important source is the enemy itself. Have you taken this into consideration? If the answer is yes, what is the approximate ratio?

ABU EYAD: Our basic emphasis was on training. The enemy's arms is a basic principle in guerrilla warfare. This was, still is, and will continue to be a part of our evaluation. But, in order to be realistic, I should declare that we consider the amount of arms captured from the enemy far below the required quantity. It does not form more than 10 percent of our arms. Naturally such a percentage is double what it was once. We have taken this into account.

KHOULI: With your permission, let us go back to the general trend of the conversation. How did you face the complex situation directly after the defeat?

ABU EYAD: Our basic emphasis was on guerrilla warfare training, on the one hand, and reorganizing the cells which had existed during the Arab rule, I mean in Jordan, and establishing new cells to confront the requirements of the new situation after the whole of Palestine had fallen under the Israeli occupation. The number of people who joined the resistance movement was greater than expected, and the enthusiasm of the people enhanced our activity. We can say that the phase of training and organization of cells was completed precisely, on 29 August 1967, and a new phase of organized resistance operations on a grand scale was embarked upon.

KHOULI: Why specifically 29 August 1967?

ABU EYAD: Prior to this date we had completed a great deal of training. We had organized our main cells and moved the largest amount of arms possible from the Arab occupied territories.

Here I would like to clarify an important point. We could have postponed the starting of organized resistance on a wide scale for a few weeks after 29 August in order to complete the training of the greatest number, enlarge our cells, develop more and make more than one level of our organizations politically aware, but we were forced to start our operations on that date in Jerusalem, Tul Kann, and other places.

KHOULI: Why?

ABU EYAD: For a number of important considerations. First, it was not healthy from the political, military, and psychological points of view to freeze the organizations and the fighters after the degree of training we had reached. Second, freezing with no movement made us more vulnerable to dangers. Third, the enemy began to sense and hear about a number of our secret bases.

For these reasons we decided to strike so that the enemy could not surprise us with a counter-attack. Actually we started, and Al-Fateh continued, to fight alone until December 1967. Our brothers in PFLP started their armed struggle in the first half of January 1968. Of course following that date the operations continued and the establishment of small organizations continued until we reached the situation which I have discussed earlier. These are, as far as can be published, the principal points with regard to the formation, ideology, and action of Al-Fateh.

KHOULI: Permit me here, before we proceed to another subject, to ask a question; How was the decision taken to start organized resistance on 29 August 1967? Who took the final decision? In other words, was this decision adopted on political grounds and a comprehensive analysis of the situation or was it taken on military grounds to prevent a counter-attack by the enemy and to unfreeze the cells and fighters? Who took the decision: the political leadership or the fighters? If it is possible I hope that the answer will cover a more detailed definition of the relationship between political action and military action in Al-Fateh?

ABU EYAD: I am grateful for being given the opportunity through this question to explain Al-Fateh's understanding of such an important question. Evidently you are aware of the accusation that Al-Fateh is only interested in military action; that it is composed of a group of adventurers— and this was actually said—who are only interested in hitting, killing and frightening the enemy; and that Al-Fateh is a prisoner of this traditional circle which it cannot overcome to indulge in political activities.

I am still unaware of the reasons on the basis of which such an accusation is made. Is it possible that military action in an armed resistance, a guerrilla warfare, or a liberating movement be separated from political action? On the whole we in Al-Fateh clearly recognize that military action is of no value if it does not serve a political program and is not a part of a comprehensive political plan. The first nucleus of Al-Fateh was formed on a political basis which rejected a specific political situation and developed its own political beliefs, which they believed, and still believe, will lead to the accomplishment of their aim. Out of the political attitude of Al-Fateh emerged the military action of the armed resistance movement as a concrete manifestation of such a line. Military action follows Al-Fateh's political orientation. We thus believe that we have placed political action in its right place. We in Al-Fateh struggle in the political and military fields. Either one of these two fields serves the other within the general framework of the strategic plan of Al-Fateh. Thus we do not separate or distinguish between political and military action. To ensure the implementation of such a policy we do not admit to the armed struggle movement any fighter unless he is recommended by the political organization.

KHOULI: Does this imply that all the fighters in al-'Asifah have been members in the political organization of Al-Fateh and the latter has recommended them for military action?

ABU EYAD: This is the principle we follow and apply. But in order to be honest with you, there have been exceptions to this rule for special reasons and on the basis of our political evaluation. I do not deny that in spite of the fact that we have been forced to do so and it has erased us some trouble which I cannot divulge and discuss right now. Yet such an exception has strengthened our belief in the necessity to adhere to the general rule, namely, that a member in Al-Fateh is in the first place political and in the second a fighter. The exception took place in the first difficult phase of the development of Al-Fateh, following the defeat, when we were forced to accept volunteers for direct fighting without their passing through the membership of its political organization. Almost two months after the battle of al-Karameh we reapplied the general rule, now no fighter is accepted unless he is recommended by the political organization. This clarifies the point that the political organization and mentality is at the head.

KHOULI: A question for clarification. For example, when an operation is thought of, the fighting unit might have an idea ... Can its military leadership carry it out directly or has it to discuss its political implications in addition to the military ones? Thus will the final decision be taken by the political leadership?

ABU EYAD: It might be helpful if I answer this question by giving you a specific example which up till now has been a secret. When we decided to embark on organized armed resistance on a wide scale, our brothers inside the occupied territories demanded that it should start on 20 August 1967, yet those who were outside the occupied territories thought otherwise. What did we do? We called all of the political leaders, including those of the occupied territories such as Abu 'Imad, in order to discuss carefully the problem from both the political and military points of view. We requested the leadership inside the occupied territories to postpone starting operations until the leadership took a decision. The discussions lasted for nine days and it was decided to start military operations. For that reason operations started on 29 August. This explains that we do not carry out military action except in the light of comprehensive political orientation.

Operations carried out by the resistance movement are military in nature yet they are political and have definite political aims. If they were simple military operations, then they would become demagogic and the work of adventurers. These false impressions might have resulted from our emphasis, in the face of the political circumstances, that our method in the struggle is that of armed struggle. Will you be amazed if I tell you that in Al-Fateh there is no professional military man or leader. There is no fighter in Al-Fateh who is not a university student, an engineer, nationalist intellectual, or a worker. We do not have classical military men. Some people considered this situation a short-coming which Al-Fateh should be criticized for. Our differences with some of our brothers in the Palestine Liberation Army (PLA) pertained to this point. They used to ask us: Where are the officers? Where are the lieutenants? Where are the captains? We told them that we are fighting a war of liberation in which the fighters and the leaders learnt the tactics of war from the war itself. Unless they become an army and a leadership, a true and active force through practicing and leading armed struggle over a long period and according to plan. We do not have a military leader who is a graduate of a military college. All the leaders were trained during the war and learnt the art of war from the war with the enemy, itself.

In the general command of Al-Fateh, within the central committee, there is a distribution of responsibility. There are colleagues who have political responsibilities and others military. Yet all of them represent one unit. In 1963, when we started our activity, we issued a political statement; and in 1967 we did the same.

1 would like to take this opportunity to clarify one point, in Al-Fateh there is nothing in the name of the military wing as reported by the newspapers and broadcasting services.

KHOULI: How is this? What about al-'Asifah?

ABU EYAD: This is precisely the point. How did the word al-'Asifah emerge? The principle and only thing we have is Al-Fateh. Yet when we embarked upon our military operations in January 1963, the majority of those who attended the congress which we called for this purpose supported the view that operations should be started. The minority which opposed this view suggested that operations should be carried out under another name so that if they fail, Al-Fateh would not be affected. Consequently we used the name of al-'Asifah. We did not announce that al-'Asifah was actually Al-Fateh except after the 10th military communiqué and the success of the operations. We decided to continue the use of the name al-'Asifah since it has become a historic one, but in reality Al-Fateh and al-'Asifah are synonymous.

KHOULI: Can we know something about the organization of Al-Fateh, the nature of the relationship between the commandos on different levels from the base to the top, if it is not to be kept secret?

ABU EYAD: The organizational structure of Al-Fateh is actually a secret. Yet I would like to assure you that relationships have developed, since the secret development of Al-Fateh, from a narrow form of centralization into a revolutionary democracy governed by specific organizational regulations to which all members adhere from the base to the top.

KHOULI: There is another point. I have noticed through my contact with you that you are all careful in portraying the nature of collective leadership in Al-Fateh. Then you decided to appoint Abu 'Ammar as the official spokesman of Al-Fateh. What is the principle idea behind this decision and how does it reflect itself on the principle of collective leadership and its implementation?

ABU EYAD: As you have pointed out, collective leadership is a basic and essential principle of Al-Fateh. This conclusion was not reached as a result of being outwardly fascinated by revolutionary expressions, but as a result of the suffering that we and our youth have gone through. Individualism was one of the causes of failure, hesitancy, etc.. The principle of collectivism, especially with regard to leadership, expressed our extreme reaction against the principle of individualism in all its forms. Al-Fateh may have succeeded in maintaining its unity and cohesiveness as a result of its adherence to the principle of collectivism. Al-Fateh was originally a secret movement and its leaders were unknown. Their names remained secret. If it were not for the necessity of personal contacts to carry on the work, none of its members would have been publicly known. We were forced to announce a number of the names of its members. A section of our leadership, who might be better and more virtuous than those of us whose names are known, remains secret. Moreover, the widening scope of action and responsibilities compelled us to put forward to the masses an official responsible man. This is especially so since in Beirut pamphlets and communiqués began to be issued in the name of Al-Fateh, at a time when it had nothing to do with them and they did not express its point of view. Who could stand up and declare publicly to the people in the name of Al-Fateh what belonged to it and what did not? There was no one.

Moreover, the Israeli broadcasting service and press began to stress the name of Abu 'Ammar as one of the leaders of Al-Fateh in the occupied territories. In addition he was a commando who carried both political and military responsibilities. At one of its meetings the leadership chose him as the official spokesman of Al-Fateh. He was not present at the meeting and knew of the decision as others did. There is a special reason for choosing Abu 'Ammar, besides other reasons pertaining to his long standing struggle, and that is of us all he is the least garrulous. Actually the idea was to announce three names as the official spokesmen of Al-Fateh, but they all refused. Since Abu 'Ammar was the only absent one, he was chosen. The decision was announced publicly and he could not but accept. Evidently any member of a liberation movement prefers secrecy, unless it is necessary to act otherwise. You are aware of the difficulties we encountered in nominating colleagues of ours in the leadership to the executive committee of the PLO in its new form, because this implied the disclosure of their names. Thus, there is no relationship between nominating Abu 'Ammar as the official spokesman of the movement and the collective leadership. It was merely an answer to urgent necessities.

KHOULI: You explained in your discussion that military action is subject to and in the service of the political programs of Al-Fateh, can we know the main characteristics of these programs?

ABU EYAD: We cannot discuss the political programs of Al-Fateh without including the objective circumstances pertaining to its establishment and through which it operates. Generally speaking, it is a national liberation movement which works for the realization of the Palestinian people's potentialities through their armed struggle for the liberation of all of Palestine from the imperialism of Zionist colonization. Al-Fateh has declared from the start that it is a national liberation movement. This implies that Al-Fateh considers itself to be a part of the whole Arab revolution, the signs of which are beginning to appear in certain parts of the Arab homeland. Moreover, Al-Fateh considers itself to be a part of the progressive world movement against imperialism, in spite of the fact that the actual conscious application of this clear political content is limited to Palestine. This is caused by objective circumstances which are known to the Arab citizen.

Al-Fateh is criticized, and this may indirectly shed some light on its political line, because it calls only for the liberation of the land and does not tackle the problem of man and society. We say that this is nonsense. Liberation of the land cannot be achieved except through the liberation of man. A revolution cannot raise the banner of liberation and practice the method of armed struggle, unless it is a progressive revolution. We have never heard in the history of the world of a rightist who carried arms in the face of imperialism. In other words, since Al-Fateh, at the phase of its formation, admitted and accepted grouping all of the Palestinian youth who were engulfed in Arab politics and were members of different parties in order to express their sufferings as Palestinian refugees, it opened the way, without complications, for this youth to reconsider their unproductive political activity and practice productive, effective and armed political activity. Al-Fateh opened the door for the youth who believed in the theories and ideology which might belong to this front or that, to group them within the framework of armed struggle. Armed struggle purifies the soul, wipes out sensitivity and makes them follow a truly revolutionary progressive course of action. Thus Al-Fateh from the beginning was interested in grouping people from the extreme right to the extreme left. Through interaction within the revolution and through armed struggle the true revolutionary youth will emerge.

KHOULI: What were the conditions for their joining Al-Fateh?

ABU EYAD: The Palestinian youth had to dissociate themselves from their ideologies and party affiliations and believe in liberation. This was the basic condition. At this point we should differentiate between strategy and tactics. The past and present announcements of Al-Fateh may be considered as a tactic more than a long-range strategy. For example, the question of non-interference in the internal affairs of the Arab states to which Al-Fateh is committed has aroused criticism such as that of being a rightist slogan. I believe that this slogan is, objectively speaking, sound. It requires of Al-Fateh to be disinterested in who is the prime minister of this state or that. In reality there is an interconnection between Palestinian action and Arab action, and for this reason we have always declared that we are part of the Arab revolution. From where did this interconnection stem?

We believe that the progressive slogans of the Arab nation cannot be achieved except through the war of Palestine and its liberation. Even socialism and unity cannot be achieved except through a true war of liberation of Palestine because Arab efforts are of necessity directed to that course of action. This is the case irrespective of whether such production is fruitful or not yet. The most important thing is that Arab efforts in the field of production must be directed to the war of liberation. How can we build an advanced social life in our countries at a time when all our material efforts (money and means of production) are channeled towards the war machine against the aggressive colonialist enemy? From here the slogan of non-interference in the internal affairs of the Arab states stems. It does not imply non-interference between the Arab states and Palestine. Thus it helps in bringing the objective circumstances of the Palestinian Liberation movement to fruition by grouping the Arab forces with no diversionary side issues. At the same time it creates a revolutionary atmosphere along the Arab borders with Israel and among the Arab people living near the borders. Such a revolutionary atmosphere may spread all over the Arab world. Thus Arab hopes and progressive thoughts will be achieved through a revolutionary atmosphere along the Arab borders with Israel and among the Arab people living near these borders. Such a revolutionary atmosphere may spread all over the Arab world. Thus Arab hopes and progressive thoughts will be achieved through a real war inside Palestine itself. If it is necessary to give examples, we can take Jordan or Lebanon in which the national and progressive forces, irrespective of their differences, can move. Another example is the idea put forward by some that the "petit bourgeoisie" has failed and does not have the right to struggle. Al-Fateh has by-passed these matters as a result of its experiences. It said that every Palestinian has the right to participate in the war of liberation, but the leadership of Palestinian action must be in the hands of honorable national people who will not sell or bargain or transfer this action for the benefit of any reactionary forces. The leadership could limit action to a certain class. But such action is not the privilege of any one class, in addition it would weaken the liberation movement. There are classes and groups which were not known at the time of Karl Marx. Did Karl Marx discuss the question of the class of refugees that has emerged among the Palestinian people? The refugee was a laborer working in his country but now is unemployed. There are refugees who were peasants but now are unable to do this work. How can we evaluate this and that. Evidently there is a class of refugees that imposes itself upon us and cannot be defined according to classical lines even if they were revolutionary. This is what we are facing openly and fearlessly.

There are some who criticize Al-Fateh for not adopting a Marxist-Leninist course, or something similar that is defined as progressive. I say that if we ask those who are at present propagating such a course what their background was and former practices were, we find that they are very firm Marxist-Leninists. Al-Fateh, which has not declared that it is a Marxist-Leninist movement, was the first to undertake armed struggle, offered martyrs, and opened the long way for the war of liberation. Uttering words is not enough. Action is the determining factor. We say that Al-Fateh's actions are related to progressive thought more than those who merely declare their support for such thought. The important thing in any revolution is not propagating an ideology but actual action. Ideology alone is meaningless if it is not put to the test.

KHOULI: This will lead us to discuss the social structure of Al-Fateh. If you want to explain more, I say that at the early stages of its development the more dominant feature in Al-Fateh was that of the educated intellectuals—meaning that the majority of its members and leaders were educated Palestinians. The question is: Is this still the dominant feature even after the development of Al-Fateh and the increase in its membership, or have other social groupings joined it after June 1967, such as workers, peasants, and craftsmen and thus changed this feature?

ABU EYAD: This is closely and organically linked to the principal slogan of national liberation which was raised by Al-Fateh and which it is still raising. Such a slogan is a wide one and can encompass all the national forces, groups and classes which believe in national liberation. Yet a person cannot deny the clear fact that the majority of the people who participate in the armed struggle are workers, peasants, and revolutionary intellectuals.

KHOULI: In training its members for the struggle does Al-Fateh pay attention to the political aspect alongside the military fighting aspect? Do you have the opportunity to educate political-military cadres in special schools for organizing the cadres? How is this carried out if such schools exist?

ABU EYAD: Naturally the political and military education of the cadres is an essential question in Al-Fateh. In the absence of such an education Al-Fateh would not have been able to survive, develop and be strengthened. This is accomplished within the limits of the phase of national liberation. For such a purpose our cadres are taught the Palestinian reality, problems, and aims in addition to both the Arab and international realities. We also pay great attention to the reality of the enemy. Knowing the enemy's policies, economy, parties, thought, method of living, and armed forces is a principal matter for every commando in Al-Fateh. Moreover we acquaint our cadres, without complications, with world experiences in national liberation. We believe that we should benefit from such experiences, but at the same time we believe that attaining victory necessitates that we produce from our actual circumstances a national experience which will also enrich world experience. We study the experiences of the world and we have published them in pamphlets which are regularly distributed to our cadres and discussed. As for the cadres' schools, we have such schools, but we are dissatisfied with them, and we are studying the possibility of improving and strengthening them. Some of these schools have been closed for reasons which are beyond our control, and that was during the stage of transferring our activity and its leadership from Damascus to Jordan.

KHOULI: Actually the spatial movement you have discussed reminds me of certain opinions uttered about the Palestinian resistance, which I do not personally agree with, but I will put them forward in order to know your opinion about them. A summary of these opinions is that resistance, or guerrilla warfare, or a liberation revolution must stem from the occupied territories. According to such views the Palestinian resistance movement is located outside the occupied territories. Naturally these ideas are classical and do not take into consideration the nature of the circumstances of the Palestinian movement. I do not want here to expose in detail my opinion, but I would like to get acquainted with your opinion and the extent to which the forces of the Palestinian people can be mobilized inside and outside the occupied territories.

ABU EYAD: These opinions evidently confuse two things. In the first place there is a difference between the leadership of the armed liberation and the revolution. It would be true to say that some of the leaders are outside Palestine—that is to say they are located outside it. But the revolution itself—both in terms of people and the way it is carried out—stems from and actually exists inside it. This is historically known and a natural phenomenon of all the national liberation revolutions.

As for our action or revolution, objectively speaking, the Palestinian people are carrying out, under objective circumstances, a revolution which differs from the rest of the world revolutions. Why? Because the people, as it is clear, are socially, politically, and geographically dispersed. Such a situation imposes on us the application of methods for the struggle. In spite of that—within the general framework—ours is not an innovation among the world revolutions. Let us, for example, analyze the Yugoslav revolution. This revolution had wide stretches of land, and areas fortified by their geographical position, at its disposal—it was in the Blade Mountain as far as I remember that the leaders of the revolution headed by Tito were to be found, i.e., inside Yugoslavia. Another example is the Algerian revolution whose leadership was found outside the country in spite of the nature of the wide land and geographic fortifications, and in spite of the fact that the Algerian people were all inside the country. This did not arrest the revolution and prevent it from attaining victory.

In our Palestinian revolution we are located both inside and outside the occupied territories. This is natural. In the inside we are in our occupied country, because we do not recognize the Zionist-Israeli entity. Thus our revolution is in a natural form and cannot be compared—as in some foreign newspapers—with the French resistance, which was led from London, against the Nazi occupation. Only a few meters separate the leadership which is located outside, from the occupied territories.

Colonial Zionist imperialism has expelled a great number of our people from part of their land. By virtue of such expulsion, those who were not expelled and kept their land will initiate resistance. From where will the revolution emanate? It will emanate from the West Bank and the Gaza Strip. These are two parts of Palestine. We do not recognize a land called Israel. The revolutionary movement must be located in it because we consider it, in its totality, Palestine. Israel with the whole of the Arab land bordering Palestine constitutes one unit, the land of the Palestinian revolution. Our bases are located in this area, and we have many bases inside the occupied territories. If it were not for these bases, we would have been unable to carry out any military action. In the absence of such bases, the revolution would be completely isolated. The principle bases are those located inside the occupied territories, and those which are located outside constitute a continuous source of supply for the revolution by virtue of the Palestinian people's circumstances, which I have already discussed.

KHOULI: Don't you think that the Arabs inside Israel have been continuously neglected and that the difficult circumstances under which they are living have not been appreciated?

ABU EYAD: The truth is that I cannot say that there was any negligence or lack of appreciation. The evidence is our recognition that the best of our modem poetry is that of our brothers in the occupied territories, e.g. Samih al-Qasim, Mahmud Darwish, Tawfiq Zyad, etc. All of them have contributed to the enrichment of the Arab revolution in general, and the Palestinian revolution in particular, by their humanitarian, honest, and good words. This is the diet of revolutionaries in their struggle.

At the same time we appreciate their conditions and we do not attempt, either directly or indirectly, to provide the Zionist-Nazi force with motives to torture them more. Such is the nature of the torture which they are facing courageously that we do not ask them to carry arms and they are not requited to do so.

At the same time we deeply appreciate the demonstrations of the Palestinians—men and women—in Nazareth and the surrounding areas of the Galilee District. This proves their adherence to the land and country in spite of the suffering, terror, arrest, imprisonment, eviction, confinement to quarters, confiscation of property, etc., inflicted upon them by the Zionists. For this reason we do not endeavor to organize them according to Al-Fateh's system of organization.

KHOULI: What about the Palestinian people in the post-1967 occupied territories?

ABU EYAD: Here I do not need to say more than that they are being mobilized. Evidence will be found in daily demonstrations and the numerous different forms of passive resistance to the occupation. At this point we should mention, with great appreciation, the role of the Palestinian women which has reached the level of armed resistance. The Israeli prisons are full of thousands of the sons and daughters of our people who reject occupation and resist it in every way and bear all kinds of psychological and physical torture. In this connection I would like to tell you of an incident which took place more than two months ago in Nablus. Under pressure from world public opinion the Israeli authorities permitted a Red Cross delegation to visit our imprisoned sisters in the jail of Nablus.

They received the delegation with a song, "My country, my country, Al-Fateh is the revolution against the aggressors." The prison guards were unable to stop them. The representatives of the Red Cross could not hide their impression.

Actually one of the most important results of the armed Palestinian revolution is the emergence of the Palestinian woman and her role as a commando equal to the Palestinian man in armed action and sacrifice. The important feature in all this is that the Palestinian woman, through the revolution, was able to overcome all the traditions according to which she was brought up in old Palestine. Nothing stands in her way for the liberation of her country, neither death, nor imprisonment, nor torture. Thus, the Israeli intelligence services, which have depended in their psychological propaganda on old traditions against the progress of the Palestinian woman in the field of struggle, failed because in reality the Palestinian people—men and women—have overcome these traditions. The enemy has propagated accusations of assaulting honor, etc., but this did not prevent women from joining the revolution *en masse* and carrying arms against the enemy.

KHOULI: This is natural because national armed struggle always achieves real equality between man and woman through struggle and resisting the enemy. This took place in the colonized or occupied countries which had been under-developed in social relations and in which armed liberating revolutions broke out such as Algeria, the under-developed areas of Yugoslavia, the under-developed southern areas of Italy and now Palestine.

ABU EYAD: This is true.

KHOULI: With your permission, let us move to discuss another point. From reading Al-Fateh's statements and documents, and through discussions with its leaders, it becomes clear that Al-Fateh is intent on careful distinction between Judaism and Zionism, and although it fights Zionism it does not harbor any animosity towards the Jews as human beings and Judaism as a religion. What is the practical meaning of this?

ABU EYAD: The meaning is that the Palestinian revolution is a revolution against racism, fascism and colonialism. Thus it is totally purified from racism, fascism and colonialism. On this basis it does not act or carry arms against the Jews as human beings and people. Al-Fateh is against the fascist, racist Zionist movement, which practices colonial imperialism in the homeland of the Palestinian people. Thus Zionism is a colonialist movement closely linked with imperialism. This is the movement, with its concepts and entities, which polarizes our animosity and which we confront until our last breath. The strategy of the Zionist movement is based on:

>1. Exploiting what happened to the Jews, as individuals and groups—in Europe at the hands of the Nazis—to nourish the complex of persecution among them in order to enmesh them in the traps of Zionism. Under the influence of this complex, and for other reasons, the Zionist movement pushes the Jews to join its organizations and emigrate to Palestine awakening in them the evil feeling of revenge.
>
>2. The Jews cannot be absorbed in Palestine without expansion, not only at the expense of Palestine but also at the expense of Palestine's neighboring Arab countries.

These two elements of the policy of the Zionist movement are continuously interacting with each other. The proof is that whenever immigration to Palestine reaches a low ebb or is obstructed, Zionism and its organizations create secret societies composed of its terrorist members. These embark on campaigns of persecution of the Jews in order to terrorize them and deepen the persecution complex among them, thus forcing them to immigrate to Palestine. It has been possible at certain times to expose the reality of these organizations and their organic association with the Zionist movement. This happened in Brazil and other parts of the world where anti-Semitic movements made their appearance. As a result we talk and act on the basis of a deep awareness of the necessity of distinguishing between Judaism and Zionism. We are true to our long Arab history and traditions. In the gloomiest ages the Arabs and Jews lived in peace and equality without any kind of prejudice. Since the Zionist movement's interference in the affairs of the Jews and Arabs it has poisoned the atmosphere, planted obstacles and practiced, against our people, all the barbaric methods it had learnt from Nazism, in addition to its colonialist usurpation of our homeland and the eviction by it of the Palestinian people. In the name of "the chosen people of God," Zionism has implemented its racist colonialist plan.

Zionism's endeavor to exploit religion to the maximum is very clear, it thus forged and counterfeited religious books to prove to worldwide Jewish populations that their place is in Palestine. In this context, all the non-religious Zionist parties, such as Dayan who declares that he is non-religious, concurred in rushing to the Wailing Wall to exploit religion and the appearance of religion in order to convince the Jews. From here we realize that the question of Judaism and the Jews is separate from that of Zionism and its colonialist racist movement. Thus when we declared that through our struggle we aimed at the establishment of a Palestinian democratic state, it was not a tactic but a true and honest manifestation of our strategy. This is based on our conviction that among the Jews there are individuals of a good caliber with whom we can live in peace. In our opinion those who are fighting against our way of thinking are the Zionists. Take for example, the Zionist Israeli newspapers. After every operation we carry out, they publish comments on it in the following manner: "These are the terrorists of Al-Fateh who want to establish a Palestinian democratic state." They always do that even if we are not responsible for the operation.

KHOULI: What does Al-Fateh exactly understand by "Palestinian democratic state"?

ABU EYAD: We have always believed and declared, and will continue to declare, that armed struggle is not an end in itself. It is a means for a great humanitarian aim. Since 1917 Palestine has been subjected to war, revolutions, and bloody fighting. The time has come for this land and its people to live in peace as other human beings. We carry arms in order to achieve a truly peaceful settlement of the problem, and not a false settlement based on the imposition of aggression and racism. Such peace cannot be achieved except within the framework of a democratic state in Palestine. What are its details? I believe that through the development of the struggle and fighting the details of such a state will be drawn up. But this is the wide strategic course which will encompass all these details.

KHOULI: Within the framework of this wide strategic course will the Palestinian democratic state accept the Jews as equal citizens with the Arabs?

ABU EYAD: Of course we accept the Jews as equal citizens with the Arabs in everything. The meaning of the Palestinian democratic state is very clear. It only aims at eliminating the Zionist racist entity in Palestine.

KHOULI: For the sake of more clarity, will Al-Fateh guarantee in word and deed the right to citizenship in the Palestinian democratic state to the anti- Zionist Jews who will declare their agreement with Al-Fateh's aim of establishing the new Palestinian democratic society? Is the right to citizenship guaranteed to the anti-Zionist Jews whether they have been in Palestine before or after 1948?

ABU EYAD: I repeat that this right will be guaranteed by Al-Fateh, as a liberation movement with humanitarian dimensions, not only to every anti- Zionist Jew but also to a Jew who has purified his soul of Zionist ideas, meaning one who has been convinced that Zionist ideas are alien to human society.

KHOULI: How does Al-Fateh view Israeli society? Does it still view it as a conglomeration of racism, colonialism, reaction, and aggression? Or does Al-Fateh see the emergence of certain progressive forces and tendencies in Israeli society—even if they are small and weak—opposing aggression, Zionism, and racism? If Al-Fateh is aware of the existence of such forces and tendencies, what is its opinion of and attitude towards them?

ABU EYAD: There is no doubt that Israeli society, in its present form, is a colonialist, imperialist, and racist society. We are attempting with all the means at our disposal to liquidate such a society and create its substitute, namely, a democratic anti-racist society open to humanity and the world. Actually Israeli society is closed to humanity and to every progressive movement in the world. Israel has not supported any liberation cause in the world. Thus when we said that we want to live with the Jews in a non-racist democratic Palestine, we primarily call on the progressive forces, if they exist, to strengthen their stand. There are certain forces in Israel which claim progressiveness, but in reality they are false, Zionist, racist, and imperialist.

Yet this does not prohibit us from saying that there is a small nucleus of progressive forces which have started to emerge and we sense their existence. They call for the liquidation of the Zionist entity, and we are sure that if their voices were heard and met with a positive reaction, they would suffer even more torture and persecution than that suffered by Al-Fateh. The truth is that there are signs of progressiveness, small beginnings. We hope and wish that such beginnings will grow and assert their belief in the right of the Palestinian people to live on their land. When I say the Palestinian people I mean all the people with all their sects: Christians, Muslims, and Jews; but without the Zionist entity that is linked with colonialism. A country in which there will be no racism, no Zionism, and no religious fanaticism.

KHOULI: In accordance with the principle of frankness which we have agreed on, I permit myself to ask the following question: Some people say—in spite of their appreciation of Al-Fateh's valor and its leadership of the Palestinian armed struggle—that it is concerned with making propaganda about itself and its action so that it has begun to appear in papers and broadcasting services to be of a greater stature than it really is. What is your opinion of such an accusation?

ABU EYAD: I do not want to start by declaring that such a statement is un-objective and contrary to the truth. But let us view the matter step by step and unemotionally. Has Al-Fateh started to concern itself with the propaganda aspect? The answer is yes. But if one says that the interest of Al-Fateh in propaganda is superseding that of the military aspect, then there is a basic error in the analysis in which such statements are uttered. Why? Because the question of propaganda for us, as a resistance movement, is one form of political action which complements and accompanies military action. Thus it is not action merely for the sake of propaganda. Propaganda basically revolves around persons; we refuse and resist this because it harms our struggle and movement. If this has happened—unfortunately it is happening—it is not Al-Fateh's fault but that of certain Arab journalists and newspapers whose enthusiasm and the necessities of incitement in journalism have blinded them.

We in Al-Fateh do not agree with the journalists on that point and we have told them our opinion more than once; actually at times we have told them that such incitement is a disease and some Arab newspapers should get rid of it. Abu 'Ammar, in his capacity as the official spokesman of Al-Fateh, expressed frankly our stand *vis-à-vis* this question, and his opposition to publishing his picture—if the occasion arises or in the absence of it—at a time when they avoided publishing anything about the fighters as a group and a movement. I would like to assert once again that publishing the picture of the leaders will harm our work because it hinders their freedom of movement. The three or four members of the leadership whose pictures have been published are greatly distressed. This is not an attempt to defend—thank God my picture has not been published—but it is the actual truth with regard to the necessities of work. On the other hand, I would like to assure you that publishing the picture of one or more of the leaders of Al-Fateh does not create any kind of sensitivity because the structure of collective leadership of our movement is so deep that the individual melts in the group. Thus the picture of Abu 'Ammar or any other member, as far as we are concerned, is that of Al-Fateh as a whole.

KHOULI: You have said that information for Al-Fateh is not propaganda but political activity, what do you mean by that?

ABU EYAD: I mean that it is a part of the whole bottle of liberation, because the battle is not merely military statements which are announced and published without a continuous effort to explain Al-Fateh's thought and aims. There is an important matter which should not be neglected, namely that before the June war we met with great obstacles in the dissemination of information. All means of informing and contacting the Arab masses to explain our ideas, aims and methods of struggle were closed in our faces. Now these vistas have been opened and we have had to put ourselves forward to the masses and deepen our political ideas and the principles of our struggle, otherwise we would be greatly neglecting the rights of our movement and the Palestinian struggle as a whole. This required contacting people, disclosing names, etc. As for the fact that certain newspapers have deviated—and I stress the word deviated—in presenting all this for the purpose of incitement or individualism; this is not in the least the fault of Al-Fateh.

KHOULI: If Al-Fateh's information is a political activity directed at the non-Arab people of the world, namely, the capitalist and socialist people, what are Al-Fateh's principal broad lines in this field?

ABU EYAD: The principle broad lines are based on presenting Al-Fateh to the world as a national liberation movement hostile to racism and colonialism, and one which, in its struggle, distinguishes between Judaism and Zionism. Thus our movement is a part of a humanitarian movement, whereas Zionism, which we have taken it upon ourselves to fight and liquidate, is the enemy of humanitarianism and not of the Arabs alone.

If you review what has been published lately about Al-Fateh in the foreign press—whether in the West or East—the success of Al-Fateh's plan will become clear. If we—and this is not our fault—have failed with regard to the press of the socialist camp which has not clarified Al-Fateh's aims in a satisfactory manner, the fault is not ours but theirs. I am saying that with regret and I am not attacking or alluding to the socialist camp or its press.

KHOULI: Does Al-Fateh, within the framework of its plan of political information, envisage winning world Jewish public opinion which is against colonialism and Zionism? If this is the case, what steps have so far been adopted in this field?

ABU EYAD: Naturally we are concerned with this. Our concern stems from our principal point of view which distinguishes between a Jew and a Zionist, Zionism and Judaism. Thus we try to have relations with all the Jews who do not participate in consolidating the Israeli colonialist, racist, closed society—the Zionist society. I shall give you practical examples to prove the true meaning of my words. In January 1969 the Second International Conference in Support of the Arab Peoples was held in

Cairo. All the departments, forces and Arab and foreign individuals—among whom there were Jews—who attended the conference were of the opinion that Al-Fateh's stand *vis-à-vis* this problem saved the conference, since it urged every progressive Jew, outside or inside Israel, to work for the liquidation of Zionism and its entity, and called for the establishment of the Palestinian democratic state.

Another example. In February 1969 the Palestinian Theatrical Troupe gave a play in Rabat in Morocco for the benefit of Al-Fateh. The Moroccan police forbade the Moroccan Jews from attending the play to protect their lives against the enthusiastic Moroccan masses. Our friends over there took it upon themselves to protect the lives of the Moroccan Jews and convinced the policemen to allow them to attend the play and see for themselves, through the play, the reality of the racist and non-humanitarian nature of the Israeli state. During the play the Moroccan citizens contributed to Al-Fateh expressing their support for its armed struggle. Among those who contributed was a Moroccan Jew, Ibrahim al-Sarafati, a professor in the School of Engineering at Muhammad Fifth University. He contributed one thousand dirhams as a token of his support for Al-Fateh in its struggle for the establishment of a democratic state in Palestine. He wrote us a letter in French explaining his stand and the reason for contributing to Al-Fateh in particular. His wife translated it to Arabic and gave her wedding ring to the resistance movement struggling against Zionism and its racist entity. Such stands towards Al-Fateh have become popular in a great number of European countries.

This Arab orientation towards the Jews who are against colonialism and Zionism, in addition to being an un-tactical action, could not have taken place if Al-Fateh had not carried arms. Through the armed struggle for liberation such an orientation was possible. If such a call had been put forward before Al-Fateh's armed struggle, it would have been fiercely opposed by Arab public opinion in general, and Palestinian public opinion in particular. The liberation weapon of Al-Fateh and its strength in the political and military fields gave this strategy the opportunity of being implemented.

KHOULI: This is, to a great extent, true. 1 have other remarks which I would like to discuss with you in order to know Al-Fateh's opinion. From the time Al-Fateh embarked upon armed struggle in January 1965 up until 1967, I can distinguish two phases in its history: first, the difficult phase of the starting point before June 1967 when Al-Fateh was isolated as a result of the press blockade and accusations of adventurism.

ABU EYAD: Unwillingly.

KHOULI: Naturally. After June the blockade was removed, and the Arab masses and nation became aware of the existence of Al-Fateh. This was followed by the battle of al-Karameh, March 1968, in which Al-Fateh proved itself politically and militarily. From that date the great and important phase of resisting the enemy started. Can you, through these two phases and the experience of August 1968, explain what Al-Fateh has precisely gained? Has the totality of the experience gained resulted in particular changes with regard to Al-Fateh's methods of resistance and activity?

ABU EYAD: With regard to the first phase Al-Fateh has benefited from organizing its cadres, or what we can call "the nucleus of the real Palestinian struggle" which gave birth to the growing forces of the armed resistance movement. The most important thing which we have concentrated on and acquired from experience, during this phase, is educating the guerrillas to reject individualism and egoism, adhere to the group, get used to the most difficult work pertaining to the struggle, and offer sacrifices in difficult circumstances. In this phase you would start a battle and only few would support you, even the forces which were supposed to be our heirs did not support us at this time. Thus Al-Fateh was able to get rid of all the diseases of society, such as individualism, showing off and substituting action with futile discussions. When the post-June war phase began Al-Fateh had benefited from the earlier phase and was ready to confront it with cadres that were politically and militarily aware, in spite of all that certain errors were committed. Such mistakes could be traced back to the opening of Al-Fateh, after the June war, to the Palestinian and Arab masses on a scale that its organizational and military apparatus was not yet ready to cope with. We went through a phase full of problems and difficulties which we had to overcome before we could enter the phase of wide-scale organized resistance in August 1968.

In all these phases there is one truth which has been revealed through beneficial experience, namely that a vanguard group, who believe in something stemming from the will of the people, on which they insist and for which they struggle, will be able to fulfill their aims despite the sacrifices and difficulties. I do not know if I have fully answered your remarks or not.

KHOULI: I think you have, but let us complete the picture. On the basis of Al-Fateh's position as a symbol of the aimed Palestinian struggle internationally speaking, what does Al-Fateh have to say to the Palestinian people in general, and the other resistance organizations in particular?

ABU EYAD: I do not have any objections to answering your questions. But I fear that in answering this question I will appear as a preacher and adviser. Yet through my education in Al-Fateh I refuse to take such a position. I mean I do not want to stand and preach saying: My brothers this and that. With your permission, let us reformulate the question in the following manner: "What can Al-Fateh contribute in the light of the present circumstances which are witnessing the emergence of numerous resistance organizations, and how can healthy relations be established for the benefit of Palestinian action aiming at liberation in spite of the present circumstances?" Do you approve of this formulation?

KHOULI: Yes.

ABU EYAD: There is a truth which should be admitted by our brothers in the different guerrilla organizations. Such an admission should be preceded by an admission on the part of Al-Fateh to the effect that it is not an ideal and infallible organization. Since in Al-Fateh there are wrong things, it is the duty of the other guerrilla organizations and honest critical outside observers to point out the mistakes to the members of Al-Fateh who cannot discern them in order to get rid of the mistakes which any national liberation movement commits. On the other hand, our brothers in the other guerrilla organizations should admit that the colonial and Zionist departments, the intelligence services of the imperialist countries, in addition to other counter-revolutionary forces, work according to one plan to sabotage and deface Al-Fateh. Evidently they attempt to fight it directly using material and tangible means. They attempt to wage psychological warfare on Al-Fateh from both within and without. Sometimes sabotage is done by exaggerating Al-Fateh through the information media, or by attributing to Al-Fateh statements which it does not support, or by misinterpreting the essential policies which Al-Fateh adopts in its relations with the Arab states: they in these ways fight against Al-Fateh. Our brothers in the other organizations should comprehend that the destruction of Al-Fateh means the destruction of the totality of Palestinian guerrilla action, the movement of the Palestinian people, and the Arab progressive movement.

KHOULI: I believe that we have reached the point where you can explain Al-Fateh's vision of the present Arab attitude *vis-à-vis* the battle of liberation on the one hand, and the armed Palestinian resistance movement on the other? I do not know if it is beneficial to divide the discussion into phases or not? Of course, this is left up to you.

ABU EYAD: There are a number of remarks to be made in this connection. The first and basic one is that we did not fully and effectively mobilize all the Arab forces. At times and under certain circumstances—not few—we feel that certain aspects of the Arab reality are not involved in the fierce battle in all its dimensions.

KHOULI: In your opinion, what is the reason for that?

ABU EYAD: In my opinion the Arab masses' participation in the battle implies their living and objectively understanding the realities of the battle without concealment or exaggeration and that they are assigned their proper role. The role of the masses when the country is under occupation is known—mobilizing, training, and giving arms to the people, and their participation in different forms in the battle. The Arab masses, up till now, have not been given this proper role. The implication behind this is that rebuilding the regular armies is not enough if the Arab masses' role is neglected.

This is a reality which we should remember and it is not shameful to say it. The shame lies in hiding it, because we are all supposed to live for the battle. This is the first remark.

As for the second remark, it is that there is a difference between the Arab states adjacent to Israel and those far from it. If we feel the separation between those who live on the front and those who live in the city in the same country, we feel greater separation among those who live in areas far from the borders. The Arab masses who are far away should know the reality of the Zionist danger; for it does not aim at certain areas in Palestine, or this part of the Arab land or that, but it aims at the whole Arab nation. Thus the Arab individual who is living in areas far from the states adjacent to Israel does not have the right to say that the battle is not his. I believe that the Arab masses who are geographically separated from the land of the battle want to participate in the battle with all the power at their disposal.

Thus the duty of national leaders who are aware should be to develop the attitude of their government in order actually to participate in the battle. I do not say anything more than that.

The third remark concerns Palestinian resistance. Palestinian resistance is required to develop and gradually escalate its activity inside the occupied territories. These are duties which the Arab people request. But we should ask a question: Is the escalation of the resistance a mechanical action; you press a button and Palestinian resistance is escalated, you press another one it is de-escalated? No it is not a mechanical action. It is a process of interaction on the part of the Arab people, providing the fighting people with Arab expertise. Has the Arab nation provided Palestinian resistance with what it requires?

I frankly say that the Arab people are ready to help, but certain obstacles are put between them and Palestinian resistance. If the resistance has the chance to meet the Arab masses without complications and formalities, the Arab people might play a great part in the battle alongside Palestinian resistance. It is not true that Palestinian resistance is regional. When we talk about Palestinian resistance and Palestinian people we do not separate the Palestinian people from the unified Arab nation which has the same destiny. National unity does not deny the existence of an Egyptian people or Iraqi people, etc. The Palestinian people have the right to appear after 20 years of burial and after having been charged with 1,000 different accusations. The appearance of the Palestinian people implies that of the Arab people. There is absolutely no contradiction between the appearance of the Palestinian people and their being a part of the large Arab nation. Thus Palestinian resistance is neither regional nor isolationist. It demands that the Arab people with the totality of their capacities should adopt it. Take for example the question of material aid, has any Arab government allocated in its budget a sum for Palestinian resistance? I say it frankly, is there one Arab state? On the contrary, the Arab governments have begun to interfere with the popular subscriptions which the resistance movement used to carry out, by setting up government committees for the support of guerrilla action to which collection of contributions is limited. These committees are headed by a minister or a government official. The collection of contributions has been subjected to state regulations, if the state has wanted the committee to continue its work, then contributions will continue, if not, they will stop. The government has turned the collection of contributions into a new tax to be paid by the people. We believe that the continuation of the operation on this basis will hinder the interaction between the resistance movement and the Arab people which is the essence of the operation.

These are my three remarks on the Arab reality. What do we hope for? We hope that the reasons for the three aforementioned remarks will disappear and that the masses will be effectively mobilized for the battle. We do not fail to pay due regard to the danger nor to dilute the battle. What do we mean by dilution? We can dilute the battle by confusing political and military action. We should explain to the people the meaning of political action and military action. The masses who participate in the battle will not be observers, and I say the participation of the masses is possible and it is a necessity. We should believe in the role of the people's militia which can greatly hinder the enemy's effectiveness. We hope that the subject of Palestinian resistance will be given enough attention and concern, materially and financially. At the same time we should show the people the truth without deception.

KHOULI: Based on what you have said, I understand that Al-Fateh's concept of the battle of liberation is Palestinian in its initiation, Arab in its dimension and essence. Isn't it so?

ABU EYAD: Exactly. The national dimension in the Palestinian revolution is essential and basic. It is not mere words uttered in order to incite or reach the press. We cannot be separated from the struggle of the Arab nation and its struggling forces, otherwise we will be our own enemies before anything else.

KHOULI: Don't you agree that it has become necessary to manifest, in a practical way, the national dimension of Palestinian resistance in order to be able to maneuver and surmount obstacles in its way? With regard to this I have three specific points. Firstly, hasn't it become necessary to work for the establishment of a comprehensive Arab popular front to rally around one specific aim, namely the protection and support of the resistance movement? Secondly, what is the attitude of Al-Fateh to the desire of many non-Palestinian Arab nationals who want to join the resistance movement and participate in the armed struggle? The third point pertains to the question of coordination between Palestinian armed resistance and the regular Arab armies. With reference to this point, there is a view which says that Palestinian resistance cannot alone liberate Palestine, thus the Arab regular armies should out of necessity intervene. Objectively speaking, to what extent can a phase of the struggle be achieved in which the two forces and methods are used—guerrilla warfare and the movement of regular armies—without infringing the freedom of action and independence of the resistance movement?

ABU EYAD: Actually Al-Fateh has declared that one of its direct short range aims is the establishment of the Arab front. Al-Fateh is not solely responsible for the creation of such a front. It is the responsibility of all the Arab national forces in addition to Al-Fateh. Al-Fateh had made contacts, more than once, for this purpose. It seems that the multiplicity of the Palestinian organizations has obstructed the formation of the front in an organized manner.

On the information side, Al-Fateh called for the creation of an Arab front for the support of guerrilla action. Practically speaking, Al-Fateh considered a great number of the Arab youth in the Arab states, especially in the national and progressive circles, to be the front. It is true that such a front was not organized and it is necessary and our duty to organize it. But, as I have pointed out, the responsibility is that of Al-Fateh and the other national and progressive forces. Actually we have witnessed, in certain cases and at certain times, that the response of some people with regard to the establishment of the front was vitiated with unbelief as a result of the local differences existing in this or that state.

It is our duty and very necessary to think of a practical way of forming the front. I recall the proposal which you have put forward and which was published more than once in *al-Tali'ah* and *al-Ahram* calling for the convening of a preparatory conference for this front to be attended by all the national and progressive forces in the Arab homeland. What can we do when these forces are divided against each other? For example, in Lebanon the national and progressive forces have not yet been able to form a unified powerful and effective front. Each one of them wants to be the sole supporter of armed struggle, or of Al-Fateh in particular, without the participation of the others. The different trends inside the national and progressive forces in the Arab homeland are hindering the creation of the front. We hope that in the near future these forces can develop their attitudes and lessen the sensitivities and existing differences among them for the sake of the Arab struggle in general, and the Palestinian struggle in particular, and agree on a minimum program, namely supporting the armed Palestinian struggle, irrespective of the organization. The important thing is to support the concept of armed struggle for liberation in order to stop the recurrence of what happened in an Arab state against us, and comprehend the reality of our stand through this front.

KHOULI: I believe that under the present circumstances we are capable of overcoming all these problems and differences and, thus, of creating the Arab front. This is our role in the straggle. The nucleus for building the front is the Palestinian armed struggle, which has become the true and practical way for the liberation of Palestine and the establishment of the Palestinian democratic state and which is offering a great service for the liberation of the Arab homeland from the different forms of colonial bases. In the final analysis, Israel is a colonial base in the form of a state opposed to the Arab states. Thus the front should be opened to all the national and progressive Arab forces without exception and in spite of their thought and social and political tendencies with regard to the other problems confronting the Arab homeland or the individual Arab states. The most important thing is that it should support and aid the Palestinian armed struggle. I believe that the PLO can take the initiative and call for the convening of the preparatory conference of the popular Arab front.

ABU EYAD: There is no disagreement on this point. We fully support it. Al-Fateh, as a part of the PLO, can actually participate in realizing this great and necessary aim.

In your discussion you tackled the question of the non-Palestinian Arab youth volunteering to join the resistance. I take this opportunity to stress in the name of Al-Fateh that it accepts without reservation any Arab youth who wants to volunteer. We accept him, but there are obstacles put by the circumstances of Arab officialdom. If these circumstances are eliminated, we are ready, as of this moment, to accept the Arab youth among us.

In this context there is a point which should not be neglected, namely that volunteers come in great numbers, for example 12,000 volunteered from one Arab country. How could the resistance movement arm 12,000 with its present capabilities? Again the necessity for creating an Arab front which could play its role in supporting, aiding and widening the resistance movement emerges. Through the front we can organize all these matters so that volunteering will not become a hindrance but a driving force.

KHOULI: Some Iraqis and Sudanese have expressed their desire to volunteer with their arms?

ABU EYAD: Such men are welcome.

Next we come to the point of coordination between the resistance and the Arab regular armies. Our concept with regard to coordination is a specific and clear one, from which we will not deviate. Coordination in our view is, firstly, whatever is contributed to the resistance in the field of support, aid, and training. We are ready to be part of a national plan for liberation. But we are not ready to be part of a regional plan for coordination. In other words, if we find Arab regimes which have a serious plan for the liberation of Palestine and which want us to be part of that plan, we do not have any objections. But if certain Arab regimes aim at containing us in the name of coordination and maintaining their regional boundaries, we—frankly—reject this. We reject coordination if it means containment and mandate; we accept it if it means a plan on the national level of liberation.

KHOULI: You want to say that, as you respect the independence of each Arab state, you require each Arab state to respect the independence of the Palestinian armed resistance movement.

ABU EYAD: Exactly, in order not to indulge in irrelevancies. This is our concept of coordination and our view of blending guerrilla warfare with regular armies. When, in 1965, we raised the slogan of armed struggle and said that the Palestinian people want to carry out this action, we realized that blowing up a bridge could not be a determining factor with regard to liberation. Yet we realized that blowing up a bridge would recruit 10 other people to join Al-Fateh. We were aware of the fact that blowing up a bridge will enlighten 10 other people and make them believe in the armed struggle. We did not understand the struggle in terms of profit and loss. We blow up one bridge and the Zionists will blow up 10 of our bridges. The concept of profit and loss has been entrenched in our system of thinking by colonialism, to restrict our movement. We should not think, as in the past, in a manner which always fears retaliation. We believe that the Palestinian popular armed struggle should, in fighting any serious battle with the forces of Zionism, indulge in a popular liberation war on the Arab level. In the present phase and under the present Arab circumstances, we could be the losers if a regular war is waged against Israel. Yet this does not imply that the Arab states are not required to have strong armies. On the contrary we want strong armies to defend the borders. However, if we calculate the battle of Palestine on the basis of loss and gain—tank for tank, combat plane for combat plane, pilot for pilot, etc.—there is no doubt that the Zionist state in Palestine is more capable than us since it is supported by world imperialist forces, in addition to being better armed and more scientifically educated.

KHOULI: You are against mechanical calculation.

ABU EYAD: Exactly, mechanical calculation is rejected. At this point, in our opinion armed struggle is required on the Palestinian level. But it is well known that Israel does not allow itself to lose one battle, even if it is a partial one. It must always take revenge, because this false state cannot survive unless it is always victorious. Any defeat, even a partial one, will affect the morale of its people. This explains the continuous Israeli threats. Any small operation on our part will be answered by 10 in order to terrorize the Arab people and tell them that their endeavor is a hopeless one, and that the Israeli army is a legend which cannot be defeated. We should let our people get used to the idea that a conventional war is not the only kind of war they can fight. As Palestinians we hope that the capabilities of the Arab armies will be very high, and that they will coordinate with us for a dual battle in which guerrilla warfare and regular armies will have a part. Are we truly prepared for this? Or is it because we are not prepared to let the fighters feel that they are fighting in emptiness? Here lies the danger of saying that the Palestinian question will not attain victory except through regular armies. We know, and reality forces upon us this knowledge, that the regular armies cannot achieve this end now.

We must plant it firmly in our minds that the war is that of a guerrilla warfare which should be developed into a popular war of liberation in which the Arab masses by means of the Palestinian question will be prepared to confront the Zionist enemy and its policy and expansionist war. In future, things may change and the regular Arab armies become capable of fighting successfully the war of liberation. But we are living the present reality and its conditions. Thus the vanguard of the Palestinians will be the same as that of the popular war of liberation in its entirety in terms of the Arab homeland as a whole. This is mainly what frightens Israel, Zionism, and the other counter-revolutionary forces. Why? Because calculations will not be made on the basis of a tank for a tank and a combat plane for a combat plane. The calculations are based on the will of a struggling people who want to fight, defend their land, and terminate the Zionist existence. We believe that it is a long term war. We do not believe that our war will end in victory in one or two years. In the war many of our fighters will die. Thus we are not against the idea of strengthening the Arab regular armies. On the contrary they should get stronger and stronger. Yet the regular armies are not a substitute for the Palestinian people's struggle and their fight on their land. The implication behind this is that the Palestinian people's struggle is a tactical trump card in the hands of the Arab armies, or Arab regimes. If we consider it as a tactical trump card then I will be gambling with and selling these men who are dying each day for a tactical plan of certain Arab countries. This is a fundamental factor. Even the struggle of the regular soldiers falls within the framework of armed struggle. I do not want to discuss here the international circumstances and the link of the regular Arab armies, through their states, with the official international status and its effects if we declare the war to be that only of the regular armies.

KHOULI: I noticed that in your discussion of the Arab states you distinguished between the Arab states bordering Palestine and the remote Arab states. Such a distinction on your part must have the meaning that each group has a special role to play in the battle of liberation. What is your evaluation of the role of each group? What has been accomplished until now? What has not been accomplished and why?

ABU EYAD: Briefly I say that the fundamental role of the Arab states bordering the occupied territories is to shoulder whatever results from the resistance operations in the form of Israeli counter-attacks, in addition to rebuilding their armed forces and modernizing their armies. This is what is happening to the UAR, Syria, Jordan, and Lebanon. They are supposed to shoulder the Israeli counter-attacks. Israel tells lies when it claims that it is attacking guerrilla bases in the East Bank or other places. Actually Israel attacks civilians, their cars, and homes in order to intimidate the Arab masses, in Jordan for example, and attempts to make them believe that support for the commandos is futile and will cost them great sacrifices. Israel knows that it cannot destroy all the bases of the commandos because it does not know and will never know their location. Furthermore, Israel attempts to make world public opinion believe in the futility both of resistance itself and of any world feeling for it. What is required of the Arab states bordering Palestine is the following: to mobilize and strengthen their armies, to mobilize and organize the masses for the battle, and to prepare themselves to bear the consequences of the resistance movement. This was the case with Algeria and Tunisia with regard to the Algerian resistance movement. Egypt also in 1936 shouldered the consequences of its support for the Algerian resistance and successfully confronted the tripartite aggression on the Suez.

As for the remote Arab states their role centers on continuously providing financial aid. They are not supposed to direct danger so they should compensate for not having to mobilize their armies by mobilizing the masses and providing the bordering states, in addition to the resistance movement, with the necessary financial assistance. We are confronting a Zionist state which receives substantial and continuous assistance from imperialism and world Zionism.

KHOULI: Let us have a look at the international attitude *vis-à-vis* the problem and the battle of liberation after the two years which have elapsed since the June 1967 defeat. What is your analysis of the present international position of the Palestinian aimed struggle? Has it proved its existence and forced the world to recognize it?

ABU EYAD: Actually this question has been always buzzing in our minds. All the people of the world only respect strength. And I do not mean by strength the mere possession of vast military equipment, I mean the determination and resolution of groups of organized people to strive for their right at any expense, summoning up their inner forces. It is my belief that on the basis of this understanding in the last two years we have made up for the past 20 years when all our activity and propaganda centered on the wretched refugees queuing at UNRWA soup kitchens. This picture of refugees has been transformed into one of fighters carrying arms to win their freedom. At the outset many asked what can such a weak few do in the face of a state so strongly supported by imperialism and which has defeated Arab armies. We were accused of adventurism. But now the world and its political information have become interested in us after Palestinian resistance has proved that it is a growing and effective force in the area, politically and militarily. They are now facing a new political development in the area. A force which is carrying arms to liberate its arms to liberate its homeland.

We know the world is almost divided into three parts: the countries of the eastern camp, those of the western camp, and those of the third world. As far as we are concerned, I believe that we have succeeded in different degrees and up to an extent, in explaining our case in these three camps. The support of the peoples of the world is continuously growing. The Second International Conference in Support of the Arab Peoples, which was held in Cairo on 23 January 1969 and in which a number of forces of differing tendencies participated, was a great test for the strength of our movement and struggle. The delegates who attended the conference expressed their support for the problem as put forward by Al-Fateh. Naturally this did not result from a plan drawn up for the conference but was a positive result of political effort prior to the convening of the conference. We are now hoping that the information media in the socialist bloc and the countries of the third world will show more readiness to present our case. Isn't it strange to find the means of information in the western countries more open to us than that of the socialist countries?

KHOULI: How do you explain this phenomenon?

ABU EYAD: I relate it to the inadequacy of the Arab progressive forces, which are supposed, in this context, to carry the burden of the Palestinian socialist resistance movement to the country as a whole.

KHOULI: I think that this explanation is insufficient. Why don't you explain it on the basis that the resistance has not seriously put itself forward in this sphere? In other words, why do you only explain it by blaming the others and denying that you have also erred?

ABU EYAD: What does the other side accuse us of?

KHOULI: They say that you distinguish, in an un-objective manner, between political action and military action, and that you always prefer military activity to any political activity. Furthermore, you make the accusation that any political activity, exerted for the sake of the Palestinian problem at different levels and within the scope of securing the national rights of the Palestinian and Arab people, is bargaining.

ABU EYAD: I believe that the problem is different. The question of the remissness of the socialist information media with regard to the resistance is a reality. I would like to assert that our discussion of this point is initiated by reprimand and argument and not intimidation or attack on the socialist bloc, to whom we have friendly feelings and appreciate the huge and valuable assistance they offer to certain Arab states. But we would not be friends if we did not discuss the issues frankly. I think that this remissness is related firstly to the Palestine question itself because the socialist camp's stand, at the beginning, was not proper and was un-objective. The reasons for such a stand could be traced in the unfriendly relations we had with this camp because of our circumstances, especially in the years 1947, 1948.

In addition the Arab communist parties failed to explain the reality of the problem and situation. The socialist camp was of the opinion that a progressive revolution could only be launched with the support of around 60 per cent of the local inhabitants. Since this was not the case in Palestine, the socialist camp did not recognize the Palestinian revolution. Let us suppose that the socialist camp wanted now to apply this theory to the present situation in Israel, it would find that the number of the local inhabitants who wanted the revolution and the elimination of the Zionist entity would not total 60 percent. We are of the opinion that such a view of the Palestine question is not sound. The subject is primarily that of the existence of a racist fascist state as a result of an outright and direct usurpation of the land of another people through colonial imperialism. The essence of the problem is that colonial imperialism was able through the methods of the fascist Zionist movement to expel and drive out the indigenous inhabitants in a manner similar to what is happening in Rhodesia and South Africa. This is the real problem which the socialist camp did not comprehend very well. In addition, we did not seriously attempt to make the socialist camp understand it.

KHOULI: In your opinion the failure was both their responsibility and our own. How can we overcome it?

ABU EYAD: There is no doubt the failure was the responsibility of both them and ourselves. There are two important points to be considered here: Firstly, the attitude of the socialist camp towards the Palestine problem. I believe that one of the basic reasons behind the weakening of the communist parties in the Arab world is their wrong stand *vis-à-vis* the Palestine revolution, by limiting its development and expansion and by alleging that the number of those supporting it do not constitute a majority. This might not apply to the Communist Party of Egypt but it applies to the other Arab countries.

KHOULI: It applies to Egypt.

ABU EYAD: The second point is that the socialist camp, after the June war, did not attempt to understand the reality of our attitude towards the November 1967 Security Council resolution.[7]

KHOULI: Here you should explain why Israel rejects the implementation of this resolution.

ABU EYAD: Israel simply rejects this resolution because the victorious wants to achieve results from its aggression which it has not yet achieved. The aggression—as understood by our enemy—aimed at terminating the existence of anything called Palestine and Palestinian. The enemy could have made many of the Arab regimes fall. It could have put the Arabs in a position of defeat and surrender so that they would accept its existence. All these matters were not accomplished as a result of the aggression. Thus, victory was one of paper and maps but not a real one. The Palestinian resistance movement grew and became stronger. Certain regimes which were supposed to fall did not do so. Many other things, the peace treaty which the enemy requested was not agreed to by any Arab country. I think that the positiveness of the Khartoum Summit Conference was expressed in the decision calling for no peace, no recognition, and no negotiations. Thus the aggression did not achieve anything. The Security Council resolution calls for withdrawal; it is true and natural that the Israelis do not want to withdraw, not even with secured boundaries. The Arab governments might accept on paper the concept of secure boundaries, but in reality the Israelis want more guarantees. What are

---

7   Ed. Note: The UN Security Council unanimously adopted Resolution 242 on November 22, 1967, following the conclusion of the Six-Day War. The Resolution asserted the "inadmissibility of the acquisition of territory by war and the need to work for a just and lasting peace in the Middle East in which every State in the area can live in security," and also called for the "Withdrawal of Israeli armed forces from territories occupied in the recent conflict." The full text of the Resolution is contained in the later pages of this volume.

they going to lose? They are occupying territories which might solve their economic problems, since the reality of the Zionist aggression is always linked with Israel's daily requirements. If we go back to the Israeli official yearbooks, we find that in 1956 unemployment totaled 36 per cent; in 1967 it totaled 39 per cent. In both cases they had to wage wars to curb unemployment.

KHOULI: Can't we say that the Palestinian resistance movement fears that if the Security Council resolution was implemented—and I think that this will not be the case—the attitude of the Arab governments, or a number of them at least, might change with regard to the resistance movement?

ABU EYAD: Actually I did not, purposefully, tackle the question that one of the conditions of the colonialist countries for the implementation of the Security Council resolution is the liquidation of Palestinian resistance. But—and I am not being conceited—it has become a popular movement and cannot be liquidated. It cannot go backwards.

KHOULI: At least it will be faced with unsettling problems?

ABU EYAD: Even so, at present the Palestinian resistance, in spite of the numerous loopholes within it, has become the property of the Palestinian people and all the Arab people. It is not feasible to destroy a movement which has such deep roots, which has been adopted by the masses, and which belongs primarily to the logic of the present age. Of course, when colonialism thinks of implementing the Security Council resolution, it does so according to its own wants and interests. These require the destruction of Palestinian action and guerrilla action, even if by putting forward, the outward form of our alternative. Consequently, we hear, every now and then, of the idea of the Palestinian state which aims at aborting the liberation movement of the Palestinian people and their armed resistance. That is a Palestinian state which is completely subordinate to Israel and colonialism to be established on the West Bank and the Gaza Strip with a corridor connecting these two parts. That will end the fighting. You want a Palestinian state. Here is the Palestinian state and the war is over. According to our sources of information on the discussion of the four great powers in New York, such a "forged Palestinian state" is under consideration. The strange thing is that the American delegation is the one presenting and defending this project.

KHOULI: What is so strange about that?

ABU EYAD: The strange thing is that, in the past, the Americans have been refusing to recognize the Palestinian people and now they are showing such interest in the Palestinian state.

KHOULI: Exactly as they understood the destiny of socialism in Czechoslovakia. Why don't you have a dialogue concerning these questions and differing points of view with the socialist camp?

ABU EYAD: What I can say is that we have asked them, and we are still asking, to have such a dialogue. We are always ready to have a dialogue with all the world forces. We are open to every kind of unconditional aid and discussion. But, as you know, the opening from one side is insufficient. It should be from both sides.

KHOULI: Alright. What is the attitude of the states and peoples of the third world towards you?

ABU EYAD: Actually their attitude is one of great and growing support. Naturally the internal problems of the third world limit its capabilities. We realize that.

KHOULI: As for the peoples of the capitalist world?

ABU EYAD: We are continuously winning over friends from among them. We cannot say that we have won the support of a great and important part of public opinion, but it is continuous, especially in the Scandinavian countries, France and Britain. The new left supports us totally.

KHOULI: Last week while discussing the resistance with foreign journalists, some of them said that if the present situation continues as it is in the area and Palestinian resistance continues in its rejection of any peaceful solution, the area will blow up and this time it will lead to a world war. In their opinion the Palestinian resistance movement should realize its responsibility concerning the question of world peace.

ABU EYAD: We are puzzled with these people. At times the resistance is weak and carries no weight, and it is not necessary to contact it to know its opinion and position. At others its role grows to such an extent that it begins to threaten world peace!

These people should define their position concerning the resistance. Is it weak and unworthy of contact? Or is it a primary movement and of weight in the area?

Moreover, is our armed resistance against a racist-fascist enemy which occupies our homeland, a threat to world peace, or a threat to colonialism and racism, the cause of wars? We are a liberation movement. Why are such words concerning world peace not uttered with regard to, e.g., the Vietnamese liberation movement? Vietnam also could be regarded as a cause of a world war. Why are we alone accused of threatening world peace? What threatens world peace is the continuation of the squandering of the right of the Palestinian people to their land and country, and the continuation of the Zionist colonialist entity in our country. Peace and progress will not be realized in our country unless the Zionist entity is liquidated from the Arab homeland. The peoples of the world should comprehend that when the Palestinian people carry arms, they are working seriously for peace in the world.

KHOULI: Meaning that Palestinian resistance is causing a liberation war to burst out against colonialism and racism. Thus, like every liberation movement in the world, it objectively serves the question of world peace. This is true. Let us discuss another problem. It has been noticed that during the last few weeks the Voice of al-'Asifah, which belongs to Al-Fateh, has harshly and un-objectively criticized the Soviet Union. Don't you think that differences in viewpoints should not hide an important fact, namely that the Soviet Union is an important friend and objective ally of the national liberation movements in the world. And that such differences must be settled in terms of friendship.

ABU EYAD: We totally agree that the Soviet Union must be viewed as a friend of the Arabs. This friendship has been actually expressed in the form of material aid to and strong moral support for the Arab states especially after the June war. Yet this does not prevent us from declaring the differences in our viewpoints with regard to the situation. I believe that in this context there must be direct relations between the Soviet Union and the Palestinian people. The fact that the relations are indirect is not our fault.

The Soviet Union must appreciate our sensitivity to the meetings of the great powers. We have always, as a people, had to put up with our destiny being decided in our absence. In our criticism, we wanted to clarify to the Soviet Union, the friend and yet at the same time participant in these discussions, this essential point which we believe is supported by Soviet Union's principles. Our criticism was the sort that wants to bring the enemy nearer and not send him farther away.

KHOULI: Then it should have been essential that the method of criticism should have differed and not equated the Soviet Union, United States, and Britain.

ABU EYAD: No. We did not equate the Soviet Union, United States, and

Britain. Please re-read the criticism to be sure of that. We said that the United States and Britain participated in the creation of the Zionist entity and are still strongly supporting it. While the Soviet Union, the friend of the Arabs, is supposed not to maintain its previous 1948 stand *vis-à-vis* the Palestine question.

KHOULI: Now I would like to get acquainted with your outlook concerning the enemy. What was it prior to and after the implementation of armed resistance?

ABU EYAD: From the start, I would like to clarify a general element. The Zionist movement has attempted, and is still attempting, to convince the Arabs and its followers that it cannot bear any defeat whether in a partial battle which would have psychological repercussions on its people, or in a great battle which would lead to the liquidation of the Israeli entity and Jewish masses. It has succeeded in this attempt to a great extent. It is noticeable—with regret—that in the same way that we minimized the ability of the Zionist soldier before 1948 by portraying him as a non-fighter and a coward, so now have we exaggerated the picture of this soldier after the June war.

We feel that the individual in Israel, as far as being a man is concerned, especially the soldier—if we exclude the leaders who work within the framework of the Zionist colonialist movement plan—is not convinced of the war except from the viewpoint of self-defense. If we were able, through our behavior, to reach the heart of this individual and convince him that we are truly not butchers who want to slay him and throw his women and children into the sea, as Zionism portrays us, we can make a psychological separation between the human being and the Zionist, the Jewish soldier, and military Zionist colonialist establishment.

We have proposed to the Arab governments that they announce officially that they are ready to receive all the Arab Jews who have immigrated to Israel, that they will return to them all their property and civil rights, and treat them as Arab citizens equal to the other Arab citizens. I believe that if we succeed in this, and clarify our humanitarian stand *vis-à-vis* the Jew as a human being, we are sure that the military Zionist colonialist establishment will be automatically defeated. The Jewish soldier who is under the influence of the belief that if he does not fight and shed Arab blood, he is bound to get killed and die, will lose such a belief. We have been made profoundly aware of this implication. After the Karameh battle 300 Israeli officers and soldiers were tried for refusing to participate in it. It is regrettable that, in our newspapers, we distorted the attitude of these soldiers and officers by accusing them of being cowards and running away from the battle. If we had looked carefully into the matter and reviewed what they had written before and after the battle we would have discovered the great humanitarian implication behind it, namely that they were not convinced of the war of aggression, nor even of the destruction of Palestinian resistance. On this basis, if our propaganda is able to express the reality of our humanitarianism, and can convince the Jewish soldier and officer, and the Jewish human being in general, that our resistance under no condition aims at him but aims at Zionism and its entity, the myth will disappear, and our battle for the liquidation of Zionism and its entity will become easier and possible with fewer sacrifices.

Perhaps in my discussion 1 have concentrated on the military aspect and its establishments. In fact this is the enemy's source of strength and weakness. We have recently met a foreign progressive journalist who has come from Israel, we asked him: What are your main observations? He said that there is a basic understanding among progressive and sometimes unprogressive circles, even if their size is small, of why the Palestinian carries arms and resists. The Israeli intelligence services are after these people and constantly watch them. It is regrettable that our newspapers do not know much of what is happening inside Israel, and this in turn makes the Arab citizen ignorant with regard to these important facts. The implication behind this is that the truth about the Palestinian resistance has reached the Jewish human being, and it is not strange any more that a Palestinian throws a bomb at an Israeli patrol. On the contrary, the attitude of the Zionist military authority with regard to blowing up Arab houses and the maltreatment of captives and prisoners has become strange and is sometimes condemned.

Our view of the enemy covers the social structure and the social situation within it up till now Israeli Zionist society has not experienced a real sense of belonging or assimilation. It is an alliance of interest based on confronting danger as portrayed by Zionism. The only thing that unites a Jew coming from Syria with one from Iraq or Europe is a feeling of persecution and the necessity to be grouped together to face the danger. Such a society cannot be humanitarian, nor is it capable of any permanence. The eastern Jews are, generally, treated as second class citizens. There is obvious discrimination between them and the European Jews (Ashkenazi). Harmony between the two groups is difficult and does not exist at all at some levels. Only the European Jews are first class citizens and enjoy all privileges; they alone occupy high positions such as ministers, army commanders, senior officers, ambassadors, and high offices in ministries and establishments. Do you know that the Egyptian Jews live almost in isolation? The majority of them were grouped in Beersheba, which is located in the south. Such a phenomenon is not accidental. It reveals the sectarian divisions within the Zionist society despite superficial appearances to the contrary.

On the whole these factors, and others which we do not want to reveal, guide us in our complicated plan to confront the enemy objectively. In other words we must know the enemy as it is in reality and not as we imagine it to be. You may be sure that we calculate the enemy's strong and weak points accurately and do not overlook the dynamic relationship that exists between them.

KHOULI: I would like to thank you for the opportunity of having this dialogue with you and for the frankness of your discussion in it, and to conclude I would like to ask you a question that is often asked by some foreign friends: What is your attitude if any Jew in the world is subjected to persecution? I always replied that I would stand by him against persecution. What is Al-Fateh's answer to such a question about the persecution of a Jew inside or outside Palestine?

ABU EYAD: Our answer is clear and there are two aspects to it. If we welcome living with the Jews after the liquidation of the Zionist entity and the establishment of the Palestinian democratic state, we will stand by any persecuted Jew, and we are ready to give him a gun and fight on his side.

Constitution of the Palestinian National Liberation Movement (Fateh)[1]

[1960S]

Dear brother, comrade of the struggle:

This movement is a patriotic and historical responsibility which we all must shoulder honestly... And let's inspire all those who are faithful to Palestine with this concerted, patriotic deed... We all must confront critical times, and tolerate mishaps patiently... We all must sacrifice ourselves, our effort and time; these are the weapons of honest patriots.

Do not, therefore, dear brother, bring your march to a halt!

Proceed in your march, armed with the patriots' resolution, the true believers' determination, and the fighters' patience... Our people are in need of every second after our case has taken that long... Let's not forget for a while that our enemy is strong, and that the fight is fierceful and long... Consequently, determination, patience, confidentiality, commitment, and abiding by the revolution's goals and principles keep our march unremittingly steady and makes our road to victory much shorter.

Proceed then, my brother, forward...
to the revolution.

Long live Palestine, a free Arab state.

Fateh

---

1 Source: *Fateh Online* (accessed on March 14, 2024, online at: https://web.archive.org/web/20050912190438/http://www.fateh.net/e_public/constitution.htm, captured by *Wayback Machine* 5 Sept 2005).

INTRODUCTION TO THE CONSTITUTION

The significance of this constitution stems from its being an application of the principles of our struggle, the pedestal of the Movement. It is also an expression of the Movement's conception of its relationships with other movements and organizations, as it is the disciplinary framework which dictates and organizes the relationships among its members in a way that maintains its path and the revolution's future.

THIS CONSTITUTION REVOLVES AROUND THE FOLLOWING PRINCIPLES

1. The armed revolution we are waging has been set into orbit by the principle that it is a public revolution, and not one of a distinguished class, and that the public is capable of practicing struggle efficiently and conscientiously. The public is also the true protector of the revolutionary organization. This organization has satisfied the intimate relationship between the revolution and the public via the hierarchical structure of the Movement in which the public constitutes its solid, wide base.

With this view of the public's role in mind, the role of the organized base in the Movement is crystallized. The Movement is in close contact with the public, sharing their cares and worries and inspired by their aspirations. The public is, therefore, the sole source of authorities and the sole, honest guardian of the Movement. It is also the only party authorized to take decisive decisions, and to elect the leadership at all levels. This takes place through direct election at varying levels due to maintaining secrecy, and because of the state of geographical dispersion suffered by our Palestinian people.

2. The elected leadership assumes its responsibilities on the basis of the democratic centrality principle which warrants commitment of the lower ranks to the higher ranks' decisions. The leadership is, in turn, held accountable to its conferences and councils. Higher leaderships assume a pivotal responsibility which embodies the utter unity of the organization in different districts and institutions.

3. The Movement encourages freedom of expression and criticism within the disciplinary frameworks. This is a sacred right for all members, and no authority can deny them it. Any view or criticism within the disciplinary principles should not be taken as an indictment against a member afterwards. Free expression is the only guar-

antee to prevent the leaderships from committing mistakes or going astray, and it is the only effective method to convey the public opinion via the different bases to the Movement's leaderships.

4. The Movement firmly believes in self-criticism by all members in general and by those in authority in particular. This is important in order to attain the goal of free criticism and expression, to put an end to continual erring, and to spell out readiness to benefit from public and self criticism. By so doing, the Movement's experience will be very much developed and its path will be made much clearer.

5. In its determination on liberation and bringing about historical social changes, the Movement attempts to launch the revolutionary moral values which are on a bar with our struggle, and to create the feeling of human dignity. To this effect, the Movement tries to liberate the individual from all social ills, especially the discrimination women face, the thing that hinders their potentials and effective contributions at all disciplinary levels. This entails that the relationships among members be objective and based on the Movement's principles and constitutions. Relationships based on personal interests have no place whatsoever. The Movement, consequently, treats all members on equal footing as far as their essential obligations are concerned, and it offers equal opportunity to all faithful and active members to occupy leading positions. And while it is keen on maintaining its path, it is keen as well to get an utmost benefit from its experiences to enrich its ideology and develop its infrastructure.

6. Through its struggle, the Movement endeavors to mobilize the public in order to gain the necessary support. This task should be handled by its members. It, therefore, spares no effort to make its members set examples for others to attract the public and consolidate their faith in and loyalty to the revolutionary organization. As a result, the member has to lead a revolutionary and exemplary life which is based on loyalty, discipline, credibility, modesty, self-denial, and altruism. At the same time, he must demonstrate the highest degree of pride, rejection of reality, and conformity to the Movement's principles.

THE ESSENTIAL PRINCIPLES OF THE CONSTITUTION

1. "Fateh" is a national, revolutionary movement and its membership is top confidential.

2. The Revolution is for all the people who actively participate in it, and the Movement is its leading revolutionary organization, and hence it is the organizational force and its sole proprietor which has the right to direct its orientation.

3. The Movement constitutes one unified body which has one leadership. The rights, obligations and responsibilities are equally distributed among its members according to the Movement's principles and laws.

4. Collective leadership is the sole method of the Movement. This implies the following:

   a. Democracy is the basis of discussion, investigation and decision-taking at all organizational levels.

   b. Democratic centrality is the basis of handling responsibilities, and this involves concerted work, thinking and political participation in the Movement.

   c. Criticism and self-criticism are the basis of rectification, and punishment is not an end in itself but a means for assessment and development.

   d. The minority must conform to the majority's view, and those in lower ranks have to abide by the decisions of those in higher ranks in order to achieve discipline and unified organization which should have a unified vision, ideology and practice.

   e. The Movement firmly believes in sacred membership and freedom of the individual, and rejects vengeance, as it firmly believes in the right of any citizen to participate in the Revolution and totally rejects nullifying this right unless it can be a hazard that threatens the Movement's process and security.

CHAPTER ONE
Principles | Goals | Methods

The Movement's Essential Principles

ARTICLE 1: Palestine is part of the Arab World, and the Palestinian people are part of the Arab Nation, and their struggle is part of its struggle.

ARTICLE 2: The Palestinian people have an independent identity. They are the sole authority that decides their own destiny, and they have complete sovereignty on all their lands.

ARTICLE 3: The Palestinian Revolution plays a leading role in liberating Palestine.

ARTICLE 4: The Palestinian struggle is part and parcel of the world-wide struggle against Zionism, colonialism and international imperialism.

ARTICLE 5: Liberating Palestine is a national obligation which necessities the materialistic and human support of the Arab Nation.

ARTICLE 6: UN projects, accords, and reso., or those of any individual which undermine the Palestinian people's right in their homeland are illegal and rejected.

ARTICLE 7: The Zionist Movement is racial, colonial and aggressive in ideology, goals, organization and method.

ARTICLE 8: The Israeli existence in Palestine is a Zionist invasion with a colonial expansive base, and it is a natural ally to colonialism and international imperialism.

ARTICLE 9: Liberating Palestine and protecting its holy places is an Arab, religious and human obligation.

ARTICLE 10: Palestinian National Liberation Movement, "FATEH," is an independent national revolutionary movement representing the revolutionary vanguard of the Palestinian people.

ARTICLE 11: The crowds which participate in the revolution and liberation are the proprietors of the Palestinian land.

Goals

ARTICLE 12: Complete liberation of Palestine, and eradication of Zionist economic, political, military and cultural existence.

ARTICLE 13: Establishing an independent democratic state with complete sovereignty on all Palestinian lands, and Jerusalem is its capital city, and protecting the citizens' legal and equal rights without any racial or religious discrimination.

ARTICLE 14: Setting up a progressive society that warrants people's rights and their public freedom.

ARTICLE 15: Active participation in achieving the Arab Nation's goals in liberation and building an independent, progressive and united Arab society.

ARTICLE 16: Backing up all oppressed people in their struggle for liberation and self-determination in order to build a just, international peace.

METHOD

ARTICLE 17: Armed public revolution is the inevitable method to liberating Palestine.

ARTICLE 18: Entire dependence on the Palestinian people which is the pedestal forefront and on the Arab Nation as a partner in the fight, and realizing actual interaction between the Arab Nation and the Palestinian people by involving the Arab people in the fight through a united Arab front.

ARTICLE 19: Armed struggle is a strategy and not a tactic, and the Palestinian Arab People's armed revolution is a decisive factor in the liberation fight and in uprooting the Zionist existence, and this struggle will not cease unless the Zionist state is demolished and Palestine is completely liberated.

ARTICLE 20: Achieving mutual understanding with all the national forces participating in the armed struggle to attain national unity.

ARTICLE 21: Revealing the revolutionary nature of the Palestinian identity at the international level, and this does not contradict the everlasting unity between the Arab Nation and the Palestinian people.

ARTICLE 22: Opposing any political solution offered as an alternative to demolishing the Zionist occupation in Palestine, as well as any project intended to liquidate the Palestinian case or impose any international mandate on its people.

ARTICLE 23: Maintaining relations with Arab countries with the objective of developing the positive aspects in their attitudes with the proviso that the armed struggle is not negatively affected.

ARTICLE 24: Maintaining relations with all liberal forces supporting our just struggle in order to resist together Zionism and imperialism.

ARTICLE 25: Convincing concerned countries in the world to prevent Jewish immigration to Palestine as a method of solving the problem.

ARTICLE 26: Avoiding attempts to exploit the Palestinian case in any Arab or international problems and considering the case above all contentions.

ARTICLE 27: "FATEH" does not interfere with local Arab affairs and hence, does not tolerate such interference or obstructing its struggle by any party.

CHAPTER TWO

Organizational Rules and Principles | Commitment | Discipline | Centrality | Democracy

Public and Self-Criticism

In its organizational work, the Movement depends on the following rules and principles:

First: Commitment. This means:

Article 28:

    a. Firm belief in the case and the Movement's objectives and utter readiness to sacrifice for its sake till victory.

    b. Complete adherence to the Movement's political line.

    c. Complete conformity to the Movement's political program and to the decisions of its conferences and constitutions.

    d. Complete commitment to the Movement's decisions and defending its attitudes.

Second: Discipline. This means:

Article 29:

    a. Abiding by the terms of the essential constitution and its organizational regulations,

    b. Conforming to the organizational decisions of the leading committees,

    c. Carrying out the orders meticulously and enthusiastically, and adherence of lower ranking members to the decisions, orders and guidance of higher ranking members,

    d. Abstaining from negotiating internal issues outside organizational sessions and the Movement frameworks,

    e. Abstaining from making individual decisions or taking temperamental attitudes, and

    f. Adherence to organizational hierarchy.

Third: Central Democracy. This means:

Article 30:

    a. Central planning, leadership and surveillance, but not central execution, freedom of discussion and the right of participating in making decisions and recommendations within the organizational frameworks.

    b. Realizing democratic centrality by adopting the following organizational methods:

        1. Electing leaderships through the conferences outlined in article 42, items: d and e; article 52; article 65, item: e; article 83, item: d,

        2. Practicing collective leadership,

        3. Adherence of the minority to the majority's view,

        4. Adherence of lower ranking members to the higher ranking members' decisions,

        5. Freedom of discussion and right of participation within the organizational frameworks,

        6. Submitting reports to the electors about the leaderships' activities at every session, and

        7. Periodic reporting to higher units about all the activities carried out by lower units.

Fourth: Public and Self-Criticism

Article 31: This is one of the cornerstones according to which the revolutionary practices are evaluated in order to emphasize their positive results and circumvent their negative effects. This equally warrants the Movement's faultless process and the practice of public and self-criticism by all members and leaderships within the organizational frameworks.

Fifth: Organizational rules and principles are realized by the following methods

Article 32:

    1. When convened, the Movement's conferences (General Conference, District Conference, Region Conference) are the highest

leading authority, each according to its specialty and jurisdictions outlined in the constitution. And they have the sole authority to elect the leading committees, plan their activities, and observe and question their practices.

2. Practicing collective leadership via the committees' work, for each committee from top to bottom has to undertake its tasks on the basis of its being a complementary unit collaborating with other units in assuming its responsibilities, and that all issues must be rationally discussed through the committees and units and that all decisions must be taken in light of the legal majority.

3. The leaderships should conform to the conferences and the lower ranks to the higher ranks.

4. Achieving equality among members by their adherence to the Movement's essential constitution, regulations and decisions, and considering competence, faithfulness and sacrifice as the criteria for judging members and climbing the organizational ladder.

CHAPTER THREE

Membership: Types | Requirements | Obtaining | Rights | Continuity

Article 33:

a. The Movement's membership is a right for every Palestinian or Arab who possesses the necessary requirements, firmly believes in liberating Palestine, and demonstrates utter commitment to the Movement's essential constitution, political program, regulations and its political and organizational decisions.

b. Membership can be granted to a friend who has decided to be committed to the Movement according to a decision by the Central Committee.

Types of Membership

Article 34: There are three categories of membership:

1. Full member:

a. This is the member who has successfully completed the trial period, and is accordingly assigned as a supporter. His membership as an active member is confirmed by a decision of the Regional Committee or upon nomination by the leading organizational frameworks in the central authorities and upon consent of the Mobilization and organization office.

2. Military member: is one who has a revolutionary record. This is a member of the special organizational wing (*Asifa*) according to a special regulation offered by the Central Committee and verified by the Revolutionary Council.

b. Organizer: is one who obtains membership by a direct decree of the Central Committee, and he does not climb the organizational ladder. Once he is converted into an active member, his membership should not exceed the District Committee.

c. Supporter: is one who is nominated to join the Movement and his membership is subject to the following conditions:

1. He should meet the membership requirements outlined in article 35 except item (g) concerning the oath,

2. He should be recommended by two members who have joined the Movement for at least two years,

3. He should successfully pass a six-month trial and preparatory period during which he has to grasp the theoretical principles of the Movement and should enthusiastically perform his assignments. This equally applies to serving in the "*Asifa*" forces.

Requirements of Membership

ARTICLE 35: A member in the Movement should meet the following requirements:

a. He must not be below 17 years of age; cadets and youth have special membership regulations,

b. He must have good reputation and national credibility,

c. He must respect the people and their traditions, serve them and protect their interests and security,

d. He must be independent, not committed to any other organization or party,

e. He must have leading qualifications and demonstrate a reasonable amount of awareness and ability to assume responsibility, and have an amicable personality,

f. He must have sufficient readiness to sacrifice, self-denial and altruism,

g. He must take the following oath:

By Allah, the almighty and by my honor and beliefs I swear to remain faithful to Palestine, and to spare no effort to liberate it; I swear not to disclose any of the Movement's (FATEH) secrets and affairs; this is a free oath, to which God bears witness.

Obtaining Membership

ARTICLE 36: Members are accepted in the Movement on an individual basis according to their competence and readiness to work and sacrifice.

Rights of Membership

Article 37: The Movement's member has the following rights:

a. To enjoy all the rights cited in this constitution,

b. To have the same and equal rights and obligations as all other members,

c. To climb the organizational ladder according to the terms of this constitution and on the basis of competence, efficiency and faithfulness,

d. To have complete freedom of criticism, objection, protest, discussion, negotiation and inquiry only within the organizational sessions,

e. To criticize and cross-question any leading member within the organizational hierarchy,

f. If accused or cross-questioned, to defend himself in front of the leading committees and authorities, as well as surveillance and investigation committees,

g. To get a written reply for his queries in a month's time at the latest,

h. To enjoy protection, *viz.* he should not be fired, neglected or frozen unless he is tried and convicted by one of the Movement's courts,

i. To have the right to meet high leaderships including the Central Committee if the need arises, and

j. To have an organizational rank unless serving an organizational punishment, and his organizational ranks should appear in his record since his admission into the Movement as an active member.

Obligations of Membership

Article 38: The Movement's member has to undertake the following obligations:

a. Constant and unrelenting struggle to achieve the Movement's principles and goals,

b. Complete commitment to and application of the Movement's political line and program,

c. Application of the political constitution and carrying out all decisions conscientiously and meticulously,

d. Maintaining the Movement's organizational and ideological unity, and opposing all factions,

e. Constant and studious work to theoretically and practically elevate his education and experience,

f. Attending all meetings and paying subscriptions regularly,

g. Setting an example in altruism, courage, faithfulness, sacrifice, patience, perseverance and self-denial,

h. Continual work to maintain strong relationships with the public and to win their respect and confidence, and to constantly disseminate the Movement's principles and to consolidate the public's relationships with them,

i. Practicing public and self-criticism, and playing an active role in the organizational sessions and in the public and organizational work,

j. Constant alertness concerning the enemy's activities and the Revolution's opposing forces,

k. Keeping the Movement's secrets at the individual, committee and formation levels, and utilizing appropriate confidential methods in his work,

l. Maintaining a uniform method in work, and renouncing all individual and temperamental ones,

m. Adhering to the organizational hierarchy, and respecting the decisions of higher committees,

n. Fighting personal deceit, laziness, and temperamental relaxation as well as all harmful practices,

o. Serving the public conscientiously and faithfully, and

p. Being ready to carry out the Movement's orders to fulfill his revolutionary obligations as required.

Continuity, Suspension and Cancellation of Membership

Article 39:

a. Membership continues as long as the member continues to fulfill his tasks and obligations,

b. Membership is suspended if the member stops to fulfill his tasks for three consecutive months without reasonable excuse, or if the member requests that. Membership cannot be resumed without a decision by the District Committee for district members or by the Central Committee for others,

c. Membership is canceled if a decision to this effect is taken by the concerned committee as a result of some behavioral, political or organizational violation which entails this and determines the authority entitled to cancel the membership according to the penalty system.

THE GENERAL CONFERENCE

ARTICLE 40: The Movement's general conference is made up of:

a. Members of the Revolutionary Council,

b. 11 district representatives elected in the district conferences according to the number of areas meeting the requirements cited in this constitution and endorsed by the Mobilization and organization Office.

c. 11 representatives of the districts whose conferences cannot be convened for security purposes or failing to have quorum; such conditions are decided by the Central Committee. Those representatives are selected upon recommendation by the Mobilization and Organization Office to the Central Committee according to the organizational population.

d. District commissioners whose membership has lasted for at least ten years, and who have been appointed by a decree from the Central Committee.

e. Members of the General Military Council in the Palestinian National Liberation Army, especially *"Asifa"* forces, whose setup is outlined in the regulation appended to this constitution, and according to the decisions of the third and fourth conferences. In addition, at most 20 distinguished persons from those military forces should be nominated by the General Leadership and endorsed by the Central Committee, with the proviso that they in all should not exceed 514 of the entire population of the conference.

f. 75 "FATEH" members who are assigned duties in various departments in the independent State of Palestine and Palestine Liberation

Organization and other national and international organizations. Their membership should be through their organizational units and upon nomination by the Mobilization and Organization Office and ratified by the Central Committee. Their membership should not be below a district committee member.

g. 50 Members public organizations recommended by the Movement central offices and confirmed by the MobilOrganization Office and by a decree from the Central Committee. Their membership should not be below a district committee member.

h. 75 members of the leading bodies of central panels according to their regulations attached to this constitution. Their membership should not be below a district committee member.

i. 30 representatives of the Movement's members with the proviso that their membership is not below a district committee member.

ARTICLE 41: Requirements of the Conference Membership:

a. Membership in the General Conference has a representative nature as spelled out in article 40.

b. A member in the conference should have a five-year active membership in the Movement.

c. He should have a clean record.

ARTICLE 42: *Conference Jurisdictions*

When convened, the conference is the highest authority, and it is entitled to perform the following tasks:

a. Discussing the reports, decisions and duties of the Central Committee, and the activities of the Movement departments and institutions,

b. Endorsing the essential constitution and making any necessary modifications upon recommendation by two thirds of the present members,

c. Confirming the Movement constitutional regulations, and the political and military programs and plans,

d. Electing the members of the Central Committee by secret voting,

e. Vote of no confidence for all or some members of the Central Committee upon recommendation by two thirds of the present members,

f. Electing the Head of the Financial Supervision Committee and the Head of the Movement Supervision Committee, and protecting membership with the proviso they meet the requirements of the Revolutionary Council membership, and

g. Electing the required number for the Revolutionary Council by secret voting.

ARTICLE 43: *Holding the Conference*

a. The Central Committee calls for a regular session once every five years, and the meeting can however be put off for exceptional circumstances by a Revolutionary Council decision.

b. Upon receiving the invitation, the conference holds an unusual session within two weeks at the latest if more than two thirds of the Revolutionary Council members deem it necessary or upon request by the Central Committee. The agenda should include the topics that necessitated the session.

c. Sessions are deemed legal if two thirds of the members are present, provided that all members have been informed in writing two weeks prior to the meeting. If quorum is not maintained, the meeting will be put off two days, and then convened if more than half of the members are present.

THE GENERAL COUNCIL

ARTICLE 44: The General Council is made up of no more than 250 members of the General Conference according to the following:

a. Members of the Central Committee and the Revolutionary Council,

b. A number of district commissioners and organizational leaderships,

c. A number of military leaderships,

d. A number of the Movement's members,

e. A number of the Movement's members working in the Organization department,

f. A number of public leaderships, and

g. A number of the Movement's efficient members.

ARTICLE 45: The number of members in the previous *article* is determined by a Central Committee's decision which has to be endorsed by the Revolutionary Council.

ARTICLE 46: The General Council has the jurisdictions of an exceptional general conference according to a special system suggested by the Revolutionary Council.

ARTICLE 47: The General Council is held upon a decision of the Central Committee and approval of the Revolutionary Council which prepares the agenda.

THE REVOLUTIONARY COUNCIL

ARTICLE 48: The Revolutionary Council constitutes the following:

a. Members of the Central Committee,

b. Head of the Financial Supervision Committee and Head of the Movement Supervision and Membership Protection Committee,

c. 50 members elected by the General Conference from its members provided that each member has 30% of the electors' votes,

d. At most 20 members representing the Military Council of "FATEH" according to the special charter of "*Asifa*",

e. At most 15 highly competent persons selected by two thirds of the Central Committee members,

f. A number of the leaderships in the occupied territories, not part of the quorum, and nominated by the Revolutionary Council,

g. 5 members from other territories who are part of the quorum when attending the meetings, nominated by two thirds of the Central Committee members, and

h. At most 15 controllers from the Movement's competent members, nominated by the Central Committee and endorsed by the Revolutionary Council.

ARTICLE 49: A nominee for the Revolutionary Council has to have been a district committee member or a member of other equivalent forces and institutions for at least 10 consecutive years.

ARTICLE 50: *Jurisdictions*

When convened between two sessions of the General Conference, the Revolutionary Council is the highest authority in the Movement. Its jurisdictions are:

a. Following up and executing of the General Conference decisions,

b. Monitoring the operation of the central departments and the Movement's conditions in different districts,

c. Monitoring the Movement military affairs which do not run counter to top confidentiality,

d. Discussing the Central Committee's decisions, operations and reports, and taking appropriate decisions accordingly,

e. Adequately interpreting the terms and regulations of the essential charter in case a dispute in this respect arises,

f. Electing members of the Financial Supervision Committee and those of the Movement Supervision Committee via secret voting within six months at the latest, and

g. Discussing the reports of the committees emanating from the General Conference and taking appropriate decisions in this respect.

ARTICLE 51: At the beginning of its session, the Revolutionary Council elects from among its members a secretariat consisting of a secretary and two deputies via secret voting. The secretary should be a full-timer and should not be a member of the Central Committee.

ARTICLE 52: The Revolutionary Council devises its bylaw which is approved by the majority of members.

ARTICLE 53: In case quorum is not maintained in the Central Committee, the Revolutionary Council is called to meet within two weeks to elect two thirds of its members by secret voting in order to maintain quorum.

ARTICLE 54: If vacancies in the Central Committee are not occupied within three months, the Revolutionary Council is called to an emergency session during which vacancies are occupied by its members through secret voting, provided that each candidate should be elected by absolute majority.

ARTICLE 55: Vacancies in the Revolutionary Council are occupied by competent members who meet the requirements of the Revolutionary Council membership.

ARTICLE 56: The Revolutionary Council is entitled to fire or freeze one or more offending members of the Central Committee, and this is decided by two thirds of the members provided that the number of fired or frozen members does not exceed one third.

ARTICLE 57: The Revolutionary Council is entitled to fire or freeze one or more of its members if an offense is committed, and this is decided by the majority of two thirds of its members.

ARTICLE 58: The Revolutionary Council holds regular sessions once every three months upon an invitation by its secretary, and it can hold exceptional sessions upon a decision by the Central Committee or a written request addressed to its secretary by two thirds of its members.

ARTICLE 59: Quorum is maintained if two thirds of the Revolutionary Council members are present provided that they have been officially notified three days prior to the meeting, and if quorum is not maintained the Council will convene by absolute majority 24 hours after the set date.

ARTICLE 60: Decisions of the Council are made by the absolute majority of the present members except in cases otherwise stated, and voting is by raising hands unless the Council decides otherwise.

THE FINANCIAL SUPERVISION COMMITTEE AND THE MOVEMENT: SUPERVISION AND MEMBERSHIP PROTECTION COMMITTEE

ARTICLE 61: Heads of these committees are elected directly by the Conference upon nominating some of the candidates by the Central Committee.

ARTICLE 62: A special charter for each committee is devised and is endorsed by the Revolutionary Council in its first session after submitting it.

THE CENTRAL COMMITTEE

ARTICLE 63:

    a. The Central Committee is made up of 21 members as follows:

        1. 18 members from the Conference elected by secret voting.

        2. 3 members appointed by the Central Committee provided that they get two thirds of the votes.

3. An additional number of the occupied territories leaderships, not part of the quorum, nominated determined by the Revolutionary Council.

b. The Central Committee selects a political office from its members with the proviso that they do not exceed 11 members.

c. The Central Committee determines the jurisdictions of the political office in its internal charter.

d. All members of the Central Committee have equal rights, obligations and responsibilities.

e. The Commander-in-Chief chairs the Central Committee meetings and runs its sessions' in accordance with the regulations of its internal charter.

ARTICLE 64: The Central Committee selects a secretary and two deputies from its members.

ARTICLE 65: A candidate to the Central Committee should have been a member in the Movement for at least 15 consecutive years, and he should have served as a secretary of a district committee or any equivalent job in the departments and forces, and he should obtain 49% of the votes.

ARTICLE 66: The Central Committee convenes at least once a month to discuss the performance of all Movement departments and issue the necessary decisions and recommendations. Each of its members should be responsible for what he has been practicing during the period between meetings. Exceptional sessions can be convened when the need arises.

ARTICLE 67: The Central Committee is unanimously in charge of all the Movement's activities.

ARTICLE 68: Quorum is maintained if two thirds of the members are present, and once this is impossible, the meeting holds if half plus one of the members attend 24 hours after the assigned date.

ARTICLE 69: Decisions of the Central Committee are taken by absolute majority unless otherwise stated in the essential constitution.

ARTICLE 70: Vacancies in the Central Committee are occupied for death, dismissal, resignation or handicap purposes by members of the Revolutionary Council provided that they obtain two thirds of the votes. The elected member should be performing his duties during the period from the conference to the time of employment.

Responsibilities of the Central Committee

ARTICLE 71: The Central Committee assumes its responsibilities as the executive body of the General Conference. These responsibilities are as follows:

a. Carrying out the decisions and the political, organizational, military and financial plans of the General Conference and the Revolutionary Council as well as executing the political program endorsed by the General Conference,

b. Discussing the disciplinary violations and misapplication of the essential constitution and taking the appropriate procedures,

c. Undertaking daily operations and directing the internal, external, political, military and financial policies of the Movement as well as practicing leadership responsibilities in all aspects,

d. Leading the Movement in all public and official Palestinian, Arab and international affairs,

e. Maintaining solidarity within the Movement and applying the essential constitution,

f. Calling the General Conference to convene, preparing its agenda and submitting detailed written reports about all its activities,

g. Supervising issuance of the Movement data, newsletters and studies,

h. Setting up the Movement security court, devising its internal charter and endorsing and verifying its terms. In case of a death penalty, verification is maintained by two thirds of the votes,

i. Endorsing appointment of the Military Council members who are nominated by the Commander-in-Chief by two thirds of the votes. Re-voting is handled once a year,

j. Endorsing appointment of members of leading bodies of the central and administrative departments and the Movement central offices by two thirds of the votes. Re-voting is carried out once a year,

k. Appointing qualified members and controllers as cited in the constitution by two thirds of the votes, and

l. Naming "FATEH" members in the Palestinian National Council.

ARTICLE 72: The Central Committee devises a special internal charter to organize its operations within three months at the latest.

ARTICLE 73: During its meeting after the General Conference, the Central Committee distributes tasks on its members according to the specific specializations determined in the internal charter which includes all activities and responsibilities.[2]

---

[2] **Ed. Note:** Here, the archived text jumps to article 93 directly from article 73. For a continuation to article 74, the reader can jump to chapter 5 (articles 74-92), and then back to chapter 4; otherwise the text preserves the original format.

CHAPTER FOUR
Areas

ARTICLE 93: The term "area" is given to the base organization which consists of at least four branches. An area maintains this capacity according to a decision by the Mobilization and Organization Office and upon a recommendation of the district committee.

First: The Area Conference

Formation

ARTICLE 94: The area conference is set up as follows:

    a. The area committee members,

    b. Members of the branches committees,

    c. Members of the area committee during the previous conference,

    d. Five active members nominated by the area and endorsed by the district committee if it deems necessary, and

    e. A representative of each of the public organizations in the area.

Jurisdictions

ARTICLE 95: The area conference assumes the following jurisdictions:

    a. Discussing the decisions and operations of the area committee, and calling its members to account,

    b. Discussing the circumstances of the organization in the area,

    c. Discussing general issues in the Movement and the district, and submitting the necessary recommendations, and

    d. Electing five of the area conference members by direct secret voting provided that their membership has lasted for at least three years. The district committee is entitled to add two other members when necessary.

ARTICLE 96: The district committee selects the secretary of the area committee from the elected members.

ARTICLE 97:

    a. The area conference convenes once biannually, and it should meet before the district conference.

b. It can hold emergency sessions upon a decision by the area committee and the approval of the district committee.

ARTICLE 98: In areas where elections are impossible for security circumstances or failure to meet the organizational requirements, the district committee nominates a list of the area committee members which will be endorsed by the Mobilization and Organization Office.

Requirements of the Area Conference

ARTICLE 99:

a. Membership in the area conference is contingent upon the representational quality cited in article 94.

b. The member should have a clean record.

SECOND: THE AREA COMMITTEE

ARTICLE 100: The area committee holds weekly meetings, chaired by the area secretary. According to circumstances, emergency sessions can be held, and they follow the terms cited in the meetings of the district committee as regards quorum and voting.

Jurisdictions

ARTICLE 101: The area committee assumes its jurisdictions in its capacity as the executive leadership in the area. Such jurisdictions are similar to those of the districts within the area boundary.

ARTICLE 102: After a legal investigation, the district committee is entitled to freeze or revoke the membership of almost two of the area committee members. And if there is a need to freeze or revoke the membership of more than two members, the district conference is called to an emergency meeting to elect a new area committee.

ARTICLE 103: If an organizational necessity arises, the area committee can make any change in the committees of wings, chains and cells.

ARTICLE 104: The area committee appoints secretaries of cells, chains and wings, but secretaries of branches are appointed by the district committee upon nomination by the area committee.

CHAPTER FIVE

THE MOVEMENT LEADING ORGANIZATIONS
PART TWO
DISTRICT CONFERENCE | DISTRICT COMMITTEE | AREA CONFERENCE

AREA COMMITTEE

ARTICLE 74:

a. The term district is given to any branch of the organization within the boundary of a country. A district includes three organizational areas or more which meet the requirements cited in this constitution.

b. A district consists of organizational areas which have a hierarchical structure including branches, wings, chains and cells.

c. The organizational unit which exists in unfavorable conditions does not have to follow this hierarchy after having approval from the Mobilization and Organization Office.

d. The leading committee of any organizational unit has the appropriate leading rank according to the number of its members in the district. It directly follows the Mobilization and Organization Office, and it has the responsibilities of a district committee.

e. An organizational rank can be gradually promoted to a leading committee or any of the base organizations in districts where the sufficient number necessary to constitute an area is not available in order to set up an area with all its branches. This takes place in view of seniority, efficiency and activity and upon a decision by the Mobilization and Organization Office.

f. The cell is the basic organizational unit in the Movement.

ARTICLE 75: New cells are set up upon the approval of the district committee and the nomination of the area committee. In case there is not a district committee, a cell can be formed according to a decision by the concerned leading committee in the respective district.

ARTICLE 76:

a. Militia is the armed organization within the base framework as outlined in article 91.

b. Militia forces are formed in the districts which have favorable conditions.

c. The leadership and formation of militia is subject to the military laws of "Asifa".

d. The General Leadership of "Asifa" forces devises the charter of militia, and this must be confirmed by the Revolutionary Council.

District Conference
First: Formation

Article 77: A district conference is formed as follows:

a. Members of district committee,

b. Members of areas committees,

c. One member representing a public organization in the district which has a movement office. This member is chosen by the concerned office,

d. Former members of the district committee during the previous conference with the proviso that it carries out its assigned tasks,

e. A number of active members of the Movement selected by the district committee provided that the number does not exceed 10%, and

f. One member from each central office in the district working through the district committee.

Second: Responsibilities

Article 78: The district conference assumes the following responsibilities:

a. Discussing the report, decisions and operations of the district committee, and calling its members to account,

b. Discussing the area conditions, decisions and operations,

c. Devising the organizational and political plans of different tasks and the external relations with other political authorities, public organizations, thinkers, politicians and journalists within the strategy endorsed by the General Conference and the Central Committee's decisions, and

d. Discussing the general issues of the Movement and making the necessary recommendations.

e. The district committee also elects four thirds of the required number from whom the Central Committee selects the members of the district committee while the rest remains as stand-by. In case of a vacancy, the Central Committee selects the required number from the stand-by members.

Requirements of District Conference Membership

Article 79:

a. Membership in the district conference committee is contingent upon the representational quality cited in article 77.

b. A member in the district conference should have spent three years at least as a Movement member.

c. He should maintain a clean record.

Article 80:

a. A district conference convenes once biannually.

b. A district conference can be called to hold an exceptional session upon decision by the district committee and approval of the Mobilization and Organization Office.

Article 81: In districts, where elections are impossible to conduct for security purposes or failure to meet the organizational requirements, the Central Committee can appoint a district committee and its secretary.

Second: District Committee

Formation

Article 82: A district committee consists of at least five and no more than eleven members elected from the district conference according to item (1), article 78. The member should have spent five years as a Movement member.

Meetings

Article 83:

a. A district committee convenes once every two weeks, and is chaired by the secretary. When the need arises, exceptional sessions can be held.

b. Quorum is maintained if two thirds of the members are present, and the meeting can be put off for 24 hours if otherwise, and quorum would be maintained if half of the members could attend.

c. Decisions of the committee are based on approval of the absolute majority of the present members.

Jurisdictions

ARTICLE 84: Being the organizational leadership in the district, a district committee assumes the following jurisdictions:

a. Executing the decisions of higher leaderships,

b. Supervising all institutions and departments in the district,

c. Devising appropriate plans for all activities in the district,

d. Recommending to the Mobilization and Organization Office the freezing or revocation of the membership of at most two of its members provided that the reasons are spelled out,

e. Leading the district daily affairs,

f. Taking care of the integrity and solidarity of the Movement and co-ordinating operations among different areas,

g. Calling the district conference to convene, preparing its agenda, and submitting detailed written reports about all activities in the district to it, and

h. Preparing the members organizational map, and reporting any emergency developments to the Mobilization and Organizational Office once every six months.

ARTICLE 85: After legal investigation, the Central Committee is entitled to freeze or revoke the membership of one or more of the district committee members provided that the number does not exceed one third. And if there is a need to revoke the membership of more than one third, the district conference should be called to an emergency session.

ARTICLE 86: The district committee should report to the Mobilization and Organizational Office about a member's moving to another district after agreeing with him on the means of communication. The report should include some information about the member and his organizational rank.

ARTICLE 87: Offices of the central departments undertake their activities in the district through the district committee and in virtue of their being part of its jurisdictions. Direct expansion of the central departments offices in the district is banned.

ARTICLE 88: Tasks are distributed over the district committee members in a way that warrants controlling the operations in the district.

THE DISTRICT COMMISSIONER

ARTICLE 89:

a. The Central Committee nominates a commissioner in the districts as it deems necessary. The nominee's rank should not be lower than a district committee member with a seniority period of three years.

b. The commissioner assumes the tasks assigned to him by the Central Committee, and his relationship with the district committee by an internal regulation issued by the Mobilization and Organizational Office.

THE DISTRICT SECRETARY

ARTICLE 90: The Central Committee nominates the secretary from the list elected by the district conference. And he assumes the following jurisdictions:

a. Calling the district committee to convene and chairing its sessions,

b. Submitting monthly or instant reports to the Mobilization and Organizational Office,

c. Following up and executing the decisions, recommendations and responsibilities of the district committee,

d. Unless it runs counter to the constitution regulations, calling district conferences to convene,

e. Signing the letters, decisions and orders issued by the district committee, and

f. Signing paying orders according to the financial regulations.

THE DISTRICT BUDGET

ARTICLE 91: The district budget consists of the following:

a. Subscriptions,

b. Unconditional donations,

c. Investments and local resources,

d. The budget accredited by the Movement financial office.

ARTICLE 92:

a. The district budget is determined in a project submitted by the district committee.

b. The Mobilization and Organizational Office is entitled to verify it as stated or modify it as necessary.

CHAPTER SIX

THE MOVEMENT BASE ORGANIZATIONS

ARTICLE 105: The Movement base organizations include the following:

a. The Cell. It consists of three two five members including the secretary.

b. The Chain. It consists of two five cells.

c. The Wing. It consists of two to five chains.

d. The Branch. It consists of two to five wings.

e. The Area. It consists of at least four branches.

ARTICLE 106: In districts where security conditions are unfavorable, the district committee or the one assuming this role can overlook this hierarchy and devise an appropriate means of communication with the district committee. Likewise, the number of cell members can be lowered to two as the individual method can be followed provided that the Mobilization and Organization Office approves that.

OBLIGATIONS OF BASE ORGANIZATIONS

ARTICLE 107:

a. Providing members with a revolutionary education, consolidating their commitment and discipline, developing their awareness and experiences, and enhancing their active participation according to the programs set by the Mobilization and Organization Office,

b. Carrying out their tasks enthusiastically, and sparing no effort to achieve the Movement's objectives and embodying its principles,

c. Exerting strenuous efforts to enhance interaction with the public and winning their respect and confidence,

d. Striving continually within public organizations and maintaining commitment to their memberships, and

e. Trying hard to protect the Movement and develop its efficiency to confront and conquer its enemies

ARTICLE 108: The area committee, the branch committee, the wing committee and the cell committee assume the responsibilities of leadership, each in its organizational capacity in the following matters:

a. Leading its members according to the Movement's political program and constitution,

b. Embodying the Movement's attitudes and executing its decisions enthusiastically and fervently,

c. Upgrading its members' awareness and adherence to the Movement, enhancing their active participation and developing their experiences and potentials,

d. Developing their military and educational competence,

e. Enhancing their interaction with the public and their readiness to sacrifice for their sake,

f. Maintaining strong relationships with the public bases and winning their respect and confidence,

g. Holding brotherly relationships between bases and higher units and vice versa,

h. Observing paying subscriptions, and monitoring its members' behavioral and organizational conduct, and ensuring execution of these tasks,

i. Setting an example in sacrifice, active participation, faithfulness and team work,

j. Ensuring speed and adequacy in conveying reports, information, leaflets and others,

k. Paying adequate attention to the members' problems and taking appropriate initiatives to ensure rapid and revolutionary solutions,

l. Examining the members' work fields and identifying positive and negative aspects and taking the necessary measures,

m. Calling members to account and criticizing them for individualism or lack of seriousness, and

n. Submitting regular reports about their activities to the higher committee.

CHAPTER SEVEN

PENALTIES

ARTICLE 109: The organizational penalties aim at:
   a. Upgrading the members' morals, and
   b. Securing the Movement's integrity and getting rid of corruption.

ARTICLE 110: The organizational penalties are:
   a. Drawing attention,
   b. Rebuke,
   c. Warning,
   d. Freezing,
   e. Rank demotion,
   f. Firing,
   g. Firing with slander.

ARTICLE 111: The organizational violations are four types:

First: Firing or firing with slander and this applies to :
   1. Violation of Unit One of the constitution,
   2. Delinquency, and
   3. Illegal co operation with any other non-adversary movement and disclosing the Movement secrets to it.

Second: Freezing or demoting rank, and this applies to:
   1. Violating commitment, and this is realized by:
      a. Violating the Movement political line,
      b. Violating the Movement political program, and
      c. Reluctance to adhere to the Movement's decisions.
   2. Violating the membership protection rule,
   3. Violating the members' equality rule,
   4. Violating the freedom of expression rule, and
   5. Violating discipline, and this is applicable to:
      a. Violating the constitution,
      b. Disrespect of leading authorities' decisions,

c. Rejection of orders execution,

   d. Discussing organizational issues outside the units,

   e. Disrespect of hierarchy, and

   f. Offending the public.

7. Offending other members.

8. Disclosing secrets.

9. Offending reputation.

10. False rumors.

Third: Rebuke or warning, and this applies to:

1. Ceasing to participate in organizational activities without an acceptable excuse for at most two regular meetings and this period extends for one month, and

2. Refusal to practice self-criticism when deemed necessary by the respective unit.

Fourth: Drawing attention or Rebuke, and this applies to:

1. Coming late to a meeting without an excuse,

2. Inadequate practice of self-education, and

3. Demonstrating signs of deceit and laziness.

ARTICLE 112: Repetition of violations is a reason for imposing a stricter penalty. And if the same violations are repeated, the strictest penalty is imposed. A severe penalty is inflicted if newly violations are repeated.

ARTICLE 113:

   a. Firing and firing with slander penalties are imposed by the Central Committee.

   b. Rank demotion and freezing penalties are inflicted on area committee members and secretaries of branches by the Central Committee, the Mobilization and Organization Office and the District Committee. Such penalties are imposed on branch members or lower ranks by the area committee.

   c. A warning penalty is inflicted by the higher organizational rank.

   d. Drawing attention and Rebuke penalties are imposed by all concerned organizational ranks according to the unit the member belongs to.

ARTICLE 114: When considering violations, all concerned organizational ranks constitute investigation committees prior to passing a judgment except in case of drawing attention and rebuking penalties.

ARTICLE 115: Each penalty can be revised by the rank immediately higher than the one which has signed it in front of the Central Committee and it cannot be overruled without a decision by the Revolutionary Council.

ARTICLE 116: It is possible that each penalty is passed separately or together with other penalties issued by the Movement Court.

ARTICLE 117: A sentence for two organizational penalties due to one violation is impossible.

ARTICLE 118: No sentence can be passed without calling the concerned member to a hearing where he has the right to defend himself and prove innocent.

ARTICLE 119: If the member abstains from showing up in front of the official committee which investigates the violation, he is called a second time in a week's time, after that the session takes place whether or not he attends provided that if he has been informed.

ARTICLE 120: Penalized crimes are the concern of the Movement Revolutionary Judicial Authority, and examined by the Revolutionary Courts formed by the Central Committee according to article 71 of the constitution.

CHAPTER EIGHT

GENERAL STIPULATIONS

ARTICLE 121: The appended regulations, and those endorsed by the Revolutionary Council and transferred to it by the General Conference have the same power as the essential constitution with the proviso that they not contradict it.

ARTICLE 122: Membership in the Movement is a sacred right which can be acquired only by whoever belongs to one of the Movement leading or base units.

ARTICLE 123: Working in the Movement departments is an added task to the member, which does not entail membership, nor is it a replacement of an organizational job in any of the organizational ranks. Similarly, deputizing a member to do any task outside the Movement departments is not a substitute for the Movement organizational framework.

ARTICLE 124: During an organizational meeting, any member has the right to debate before a decision is made. Debate may be allowed after issuing the decision, and a member has the right to object to the decision after execution.

ARTICLE 125: Each member has to do some minimal military training and to be completely qualified to undertake his tasks.

ARTICLE 126: A member has to be informed in accordance with requirements of his membership, organizational rank and the job undertaken.

ARTICLE 127: A member who is sacked or is subjected to some arbitrary act without a decision by a Movement court has the right to appeal to the Member Protection Committee.

ARTICLE 128: Equality among organizational ranks in f its members. A district committee member has to handle any task assigned by the district committee, and this equally applies to an area committee member in the respective area boundary.

ARTICLE 130: A member of the Central Committee who has failed in the General Conference elections has the right to maintain his membership in the Conference and perform any tasks assigned to him by the Central Committee, and this equally applies to the member of the Revolutionary Council.

AL FATEH:
TOWARDS A DEMOCRATIC STATE IN PALESTINE[1]
[1970]

THE PALESTINE REVOLUTION AND THE JEWISH PEOPLE

It is almost a year since the Palestine Liberation Movement, Fateh, declared, officially and for the first time, a political program spelling out the ultimate objective of the liberation struggle. The declaration stated: "We are fighting today to create the new Palestine of tomorrow; a progressive, democratic and non-sectarian Palestine in which Christian, Moslem and Jew will worship, work, live peacefully and enjoy equal rights." The statement further added, "Our Palestinian revolution still stretches its welcoming hand to all human beings who want to fight for, and live in, a democratic, tolerant Palestine, irrespective of race, color or religion.[2]

The statement was repeated, explained and amplified by Fatch representatives in every international gathering attended by a Fateh delegation. The official spokesman of Fateh, Abu Ammar, was quoted by several journalists as saying that "once we defeat the enemy and liberate Palestine we will create a home for all of us."[3] Abu Eyad, one of the leaders of Fateh,

    1   Ed. Note: The document *Towards a Democratic State in Palestine* was submitted by Fateh to the Second World Conference on Palestine, held in Amman, Sept. 2-6, 1970. There were over 200 attendees, representing nearly 100 national and international organizations, national liberation movements, and included participants from the Middle East, Africa, Europe, the United States, and Asia. It can be accessed online at https://www.freedomarchives.org/Documents/Finder/DOC12_scans/12.towards.democratic.state.1970.pdf.

    2   Address by the Al-Fateh Delegation to the Second International Conference in Support of the Arab Peoples, Cairo, January 28, 1969.

    3   *Aims of the Palestinian Resistance Movement with Regard to the Jews*, published by the Palestine Research Center and the Fifth of June Society, Beirut, 1970. See also, Kadi, Leila S. 1969. *Basic Political Documents of the Armed Palestinian Resistance Movement*, Palestine Research Center, Beirut.

stated in a long interview with the editor of *Al-Taleea* that the Palestinian revolution condemns persecution of human beings and discrimination based on any form or shape and that Fateh would help Jews anywhere if they faced persecution at the hands of racists. Abu Eyad said that he would be willing to give these Jews arms and fight with them.[4] Such a statement was not just a fantastic propaganda claim, it was put into effect a few weeks later when Fateh students protected Jewish professor Eli Loebel in Frankfort, Germany, from molestation and attempted murder at the hands of Zionist German thugs last July. Fateh protected Jewish members of Matzpen [the Israeli Socialist Organization] in Germany after their lives were threatened in the same incident.

REVOLUTIONARY NEW IDEA

If this sounds a little difficult to believe, it is because of the bitterness created by the Palestine tragedy since the Balfour Declaration [1917, committed British government to sponsor the establishment of a Jewish national home in Palestine] and the Zionist penetration of Palestine ending in the uprooting and evacuation of Palestinians from their homeland in order to create "an exclusively Jewish State": Israel.

The call for an open, new, tolerant Palestine for Jews and non-Jews is a dramatic change in the Palestinian struggle, but it is hardly a new idea. Palestinians suggested the creation of such a state to the Peel Commission in 1937 [one of British commissions of inquiry sent to Palestine in response to independence struggle against British imperialism].

As for the idea of Jew, Moslem, and Christian living peacefully and harmoniously in one country, it also is a very old one. The Fateh declaration stated, "This is no utopian dream or false promise, for we have always lived in peace, Moslems, Christians, and Jews in the Holy Land. The Palestinian Arabs gave a refuge, a warm shelter and a helping hand to Jews fleeing persecution in Christian Europe, and to the Christian Armenians fleeing persecution in Moslem Turkey; as well as to Greeks, Caucasians and Maltese among others." One need not go to medieval history to elaborate on the idea.

However, what is new is the fact that non-Jewish Arab exiles who have been deprived of their homes and displaced by Jews in Palestine,

---

4 See *Al-Taleea* (Arabic Egyptian monthly journal), June, 1969. The dialogue has been translated into English; see *A Dialogue with Fateh*, Palestine National Liberation Movement, see also Kadi, *op. cit.*

can still—while holding the guns, and fighting for their land and their very existence—call for a new country that combines the ex-aggressor and persecutor.

CREDIBILITY

The idea is revolutionary, and its implications serious and pervasive. In fact it is so revolutionary that few uncommitted people can believe it, let alone support and work for it. It is the objective of this article to discuss, analyze and amplify the idea. Our hypothesis is that the creation of a democratic, non-sectarian Palestine is both desirable and feasible, and that once these two aspects are proven valid, the idea becomes credible. Credibility is very important if people are to be motivated to support the idea and work and sacrifice for it to achieve lasting peace and justice in Palestine.

EXILED PALESTINIANS

The exodus of 1948 was a stunning blow to the Palestinians. A whole nation, more than one full million inhabitants of a country, were deliberately terrorized and uprooted from their homes. They were thrown out of their country into a sea of sand surrounding it, in a period of a few months. The fact that many Palestinians knew the Zionist intentions and suspected the British of preparing for the eventual exile of the Arabs of Palestine to "the Transient Countries" did not make the blow less hard or stunning. One can hardly believe that the forced exile of a whole nation is possible in the twentieth century.

For thirty years under the British Mandate [1920-1948], Palestinians knew who the real enemy was. British imperialism and Zionist imperialism were quite linked in the mind of the people. Six bloody revolutions took place between 1919 and 1939. They were basically directed against the British occupiers.

Whatever complicity the British had in the Palestinians' fate—and it was great—the Palestinians were driven out by "Jewish" terrorists. Their uprooting was carried out through massacres such as that of Deir Yassin. Leaders of their tormentors and oppressors called for the creation of an "exclusively Jewish home" and considered them—the exiles—as fifth columnists who deserved to be excluded from this home, "their home." In their misery, humiliation and despair the Palestinians learnt to hate the Jews and everything "Jewish," everything connected with their enemy.

JEWS AND ZIONISTS

A few sophisticated leaders and most propagandists took pains to differentiate between Jews and Zionists. We are not anti-Jewish, we are anti-Zionists, it was repeated. "We are Semites and Jews are our cousins..." they stated. They sounded so unreal and phony saying: "some of our best friends are Jews..."

We are against the state of Israel, it was claimed. But the distinction was lost on the suffering "refugees," who were told by the Israelis that all Jews were Zionists anyway. Jewish pressure in the United States, Jewish money, and Jewish immigrants were making their enemy as entrenched as ever; and their hopes of an honorable return as dim as ever. No wonder bitterness prevailed and fear dominated.

Reading of the *Protocols of the Elders of Zion* [probably the most infamous piece of anti-Semitic literature ever written] became fashionable, anti-Semitic literature developed by European racists in a completely different context—*i.e.* where the Jews were the victims—became quite popular. This wave of bitterness, hate and utter confusion spread to other Arabs. It helped Zionist pressure and propaganda designed to secure the departure of thousands of Arab Jews from their homes to join the ranks of the occupying enemy. Thousands of these Jews would have stayed in their homes under different circumstances, and would have continued to live as they have had for hundreds of years in peace and harmony with their neighbors.

THE REVOLUTION, A NEW ERA

Fateh launched the Palestinian Revolution on Jan. 1, 1965, after nine years of political preparation. However, the first two years were spent in establishing a military "presence" in the Palestinian arena. It was the 1967 traumatic experience and the Second Exodus that shook the Palestinians to the core and put them solidly behind the revolution.

In the nadir of the new humiliating defeat, a new hope was rekindled. The Palestinian carried a gun and reentered home with it. He shot at his enemy's troops and jailers. A new sense of pride and dignity was emerging and rising. With the hope and the pride, self-confidence reappeared. A nation was reborn. Al-Karameh and similar victories, the sacrifices and the martyrs and the escalating struggle developed a new sense of belonging to Palestine. The revolution brought maturity to the fighters. As paradoxical as it may seem, people who fight can afford to be more tolerant. Mental and verbal violence usually accompany helplessness and despair.

A new attitude was being formed toward the enemy. Distinction between Jew and Zionist started to have a meaning. Realization that revenge was not a sufficient cause for a liberation war led to further examination of the final objectives of the revolution. The scores of intellectual liberal Jews who came from all over the world to start a dialogue with the revolution caused further rethinking.

New doctrine

Revolutionary leaders engaged in a serious study and discussion around the topic. Relearning old truths emerged. Jews suffered persecution at the hands of racist criminals under Nazism, so did "We" under Zionism. Several revealing parallels were discovered. "How could we hate the Jews *qua* Jews?" the revolutionaries were saying. How could we fall in the same racist trap?

A study of Jewish history and thought was conducted. Jewish contributions as well as dilemmas were identified. The majority of those who came over to Palestine were fleeing German concentration camps and were told that they are a people without land—going to a land without people. Once they were there, they were told that the Palestinians left Palestine of their own wish, following orders from Arab leaders in a treacherous move to perpetrate a massacre for the remaining Jews.

Further, it was discovered, new Jewish immigrants as well as old settlers were told by the Zionist machine that they had to fight to survive, that the only alternative to a safe "Israel" was a massacre or at best a little sinking boat on the Mediterranean Sea. Even Arab Jews—called oriental by the Zionists—who were discriminated against in "Israel" by the European Zionist oligarchy had to accept the argument and fight for what they considered to be their very survival. Fighting the Zionist revealed the strengths and limitations of the "Jewish" character. Jews were not monsters, supermen or pygmies. A new, human image of the Jews was being formed. Martin Buber, Isaac Deutscher, Elmer Berger and Moshe Menuhin, all spiritual humane Jewish thinkers were read and reread.

New image

The Palestinian revolutionary has freed himself from most of his old biases. Foreign visitors are amazed to discover this in the commando bases, and in the "Ashbal" camps [composed of Palestinian youth between 8 and 16] in particular. The Palestinian revolutionary is ready to die for the liberation of Palestine and will not accept any substitute to it whatever the cost. But, he is clear about the enemy, and the final goal. When several Jewish students from Europe came to spend part of their summer in a Fateh camp in Jordan, they were embraced as comrades. Fateh looks forward to the day when several thousand Jews will join its fighting ranks for the liberation of Palestine. Given the recent trend of events, this may happen sooner than most people think.

First step

The first step towards the creation of a democratic, non-sectarian Palestine has been made by the Palestinian revolutionaries. A change of attitude through relearning is taking place. The long exiled and persecuted Palestinians are redefining their objectives and are finding the goal of creating a new Palestine that encompasses them and the present Jewish settlers a very desirable one. For this goal to become feasible one should take a careful look at the other party: the Jews. How do they feel about it and what could change their mind? This topic will be taken up next.

An approach to the study of Jewish attitudes

Any attempt at studying and interpreting the attitudes and perceptions of any group of people must meet with difficulties and be subjected to accusations of bias and distortions. We don't claim immunity from such shortcomings, but we shall try to minimize their effect. Our approach will be the use of direct quotations—and documentation—whenever possible. No attempt is made here at using Marxist dialectics or purely sociological models. Political motivation is the basic frame of reference.

A final problem besets our study: Most of the attitudes and "images" studied were basically engineered by the Zionists through their propaganda machinery, and they may not have been accepted by all, or a majority, of the Jews in the world. However, one must concede that the Zionists have succeeded to a great extent in identifying Judaism with Zionism in the eyes of a vast majority of Jews, especially in the Western countries.

Nazi horrors and anti-Jewish threats in several countries helped the Zionists maintain their hold over Jewish minds everywhere. Without Jewish money, political influence, votes in certain sensitive places and overall support, "Israel" would not have survived and the Zionist imperialist occupation would not have lasted. In the final analysis, it is the power and influence of global Jewish populations under Zionist manipulation that perpetuated the tragedy of the Palestinians, their oppression, subjugation and exile. It is thus quite important to find out how do the Jews feel about the Palestinians, how do they view them as people and to what extent was this view essential to the act that led to the expulsion of the Palestinians? What is even more important; can this view be changed and how?

How the Zionists viewed the Palestinians

The early attitude of the Zionists towards the Palestinians was simply to ignore their very existence. Israel Zangwill's famous phrase about "a land without people to a people without land" epitomizes this attitude. Chaim Weizmann had a more colorful statement: "There is a country which happens to be called Palestine, a country without a people, and on the other hand, there exists the Jewish People and it has no country. What else is necessary then, than to fit the gem into the ring, to unite this people with this country?"[5]

Uri Avnery notes that T. Herzl, in his book *The Jewish State*, which launched the modern Zionist movement, dealt with working hours, housing for workers, and even the national flag but had not one word to say about the Arabs of Palestine. For the Zionists, the Arab was the Invisible Man. Psychologically he was not there.[6]

However, this attitude became obviously untenable. Palestine—it was discovered—was a prosperous country measured by the standards of the day. Its population was extensive and carried out its tasks of cultivating the soil in relative peace and made its contribution to the Arab community at large.

---

5   Ibrahim Abu Lughod, The Arab-Israeli Confrontation: Some Comments on the Future' in *Selected Essays on the Palestine Question*, Palestine Research Center, Beirut, 1969.

6   See Uri Averny's article in Jean Paul Sartre (Editor): 'Le Conflit Israelo-Arab,' in the Special Issue of *Les Temps Modernes*, June 1967. "The issue is reviewed by I. F. Stone: For a New Approach to the Israeli-Arab Conflict,' *New York Times Review of Books*, Aug. 3, 1967.

Achad Ha-am, the Russian Jew and Hebrew philosopher, tried to draw attention to this fact as early as 1891. He stated that Palestine was not an empty territory and that this posed problems.[7]

In fact Ha-am reported after a journey through Palestine in 1891 that it was difficult to find any still uncultivated farmland there.

Max Nordao, the prominent Zionist leader, hearing for the first time that there was an Arab population in Palestine, ran to Herzl crying: "I didn't know that—but then we are committing an injustice."[8]

Several reports appearing in the late 19th century and the early 20th century confirmed this fact amply. The Arab Palestinians had a prosperous citrus industry. They grew oranges of exceptional size which attracted attention as early as the 18th century.[9]

Zionist image-making subsequently turned to another theme which was to be accepted by a large number of Jews as well as Christians in Europe and America and thus became a major force in shaping the attitude of Jews toward the Palestinians. The Palestinians were "natives" or "inhabitants" who happened to live in Palestine. There people were subnormal. They lacked any national entity and civilization. Such an image was embedded in the infamous Balfour Declaration which designated the Palestinians as inhabitants who may have religious and civil rights but no political rights. They were not "real" people.

Later, however, a further character assassination of the Arabs was added. These "inhabitants" were really Bedouins, i.e., roving nomads, pillaging the fertile soil of Palestine and bringing about increasing devastation of that beautiful land of milk and honey.[10] European Jews coming to Palestine would indeed be a blessing. "For that European Jew was the carrier of a superior civilization, the master of European technology and was in a position to bestow the blessings of that civilization on the no-

---

7   See Stone, I. F., Ibid.

8   Ibid.

9   Achad Ha-am: *Am Scheidwege*, Berlin, 1923. See also John Hope Simpson: *Report on Immigration, Land Settlement and Development* (Command paper 3686, 1930), pp. 64, 66 and *Protokoll des XII Zionisten Kongresses* (Berlin, 1922), p. 304. Other sources are quoted by L. M. C. van der Hoever Leonhard, 'Het Palestina-Vraagstuk in Zijn ware gedaante,' *Libertas* (Holland) Lustrum Number, 1960.

10 See Abu Lughod, *op. cit* , pp. 63, 64.

madic population of Palestine."[11] A typical *"mission civilisatrice"* would be attempted by the Jews in Palestine.

A vivid picture of this "native" Palestinian and a depiction of the attitudes engendered by such an image is revealed by Herzl, the Father of Zionism in his famous "We must expropriate gently the private property on the estates assigned to us. We shall try to spirit the penniless population across the border by procuring employment for it in the transit countries while denying it any employment in our own country. Such process shall be carried out gently and circumspectly."[12] Herzl goes further: "If we move into a region where there are wild animals, to which the Jews are not accustomed, big snakes, etc., I shall use the natives prior to giving them employment in the transit countries, for the extermination of these animals. High premiums for snake skins, etc., as well as their spawn."[13] Herzl goes on in his Diaries discussing tasks he would assign to the "natives" before spiriting them away across the borders. He would let them drain the swamps since they are accustomed to the fever.[14] To the modern reader this all seems fantastic coming from a "Jew," a man who knows about the suffering of people because of racist discrimination. But of course Herzl was as much a European colonialist, a German imperialist, as a Jew.

Herzl himself states: "With the Jews, a German cultural element would come to the Orient. Evidence of this: German writers—even though of Jewish descent—are leading the Zionist movement. The language of the Congress is German. The overwhelming majority of the Jews are part of German culture."

And further: "if it is God's will that we return to our historic fatherland, we should like to do so as representatives of Western civilization, and the well-distilled customs of the Occident to this plague-ridden, blighted corner of the Orient."[15]

---

11   Ibid., p. 64, see also *The Complete Diaries of Theodor Herzl*, Vols. I, Il, published by the Theodor Heal Foundation, Thomas Yoseloff, New York, 1960 (Referred to later as *Diaries*).

12   Ibid., pp. 88, 89-90 for the complete passage.

13   Ibid., p. 98.

14   Ibid.

15   Ibid., Vol. 11, pp. 719. See also Razzouk, A., 'Zionism and Arab Human Rights' in *Zionism and Arab Resistance*, Palestine Research Center, Beirut, 1969. There are several editions of the *Diaries*, the one here is edited by Raphael Patai and is translated from the original German by Harry Zohn.

Image of Palestinian Leadership

Palestinians did not fit this Zionist-made image and the world was hearing about Palestinian uprisings and activism. To this turn of events, Zionist image-making had an easy answer: The Palestinians are basically docile natives had it not been for agitators and fanatics. It is dynastic and family or "tribal" struggles among the wealthy that lead to the agitations. Such struggles will cause the ruin of the common folk and make them pay the price.

The Palestinian leaders are depicted by Maurice Samuel as "an army of idlers, baksheesh artists and parasite coffee-house gossips who are mainly responsible for the existing jumpy and nervous atmosphere."[16] Any political activity in Palestine cannot be initiated by the "inhabitants" who do not understand these things anyway, but by the "agitators."[17]

Attitude towards the Palestinian "refugees"

The colonization of Palestine and the uprooting of the Palestinians was partly achieved by 1948, and completed in 1967. All the Zionist dreams and schemes came true. A Jewish homeland was created in Palestine and the "natives" have become refugees, exiles, deprived of their homes and their national rights. This great human tragedy that brought misery, humiliation and despair to a million people and later to a half-million more, was a dark stain, a premeditated crime. Image-making, however, was ready for the new situation: Palestinians had "sold their lands to the Jews and then have fled the country to prepare the scene for a massacre of all Jews at the hands of the Arab armies." Those treacherous natives were doing it again. They refused to live in peace with the European bearers of civilization. They again had to listen to the agitators who lusted for a Jewish bloodbath.

The Palestinians do not even deserve sympathy in their misery and homelessness. They must be cursed and mocked. They do not deserve Palestine. They can be absorbed in the Arab countries. Their yearning for Palestine is pathetic, foolish or misguided. They had nothing to yearn for. Their present refugee camps are probably better than their shabby houses in Palestine. They lived in tents then, and they live in tents now!! So why should they complain?

---

16 Maurice Samuel: *Foundations of Peace: The Solution of the Arab Problem Must be on the Level of Zionist Idealism*, as quoted by Razzouk, *op. cit*, p. 104.

17 Ibid.

After all, they are engaged in a "numbers game" with the U. N., falsifying records to increase their numbers so that they can swindle more U. N. rations. They are the prey of Arab demagogues and agitators who keep them as a pawn in a political game.

They cannot return to Zionist Palestine. It has been civilized and does not belong to them any more. Even if some of them return, they will be fifth columnists, saboteurs, and collaborators with the enemy. Anyway, they have been exchanged, swapped with "oriental" Jews from the Arab countries.

This image-making, built on the *"mission civilisatrice"* assumption and on character assassination of the Palestinians, continues up to the present. Palestinian revolutionaries are "terrorists." After all, the Palestinians are not capable of brave, gallant, patriotic feelings and acts. They are only fit for treachery and intrigue.

This is not the place to refute these "views" of the Palestinians, for scientific research has shown that the Palestinians did not sell their country. By 1948 the Jews had owned less than 6 percent of the land, less than 1 percent acquired from Palestinians.[18] The Palestinians did not leave their country on orders from Arab leaders but after being terrorized and forcibly uprooted by the Zionists. However, the issue at hand is how did the Jews come to accept these images and to form these attitudes?

A Jewish dilemma

The fact that Zionist propaganda was accepted by world Jewish populations and was allowed to shape the attitude of Jews towards the Palestinians is quite puzzling, in fact astonishing. There were always Jewish dissenters—and we do present their views—but they were in the minority. Jews contributed men, money, and influence to make Israel a reality and to perpetuate the crimes committed against the Palestinians. The people of the Book, the men of light, the victims of Russian pogroms, of Nazi genocide, of Dachau and other Polish concentration camps shut their eyes and ears in Palestine and changed roles from oppressed to oppressor. This is THE Jewish dilemma of modern times.

Achad Ha-am wrote at the turn of the century that Jewish behavior shows that Jews evidently learned nothing from their history. He further states: "And what are our brothers in Palestine doing? The very opposite! They were servants in the country of their exile, and they sudden-

---

18 See Sayigh, Yousef, *The Israeli Economy* (Arabic), Beirut, 1966, p. 77.

ly find themselves in a state of unbounded liberty, of unbridled liberty such as can only be found in Turkey. This sudden change has brought about within them a tendency towards despotism as is always the case when a servant becomes a master and they treat the Arabs with hostility and cruelty, curtail their rights in an unreasonable manner, insult them without any sufficient reason, and actually pride themselves upon such acts; and nobody takes any action against this despicable and dangerous tendency."[19]

In 1919, another Jew, W. Brunn, wrote: "We who are suffering persecutions throughout the world and who claim all human rights for ourselves, are going to Palestine reversing the roles."[20]

In 1923, the Jewish-American anthropologist, Goldenweiser, noted with dismay that Jews in Palestine were prejudiced against the Palestinians and considered them inferior. He reports on his visits to Jewish schools where teachers were telling him of Arab congenital stupidity and inferiority. When Goldenweiser asked a Jewish educator whether they teach this to their students, the teacher answered: but they know this by themselves![21] Arthur Koestler reports that "Each Jew, or not, regarded himself as a member of the chosen race, and the Arab as his inferior."[22]

Moral schizophrenia

This moral dilemma besetting the Jews in our time is called "moral schizophrenia," "moral myopia" by the noted American Jewish journalist I. F. Stone. Mr. Stone, who was decorated in 1948 by the Irgun [nationalist Jewish organization that carried out terrorist attacks against the Arabs], wrote a very perceptive article in 1967 from which we shall quote presently. He makes the subtle comparisons of Zionist-Nazi behavior and draws soul searching conclusions.

In refuting the Israeli argument against the reasons for the Palestinian exodus, Mr. Stone states: "The argument that the refugees ran away 'voluntarily' or because their leaders urged them to do so until after the fighting was over, not only rests on a myth but is irrelevant. Have refugees

---

19   Achad Ha-am, "Die Warheit ans Palestina" in *Am Scheidwege, op. cit*, Vol. I.

20   See van der Hoever Leonhard, *op. cit*.

21   Goldenweiser, *Jewish-Arab Prejudice*, 1923.

22   Arthur Koestler, *Promise and Fulfillment*, London, 1949, p. 34.

no right to return? Have German Jews no right to recover their properties because they too fled?"²³

Mr. Stone continues: "Jewish terrorism, not only by the Irgun in such savage massacres as Deir Yassin, but in milder form by the Haganah [regular Zionist army] itself 'encouraged' Arabs to leave areas the Jews wished to take over for strategic or demographic reasons. They tried to make as much of Israel as free of Arabs as possible."²⁴

As to the "swap" of Palestinians for "Jewish refugees" from the Arab world, Mr. Stone states: "The Palestinian Arabs feel about this 'swap' as German Jews would if denied restitution on the grounds that they had been 'swapped' for German refugees from the Sudetenland." "The Jewish moral myopia makes it possible for Zionists to dwell on the 1900 years of exile in which the Jews have longed for Palestine, but dismiss as migratory the nineteen years in which Arab refugees have also longed for it."

Homelessness, Stone states further, "is the major theme of Zionism but this pathetic passion is denied to Arab refugees."

Those who have known the effects of racism and discrimination in their own flesh and human dignity are less excusably racist than those who can only imagine the negative effects of prejudice. Mr. Stone relates a conversation with Moshe Dayan on American television on June 11, 1967, where Dayan stated then even though Israel can absorb the Palestinians in the "conquered territories" it will not do it because it would turn Israel into either a bi-national or poly Arab-Jewish state instead of the Jewish state. "We want to have a Jewish state, a Jewish state like the French have a French state." Mr. Stone comments: "This must deeply disturb the thoughtful Jewish reader. Ferdinand and Isabella, in expelling the Jews and Moors from Spain, were in the same way saying they wanted Spain as Spanish, i.e., Christian as France was French."²⁵ In conclusion Stone states: "Israel is creating a kind of moral schizophrenia in world Jewry. In the outside world the welfare of Jewry depends on the maintenance of secular, nonracial, pluralistic societies. In Israel, Jewry finds itself defending a society in which mixed marriages cannot be legalized, in which non-Jews have a lesser status than Jews, and in which the ideal is racial and exclusionist. Jews must fight elsewhere for their very security

---

23 Stone, *op. cit*. Mr. Stone's article was reprinted in Ibrahim Al-Abid (Editor), *Selected Essays on the Palestine Question,* Palestine Research Centre, Beirut, 1969, and by the Fifth of June Society, Beirut, 1969.

24 Ibid.

25 Ibid.

and existence—against principles and practices they find themselves defending in Israel. Those from the outside world, even in their moments of greatest enthusiasm amid Israeli accomplishments, feel twinges of claustrophobia, not just geographical, but spiritual. Those caught up in prophetic fervor soon begin to feel that the light they hoped to see out of Zion is only that of another narrow nationalism.

"It must also be recognized, despite Zionist ideology, that the periods of greatest Jewish creative accomplishment have been associated with pluralistic civilization in their time of expansion and tolerance: in the Hellenistic period, in the Arab civilization of North Africa and Spain, and in Western Europe and America. Universal values can only be the fruit of a universal vision; the greatness of the prophets lay in their overcoming of ethnocentricity. A Lilliputian nationalism cannot distill truths for all mankind. Here lie the roots of a growing divergence between Jew and Israeli, the former with a sense of mission as a witness in the human wilderness, the latter concerned only with his own tribe's welfare."[26]

Will the Jews change their attitudes?

It was shown, through direct quotations, that there always was a group of Jewish moral dissenters to Zionism. There was never a truly monolithic Jewish opinion. The success of Zionist propaganda in galvanizing the majority of Jews to its side is attributed not to deceit and manipulation alone. Jews must get credit for sufficient intelligence to make manipulation insufficient to sway them. Antisemitism in the West and the hypocrisy prevailing in Western societies in dealing with racial and religious issues have helped push the Jews gradually to the moral schizophrenia discussed above.

In all frankness, one must add to these factors Arab attitudes and shortcomings. Before the Palestinian revolution, anti-Jewish attitudes were prevalent in the Arab world—even though it was instigated by Jewish anti-Arab attitudes. The Palestinians could not present a reasonable, humane alternative to Zionist Israel. Jews were finding it hard to live in the Arab countries, and minority problems in several Arab countries were shedding doubt on the possibility of Jews finding security in the Arab midst without a militarist Israel. In the 1948-1967 period, Jews enjoyed security when the Palestinians and eventually all other Arabs with them were deprived of security.

---

26 Ibid.

The Palestinian revolution has provided a new set of alternatives, no security in the racist state but all the security in the new democratic Palestine.

A dialogue is developing between the Palestinian revolutionaries and the Jews, liberals, progressives, socialists and even religious conservatives. More and more Jewish friends are opening their arms to embrace the Palestinian Revolution and are being embraced by it.

The Zionists are really worrying about the new phenomenon. In an article published by the *Jerusalem Post* on July 2, 1969, the editors accused those Jews of being traitors to their own people, and consider their alliance with the revolution as most serious and threatening. It is important that the issue of Jewish moral schizophrenia be stressed, that the conscience of Jewish populations be shocked into realization of the consequences of Zionism.

It is, however, more reasonable to expect non-Israeli Jews to come to terms with the Palestinian Revolution before the Israeli Jews do. After all, Frenchmen in Paris found it easier to accept the Algerian revolution than French colonists did. But the efforts should continue in Palestine to win over Jews to the revolution.

Escalation of the revolution will have its consequences. Obviously, it is going to harden some Zionist Jews against the Palestinians, especially the oligarchy that stands to lose in a democratic, open Palestine. But escalation will have its shock effect. It will bring the realization that an exclusionist Israel can be a very insecure place indeed, and that it cannot last.

The Palestinian Revolution assumes a great share of the responsibility in winning Jews to the side of the revolution by deeds and not words alone. The revolution should not—and in fact will not—pass any opportunity to prove to global Jewish populations and to Palestinian Jews that it will stand by them if persecuted and is determined to live and create with them a new Palestine not based on bias, racism, or discrimination, but on cooperation and tolerance.

If such a campaign succeeds—both in the winning of battles and of hearts—the democratic Palestine will become credible, both desirable and feasible. What will this new country look like? What does the Palestinian Revolution really mean by democratic, progressive and non-sectarian? These are serious questions that warrant attention and therefore will be taken up in our following chapter.

Difficulties and Limitations

It is quite difficult and risky at this early stage of the revolution to make a clear and definitive statement about the New Liberated Palestine. Realism rather than romantic daydreaming should be the basic revolutionary approach. We do not believe that victory is around the corner. The revolution does not underestimate the enemy or its imperialist allies. What will happen during the years of hard struggle for liberation cannot be easily predicted. Will the attitude of Palestinian Jews harden or become more receptive and flexible? A further drift to the right, stepping up anti-Arab terrorism—in the Algerian O.A.S. tradition—followed by a voluntary mass exodus on the eve of liberation will pose a completely different problem and will be quite regrettable. On the other hand joining the revolution and working with it will lay firmer growth for the new Palestine. The revolution is striving hard to achieve the second alternative. Guerrilla operations are basically directed at the military and economic foundations of the Zionist settler-state. Whenever a civilian target is chosen, every effort is made to minimize loss of civilian life—though one would find it hard to distinguish civilians and non-civilians in this modern Spartan militaristic society where every adult is mobilized for the war. Hitting quasi-civilian areas aims at the psychological effect of shocking the Israelis into realization that the racist-militaristic state cannot provide them with security when it is conducting genocide against the exiled and oppressed Palestinian masses. In the Dizengoff street bomb [Tel Aviv], Fateh guerrillas delayed the operation three times to choose a place (in front of a building under construction) and a time (12:30 after midnight) to maximize noise but minimize casualties: The result, few were injured, but thousands were shocked and made to engage in serious rethinking. In conclusion, despite all uncertainties, there is the hope, the vision and the behavior of the Palestinian revolutionaries designed to achieve a better future for their oppressed country. Answers must be thought out and found for myriad questions relating to this future. Even if the answers are tentative, they will start a dialogue which provides the road towards maturity and fulfillment.

PROFILE OF A DEMOCRATIC PALESTINE

1. THE COUNTRY

Pre-1948 Palestine—as defined during the British mandate, is the territory to be liberated and where the democratic, progressive state is to be created. The liberated Palestine will be part of the Arab Homeland and will not be another alien state within it. The eventual unity of Palestine with other Arab States will make boundary problems less relevant and will end the artificiality of the present status of Israel, and possibly that of Jordan as well. The new country will be anti-imperialist and will join the ranks of progressive revolutionary countries. Therefore, it will have to cut the present life line links with and total dependence on the United States. Therefore, integration within the area will be foremost prerequisite. It should be quite obvious at this stage that the New Palestine discussed here is not the occupied West Bank or the Gaza Strip or both. These are areas occupied by the Israelis since June 1967. The homeland of the Palestinians usurped and colonized in 1948 is no less dear or important than the part occupied in 1967. Besides, the very existence of the racist oppressor state of Israel based on the vacation and forced exile of part of its citizens is unacceptable by the revolution even in one tiny Palestinian village. Any arrangement accommodating the aggressor settler-state is unacceptable and temporary. Only the people of Palestine: its Jews, Christians, and Moslems in a country that combines them all is permanent.

2. THE CONSTITUENTS

All the Jews, Moslems, and Christians living in Palestine or forcibly exiled from it will have the right to Palestinian citizenship. This guarantees the right of all exiled Palestinians to return to their land whether they have been born in Palestine or in exile and regardless of their present nationality. Equally, this means that all Jewish Palestinians—at the present Israelis—have the same right provided of course that they reject Zionist racist chauvinism and fully accept to live as Palestinians in the New Palestine. The revolution therefore rejects the supposition that only Jews who lived in Palestine prior to 1948 or prior to 1914 and their descendants are acceptable. After all Dayan and Allon[27] were born in Palestine before 1948 and they—with many of their colleagues—are die-hard racist

---

27   **Ed. Note:** Yigal Allon (1918-1980) was an Israeli military leader and politician, including as Foreign Affairs Minister.

Zionists who obviously do not qualify for a Palestinian status. Whereas newcomers may be anti-Zionists and work ardently for the creation of the new Palestine. In the interview referred to earlier, Abu Eyad, one of the officials of Fateh, reasserted that not only progressive anti-Zionist Jews but even present Zionists who will be willing to abandon their racist ideology will be welcome as Palestinian citizens. It is the belief of the revolution that the majority of the present Israeli Jews will change their attitudes and will subscribe to the New Palestine, especially after the oligarchic state machinery, economy and military establishment is destroyed.

3. THE IDEOLOGY

The Palestinians in the process of, and at the time of liberation will decide on the system of government and on the political-economic-social organization of their liberated country (One repeats at this juncture that the term Palestinians includes those in exile, under occupation, and Jewish settlers.)

 A democratic and progressive Palestine, however rejects by elimination a theocratic, a feudalist, an aristocratic, an authoritarian or a racist-chauvinistic form of government. It will be a country that does not allow oppression or exploitation of any group of people by any other group or individuals; a state that provides equal opportunities for its people in work, worship, education, political decision-making, cultural and artistic expression. This is no Utopian dream. For, the very process of achieving the New Palestine inherently produces the requisite climate for its future system of government i.e. a people 's war of liberation brings out new values and attitudes that serve as guarantees for democracy after liberation. Witness changing attitudes towards collective work in refugee and guerrilla camps in Jordan and Lebanon. Palestinians and other brothers joining them volunteer work and livelihoods. They are not exploited or enslaved labor. The values of human life changes. Unlike Israeli napalm raids and indiscriminate killing, Palestinian guerrillas kill sparingly and selectively. New forms of human relations emerge. No master-slave relation can be attained among fighters for freedom. Increasing awareness of the international dimensions of their problem and discovery of who backs the oppressor and who supports the oppressed create new responsibilities to the international community especially to the supporters of liberation and democracy.

Therefore, Palestinians after liberation will not accept subjugation from anybody and will not reintroduce oppression against any group for this will be a negation of their *raison d'etre* and abdication of their revolutionary existence. This is quite obvious in Palestine refugee camps in Lebanon and Jordan. After twenty two years of oppression, humiliation and manipulation by secret police and local exploiters, the camps have awakened to the revolution. In the process, the exiles have broken their bonds, have thrown out the secret police and its spies and allied exploiters and have instituted democratic self management. Medical, educational and social services are being provided locally through the revolutionary organizations in a self-help fashion that have brought back dignity and self-respect. Crime rates in these camps have drastically gone down to 10% of its pre-revolutionary magnitude. Self-discipline has replaced the police. The new militia is providing the link between the revolutionary avant-garde and the base of the masses. Democratic checks are built in. These Palestinians will not accept oppression and subjugation from anybody and will not enforce it on anybody.

Newsmen and other foreign visitors have discovered that nowhere in the Arab World can they find equally mature and tolerant people *vis-à-vis* the Jews than in the camps in Jordan and Lebanon and especially among the Ashbal: the fighting lion cubs. These young Palestinians (8-16 years) are almost totally free of any anti-Jewish biases. They have a clearer vision of the new democratic Palestine than that held by bourgeois city-dwellers. These young people are the liberators of tomorrow. They will complete the destruction of Israeli oppression and the rebuilding of the New Palestine. If the democratic and progressive New Palestine is utopia, then the Palestinian guerrillas and camp dwellers are starting to practice it.

Two Misconceptions

Several interpretations of the Democratic Palestine have sprung up in different quarters that require clarification and some corrections. An attempt will be made presently to discuss two of them that seem to be quite vital:

> 1. The call for a non-sectarian Palestine should not be confused with a multi-religious, a polyreligious or a bi-national state. The new Palestine is not to be built around three state religions or two nationalities. Rather it will simply provide freedom from religious oppression

of any group by another and freedom to practice religion without discrimination. No rigidification of religious lines is desired by the revolution. No hard and fast religious distribution of political offices and other important jobs is envisioned. The Lebanese model (where the reactionary, quasi feudalist, or commercial-capitalist hierarchy divides jobs and offices on the basis of sectarian lines to perpetuate its domination of the masses) is completely alien to the revolution.

Abu Ammar reiterated several times that the president of the liberated Palestine could be a Jew, a Moslem, or a Christian not because of his religion or sect but on the basis of his merit as an outstanding Palestinian. Furthermore religious and ethnic lines clearly cross in Palestine so as to make the term bi-national and the Arab-Jewish dichotomy meaningless, or at best quite dubious.

The majority of Jews in Palestine today are Arab Jews—euphemistically called Oriental Jews by the Zionists. Therefore, Palestine combines Jewish, Christian, and Moslem Arabs as well as non-Arab Jews (Western Jews).

2. The New Democratic Palestine is NOT a substitute for liberation. Rather, it is the ultimate objective of liberation. A client state in the West Bank and Gaza, an Avneri[28]-style, de-Zionized, or Pasteurised Israel or a Semitic Confederation are all categorically rejected by the revolution. They are all racist blue-prints to delude the Palestinians and other Arabs and continue Israeli hegemony and Palestinian subjugation. They all assume the maintenance of the basic aggression that led to the forced exile of Palestinians and the oppression of the masses. The sine qua non of the New Palestine is the destruction of the political, economic, and militarist foundations of the chauvinist-racist settler-state. The maintenance of a technologically-advanced military machine through a continuous Western capital flow and exchange of population have led the expansionist Zionist machinery to perpetuate one aggression after the other. Therefore, liquidation of such a machinery is an irreplaceable condition for the creation of the New Palestine. When the machinery of the Nazi State was liquidated, the German people were liberated together with other nations that were oppressed by Nazi Germany such as Poland, Hungary, Holland, and France. The Germans were not liquidated.

---

28   **Ed. Note:** Uri Avneri (1923 - 2018) was a German-born Israeli writer, politician, and (liberal) peace activist.

The Transition and After

It is quite logical to expect specific transitional collective accommodations immediately after liberation, and even few remaining in the normalized Permanent State i.e. some collective or group privileges besides the pure individual privileges. Jews or non-Jews for that matter would have the right to practice their religion and develop culturally and linguistically as a group, beside their individual political and cultural participation. It is quite logical for example to have both Arabic and Hebrew as official languages taught in governmental schools to all Palestinians, Jews, or non-Jews. The right of free movement within the country and outside it would be guaranteed. Palestinians desirous of voluntarily leaving the country would be allowed to do so. Immigration would be restricted in a transitional period to the return of all exiled Palestinians desirous of return. In a normal permanent state, however, subject to the agreed upon regulation and the absorptive capacity of the country immigration would be open without discrimination. Freedom of access, visits, and extended pilgrimage and tourism would be guaranteed—subject of course to the normal regulation—to all Jews, Moslems, or Christians of the world who consider Palestine a holy place worthy of pilgrimage and meditation.

Is the New Palestine Viable?

Several well-intentioned critics maintain that even if the creation of the Democratic Palestine is possible, it will not survive for long. Their basic contention is that the population and cultural balance will be heavily favoring the Jews in the new Palestine. This—in their argument—will lead either to an explosive situation, or to the domination of the New Palestine by the Jews and a possible reversion to a neo-Zionist state in disguise.

The argument is serious and looks quite plausible given the present set up, and the European Dichotomy of the "Arabs" as a backward group and the "Jews" as a modern one.

As for population, the Jews in Palestine today number 2.5 millions which is compared to 2.6 million Palestinian Arabs (Christians and Moslems) in the occupied territories before 1967 and after it, and in exile.

Birth rates and net natural growth rates are higher among Arab Palestinians compared to those for the Jews in Palestine.

Immigration, however, has been the major cause of growth in the Jewish ranks. Nevertheless one must consider the fact that 250,000 Jews have permanently left Palestine (emigrated) since 1949 in a period where relative security prevailed. Most of the emigrants were European Jews. Whereas most of the new immigrants were Arab Jews who found it very difficult to stay in their countries after the creation and survival of the aggressor settler-state of Israel.

The process of the revolution will inevitably increase the tempo of emigration especially of those beneficiaries of a racist state who will find it very difficult to adapt to an open plural society. Parallel to that development will be the increasing modernization of the Arab countries and toleration of all minorities including the Jewish citizens. Fateh is already engaged in serious negotiations with several Arab countries to allow Jewish emigrants back and to return their property and to guarantee them full and equal rights.

These factors are expected on the whole to maintain relative population balance in Palestine.

The pace of social and educational development is rising rapidly among the Arab Palestinians as well. It is estimated that the number of University Graduates among the Palestinians in exile exceeds 50,000.

Palestinians have successfully played the role of educators, professionals and technicians in several Arab countries especially those in the Arabian Peninsula and North Africa. Arab Palestinians faced this cultural challenge in pre-1948 Palestine and managed in the relatively short period of 30 years to compete effectively with the Jews in agriculture, industry, education, and even in the field of finance and banking. Armed with the spirit of a victorious revolution, hopefully in comradeship of a significant number of Jews, the Arabs of Palestine will become effective and equal partners, in the building of the New Country.

Integration of Palestine within the Arab region will add to its economic and political viability. Present Arab-boycott will obviously be replaced by economic aid and trade, a goal which the settler-state of Israel completely failed to achieve, remaining thus an American ward and protege during its entire existence.

Conclusion

The Democratic, non-sectarian Palestine still lacks full clarity and elaboration, but this is the best that can be done at this stage of the arduous liberation struggle. The Palestinians have outgrown their bitterness and prejudice in a relatively short-time through armed struggle. A few years ago, discussing this proposal would have been considered as a complete sell-out or high treason. Even today, some Arabs still find it very difficult to accept the proposed goal and secretly—or publicly—hope that it is nothing more than a tactical propaganda move. Well, it is definitely not so. The Palestinian revolution is determined to fight for the creation of the New democratic and non-sectarian Palestine as the long-term ultimate goal of liberation. Annihilation of the Jews or of the Palestinian exiles and the creation of an exclusive racist or theocratic state in Palestine be it Jewish, Christian, or Moslem is totally unacceptable, unworkable, and cannot last. The oppressed Palestinian masses will fight and make all needed sacrifices to demolish the oppressor exclusive state.

The Israeli racists are greatly irritated by the idea of a democratic Palestine. It reveals the contradictions of Zionism and bares the moral schizophrenia that besets global Jewish populations since the creation of Israel. The adoption of several significant progressive Jews of the new goal scares world Zionism. Israeli Jewish Professor Loebel and French Jewish writer Ania Francos were threatened and molested by Zionists for their sponsorship of the Democratic Palestine as the ultimate goal of liberation. The Zionists are stepping up their campaign to discredit the idea especially among the Jews. Their effort has been in vain. The force of logic and the effect of years of persecution in exclusive societies on the hands of racists are opening the eyes of Jews and others in the world to the only permanent solution that will bring lasting peace and justice to our Palestine: building a progressive, open, tolerant country for all of us.

Section III
Palestine at the UN

Text of United Nations Security Council Resolution 242 of 22 November 1967[1]
[1967]

The Security Council,

Expressing its continuing concern with the grave situation in the Middle East,

Emphasizing the inadmissibility of the acquisition of territory by war and the need to work for a just and lasting peace in which every State in the area can live in security,

Emphasizing further that all Member States in their acceptance of the Charter of the United Nations have undertaken a commitment to act in accordance with Article 2 of the Charter,

1. *Affirms* that the fulfillment of the establishment of a just and lasting peace in the Middle East which should include the application of both of the following principles:

    i. withdrawal of Israeli armed forces from territories occupied in the recent conflict;

    ii. termination of all claims or states of belligerency and respect for and acknowledgement of the sovereignty, territorial integrity, and political independence of every State in the area and their right to live in peace within secure and recognized boundaries free from threats or acts of force;

2. *Affirms further* the necessity:

    a. for guaranteeing freedom of navigation through international waterways in be area;

    b. for achieving a just settlement of the refugee problem;

---

1 Ed. Note: Source text can be found online, accessible at: https://digitallibrary.un.org/record/90717?ln=en. Accessed January 25, 2024.

c. for guaranteeing the territorial inviolability and political independence of every State in the area, through measures including the establishment of demilitarized zones;

3. *Requests* the Secretary General to designate a Special Representative to proceed to the Middle East to establish and maintain contacts with the States concerned in order to promote agreement and assist efforts to achieve a peaceful and accepted settlement in accordance with the provisions and principles in this resolution;

4. *Requests* the Secretary General to report to the Security Council on the progress of the efforts of the Special Representative as soon as possible."

ADOPTED UNANIMOUSLY
AT THE 1382ND MEETING

Political Communiqué of the 19th Extraordinary Session of the Palestine National Council[1]

[1988]

In the land of heroic Algeria and as the guest of its people and its President, Chadli Bendjedid, the Palestine National Council held its nineteenth extraordinary session—the session of the *intifada* (uprising) and national independence, the session of the martyr and hero Abu Jihad—from 12 to 15 November 1988.

The session culminated in the declaration of the Palestinian State on our Palestinian land, representing the natural culmination of a valiant and tenacious popular struggle which has continued for more than 70 years and taken its toll in the immense sacrifices made by our people in its homeland, on its frontiers and in all the camps and places to which it has been dispersed.

The session was also distinguished by its dedication to the great Palestinian national uprising, one of the outstanding battle events in the history of the Palestinian people's contemporary revolution, together with our population's legendary and epic defiance in their camps both inside and outside our occupied land.

Since the very beginning of the *intifada* and throughout the 12 months for which it has continued, the fundamental characteristics of our great people's uprising have been clearly manifest. It is an all-embracing popular revolution expressing the consensus agreement of the na-

---

1 Delivered to the United Nations on 18 November 1988 by Dr. Riyad Mansour, Deputy Permanent Observer and Chargé d'affaires of the Permanent Observer Mission of Palestine to the United Nations, and by Abdullah Salah, Ambassador and Permanent Representative of Jordan to the United Nations. Source: *Interactive Encyclopedia of The Palestine Question*, (accessed on January 25, 2024, online at: https://www.palquest.org/en/historictext/9675/palestine-national-council-19th-session-political-communiqu%C3%A9.)

tions—its men and its women, its old people and its children, its camps, villages and cities—to reject the occupation and to fight for its defeat and elimination.

This magnificent uprising has demonstrated the deep-rooted national unity of our people and its comprehensive loyalty to the Palestine Liberation Organization, the sole legitimate representative of our people—of all our people in every place where its members are gathered—both inside and outside the homeland. This has been shown by the rallying of the Palestinian masses in all their national institutions—including trade unions, vocational organizations, students, workers, farmers, women, businessmen, land owners, professionals and academics—to the *intifada*, through the unified leadership of the uprising and through the popular committees which have been formed in all quarters of the cities and in the villages and camps.

The revolutionary furnace of our people and its glorious uprising, together with the continuous and creative revolutionary momentum of our revolution at all the scenes and sites of that revolution both inside and outside our homeland, have brought to naught the wagers and delusions whereby our people's enemies hoped to give a fixed and permanent character to the occupation of our Palestinian land and to consign the question of Palestine to the labyrinths of oblivion and obliteration. Behold the generations which have been bred on the purposes and principles of the Palestinian revolution and have lived through all its battles since its awakening in 1965, experiencing the heroic defiance of the Zionist invasion in 1982 and the resistance of the camps of the revolution in Lebanon against the siege of starvation and death. And behold how these generations, the sons of the Palestine Liberation Organization, affirm the vitality and continuity of that revolution and make the ground explode beneath the feet of the occupiers, proving that the battle reserves of our people are not depleted and that its deep faith is firm and profound.

Thus we see a revolutionary symphony among the children of the rocket-propelled grenades (RPGs) and the children of the sacred stones, both inside and outside our occupied land.

Our people has defied all attempts by the enemy authorities to put an end to our popular revolution, despite all the authorities' ploys of terror, oppression, killing, imprisonment, expulsion, desecration of Islamic and Christian holy places, violation of the freedom of places of worship, confiscation of land, demolition of houses, perpetration of deliberate crimes of murder, unleashing of armed settlers against our villages and our camps, burning of crops, severing of water and electricity supplies, beating of women and children, use of stinging gases—leading to thousands of deaths and miscarriages—and conduct of a policy of obscurantism through the closure of schools and universities.

Our people have paid the price for this heroic defiance with the lives of hundreds of martyrs and the sufferings of tens of thousands who have been wounded, injured, detained and expelled. The ingenuity of our people has always throughout these trying times been ready to invent ways and means of battle which enhance its defiance and resistance, its ability to confront the crimes and practices of the enemy and, consequently, to continue its heroic and determined struggle.

By means of its defiance, the continuation of its revolution and the escalation of its uprising, our people have proved its determination to continue the struggle, whatever the sacrifices, to the utmost limits. It does so armed with a magnificent fighting heritage, an unbending revolutionary determination and a deep-rooted national unity which has been further and further strengthened through and around the *intifada*, both inside and outside the homeland, together with its all-embracing loyalty to its national leadership, the Palestine Liberation Organization, and the adherence of our people to the objectives of defeating and eliminating the Israeli occupation and attaining its inalienable national rights to return, to exercise self-determination and to establish the independent Palestinian State.

Our people have throughout this process relied on the support of the masses and forces of the Arab community, their solidarity with it and backing of it. This has been demonstrated in the broad popular Arab support received by the uprising, in the official Arab consensus expressed during the Arab Summit Conference at Algiers and the resolutions adopted at that Conference, affirming that our people is not alone in confronting the racist Fascist assault and thwarting any possibility of its isolation by the Israeli aggressors, in view of the support provided to it by the Arab community and their backing of its holy war.

In addition to this Arab solidarity, our people's revolution and the glorious uprising have enjoyed broad international endorsement, as demonstrated by the increasing understanding of the Palestinian people's cause, the growth of backing and support among the peoples and nations of the world for our just struggle and, in contrast, their condemnation of the Israeli occupation and its crimes, thus contributing to the disgrace of Israel, its increasing isolation and the isolation of its backers and supporters.

Security Council resolutions 605 (1987), 607 (1988), and 608 (1999), and those General Assembly resolutions which confirm Palestinian rights against the expulsion of Palestinians from their land, and against the repression and terror practiced by Israel against the Palestinian people in the occupied Palestinian territories, have constituted one of the strong manifestations of international public opinion's increasing support, including that of official opinion, for our people and its representative, the Palestine Liberation Organization, against the Israeli occupation and its racist Fascist practices.

General Assembly resolution 43/21 of 3 November 1988, which was adopted at a meeting devoted to the *intifada*, provides further evidence that the overwhelming majority of the peoples and nations of the world oppose the occupation and support the just struggle of the Palestinian people and its inalienable right to liberation and independence. The inhuman and abhorrent crimes and practices of the occupation have given the lie to the Zionist propaganda about democracy in the Zionist entity, which has deceived international public opinion for 40 years. The true face of Israel has been made apparent: a colonialist, racist, Fascist State based on the seizure of Palestinian land, extermination of the Palestinian people and, in addition, threats, aggression and expansionism in neighboring Arab territories.

What this means is that the occupation can no longer continue to reap its fruits at the expense of the rights of the Palestinian people unless it pays the price for doing so, either in the field or at the level of international public opinion.

Apart from those Israeli democratic and progressive forces which have rejected the occupation, condemned it, and deplored its oppressive practices and measures, Jewish groups throughout the world are no longer able to continue defending Israel or to remain silent about its crimes against the Palestinian people. Many voices have been raised within these groups in calls for an end to such crimes and for Israel's withdrawal from the occupied territories, in order to enable the Palestinian people to exercise its right to self-determination.

Among the gamut of results and effects at the local, Arab and international levels of our people's revolution and glorious uprising, there has been affirmation of the practical correctness of the Palestine Liberation Organization's national programme, which advocates defeat of the occupation, the right to return, self-determination and the independent State. It has also been affirmed that our people's struggle is the decisive factor in ensuring that our national rights are wrested from the claws of the occupation and that it is the authority of the popular masses, as represented by their committees, which controls the situation and confronts the occupation authority and its crumbling apparatus. It has also been affirmed that the international community is now more than ever prepared to help bring about a political settlement of the Middle East problem and the basis of that problem, the question of Palestine, and that the Israeli occupation authorities, with the United States Administration behind them, cannot maintain their policy of no response to the will of the international community, which is today agreed on the need to hold the International Peace Conference on the Middle East and to enable the Palestinian people to attain their national rights, including first and foremost the right to self-determination and to exercise its national independence in its own territory.

Accordingly, in corroboration of our people's defiance and its glorious uprising, in response to the will of our masses inside and outside the occupied homeland, and in faithful memory of those who have been killed, injured and detained, the Palestine National Council decides as follows:

1. WITH REGARD TO THE INTENSIFICATION AND CONTINUATION OF THE UPRISING:

a. To provide all means and possibilities for the intensification of our people's uprising, at all levels and by all methods, with a view to ensuring its continuation and escalation;

b. To support the mass institutions and organizations in the occupied Palestinian territories;

c. To strengthen and develop the popular committees and specialized cadres of the masses and the trade unions, in order to enhance their effectiveness and role, including attack groups and the popular army;

d. To consolidate the national unity which has displayed itself and taken root during the uprising;

e. To step up action at the international level with a view to securing the release of detainees, the return of those expelled and a halt to the operation of official organized repression and terror against our children, our women, our men and our institutions;

f. To invite the United Nations to place the occupied Palestinian territories under international supervision, in order to protect our masses and to terminate the Israeli occupation;

g. To call on the Palestinian masses outside the homeland to intensify and increase their support and to base such action on family solidarity;

h. To invite the masses, forces, institutions and Governments of the Arab community to increase their political, material and media support to the uprising;

i. To call on free and noble men throughout the world to stand by our masses, our revolution and our uprising in opposing the Israeli occupation, its methods of repression and organized official military Fascist terrorism, as practiced by the forces of the occupation army, armed individuals and fanatic settlers against our masses, our universities, our schools, our institutions, our national economy and our Islamic and Christian holy places.

2. IN THE POLITICAL FIELD:

Pursuant to all the preceding remarks, the Palestine National Council—in accordance with its responsibility towards the Palestinian people, its national rights and its desire for peace, on the basis of the Declaration of Independence issued on 15 November 1988, and as an expression of the humanitarian desire to strive for the reinforcement of international détente, nuclear disarmament and the settlement of regional disputes by peaceful means—affirms the determination of the Palestine Liberation Organization to reach a comprehensive political settlement of the Arab-Israeli conflict and of its essence, the question of Palestine, within the framework of the Charter of the United Nations, the principles and provisions of international legitimacy, the rules of international law, the resolutions of the United Nations—the most recent being Security Council resolutions 605 (1987), 607 (1988), and 608 (1988)—and the resolutions of the Arab summit conferences, in a manner that ensures the right of the Palestinian Arab people to return, to exercise self-determination and to establish its independent national State on its national soil, while also making arrangements for the security and peace of every State in the region.

With a view to putting this affirmation into practice, the Palestine National Council insists on the following:

a. The need to convene an effective international conference on the subject of the Middle East problem and its essence, the question of Palestine, under the auspices of the United Nations and with the participation of the permanent members of the Security Council and all parties to the conflict in the region, including the Palestine Liberation Organization, the sole legitimate representative of the Palestinian people, on an equal footing, with the provision that the said international conference shall be convened on the basis of Security Council resolutions 242 (1967) and 338 (1973) and shall guarantee the legitimate national rights of the Palestinian people, first and foremost among which is the right to self-determination, in accordance with the principles and provisions of the Charter of the United Nations concerning the right to self-determination of peoples, the inadmissibility of seizure of land belonging to others by means of force or military invasion, and in accordance with United Nations resolutions concerning the question of Palestine;

b. Israel's withdrawal from all the Palestinian and Arab territories which it has occupied since 1967, including Arab Jerusalem;

c. Cancellation of all measures of attachment and annexation and removal of the settlements established by Israel in the Palestinian and Arab territories since the year 1967;

d. An endeavor to place the occupied Palestinian territories, including Arab Jerusalem, under United Nations supervision for a limited period, in order to protect our people and to provide an atmosphere conducive to a successful outcome for the international conference, the attainment of a comprehensive political settlement and the establishment of security and peace for all through mutual acceptance and satisfaction, and in order to enable the Palestinian State to exercise its effective authority over those territories;

e. Solution of the Palestine refugee problem in accordance with United Nations resolutions on that subject;

f. Assurance of freedom of worship and the practice of religious rites at the holy places in Palestine for adherents of all religions;

g. The Security Council's establishment and assurance of arrangements for security and peace among all the concerned States in the region, including the Palestinian State.

The Palestine National Council confirms its previous resolutions with regard to the privileged relationship between the two fraternal peoples of Jordan and Palestine, together with the fact that the future relationship between the States of Jordan and Palestine will be established on the basis of a confederacy and of free and voluntary choice by the two fraternal peoples, in corroboration of the historical ties and vital common interests which link them.

The Palestine National Council renews its commitment to United Nations resolutions affirming the right of peoples to resist foreign occupation, colonialism and racial discrimination, and their right to struggle for their independence. It once again states its rejection of terrorism in all its forms, including State terrorism, and affirms its commitment to its previous resolutions in that regard, to the resolution of the Arab Summit Conference at Algiers in 1988, to General Assembly resolutions 42/159 of 1987 and 40/61 of 1985, and to the relevant passage in the Cairo Declaration issued on 7 November 1985.

3. On the Arab and international levels:

The Palestine National Council affirms the importance of the unity of the territory, people and institutions of Lebanon and of decisive opposition to attempts to partition that territory and to divide the fraternal people of Lebanon. It also affirms the importance of the joint Arab effort to help solve the crisis in Lebanon and thus to participate in elaborating and applying the solutions which will preserve its unity. The Council also affirms the importance of recognizing the rights of Palestinian citizens in Lebanon to conduct political and media activities and to enjoy security and protection, of action against all forms of conspiracy and aggression directed against them and their right to work and to live, and of the need to establish all the conditions which ensure their ability defend themselves and to maintain their security and protection.

The Palestine National Council also affirms its solidarity with the Lebanese Islamic national forces in their struggle against the Israeli occupation and its agents in southern Lebanon. It expresses its pride in the militant solidarity between the Lebanese and Palestinian peoples in opposing aggression and putting an end to the Israeli occupation of parts of the south. It further affirms the importance of promoting that relationship between our masses and the fraternal fighting masses of Lebanon.

On this occasion, the Council salutes in admiration those of our people in the camps in Lebanon and the south of that country who are resisting aggression and standing up to the massacres, killings, starvation, destruction, air raids, bombardment and sieges being conducted by the Israeli forces, the Israeli air force and the Israeli navy against Palestinian camps and Lebanese villages, being assisted as they do so by the client forces in the region. It also salutes their rejection of the settlement conspiracy, because the homeland of Palestinians is Palestine.

The Council affirms the importance of the Iraq-Iran cease-fire decision for the attainment of lasting peace between the two countries and in the Gulf region. It calls for the intensification of efforts to ensure the successful outcome of the peace negotiations and to establish peace on a firm and stable basis, affirming on this occasion the pride of the Palestinian Arab people and of the Arab community as a whole in Iraq's fraternal defiance and its victories as it defends the eastern gate of the Arab world.

The National Council also expresses its deep pride in the backing provided by the masses of our Arab community for the struggle of our Palestinian Arab people and in their support for the Palestine Liberation Organization and the uprising of our people in the occupied homeland. It affirms the importance of strengthening the relations of struggle among the forces, parties and organizations of the Arab national liberation movement, in defense of the rights of the Arab community and its masses to liberation, progress, democracy and unity. The Council calls for the adoption of all measures which will reinforce militant unity among all parties to the Arab national liberation movement.

The Palestine National Council, in addressing its greetings and gratitude to the Arab States for their support of our people's struggle, calls upon them to honor the commitments adopted at the Algiers Summit Conference to support the struggle of the Palestinian people and its glorious uprising. In making this request, the Council expresses its great confidence that the leaders of the Arab community will continue to provide backing and support for Palestine and its people in the manner which has become familiar to us.

The Palestine National Council reaffirms the desire of the Palestine Liberation Organization to maintain Arab solidarity as a framework for the organization of efforts by the Arab community and its States to confront Israeli aggression and United States support for such aggression and to promote Arab prestige and the desired Arab role, with a view to influencing international policies in favor of Arab rights and issues.

The Palestine National Council expresses its profound gratitude to those States, forces and world organizations which support Palestinian national rights and affirms its desire to strengthen links of friendship and cooperation with its friends (the Soviet Union and the People's Republic of China), the other socialist States, non-aligned countries, Islamic, African and Latin American States and other friendly countries. The Council is pleased to note the manifestations of a positive development in the positions of certain Western European countries and Japan with respect to increased support for the rights of the Palestinian people, and backing for that people. It welcomes that development and urges the promotion of efforts to extend it.

The National Council affirms the fraternal solidarity of the Palestinian people and the Palestine Liberation Organization with the struggle for liberation and greater independence of the peoples of Asia, Africa and Latin America. It condemns all attempts by the United States to threaten the independence of countries in Central America and to interfere in their affairs.

The Palestine National Council expresses the support and backing of the Palestine Liberation Organization for the national liberation movements in South Africa and Namibia, under the leadership of the South West Africa People's Organization (SWAPO), and addresses a special greeting to Nelson Mandela in his struggle against the racist Pretoria régime. It urges that the peoples of those two countries be enabled to attain their freedom and independence. The Council also expresses its support and backing for the African front-line States and its condemnation of the racist South African régime's acts of aggression against them.

As it watches with deep concern the continuing growth of Fascist forces and Israeli extremism, and the escalation of their overt calls for implementation of a policy of genocide and the individual and collective expulsion of our people from its homeland, the Council calls for the intensification of action and efforts at all levels to confront this Fascist threat. At the same time, the Council expresses its appreciation of the courageous role played by the Israeli forces for peace in their defiance and humiliation of the Fascist and racist forces and of aggression, in their support for our people's struggle and valiant uprising and in their endorsement of our people's right to exercise self-determination and to establish its independent State. The Council affirms its previous resolutions with regard to the strengthening and development of relations with those democratic forces.

The Palestine National Council also addresses an appeal to the various forums of the people of the United States to endeavor to halt the United States Administration's policy of denying the national rights of the Palestinian people, including its sacred right to self-determination. It calls upon all sectors of the United States population to work towards the adoption of policies which are consistent with international rules, conventions and resolutions on the subject of human rights and serve the desired purpose of bringing about peace in the Middle East and ensuring security for all its peoples, including the Palestinian people.

The Council entrusts the Executive Committee with the task of completing arrangements for the formation of a memorial committee in honor of the martyr and symbol, Abu Jihad, in order that the committee may begin its work immediately after the Council's session is concluded.

The Council addresses its greetings to the United Nations Committee on the Exercise of the Inalienable Rights of the Palestinian People, to fraternal and friendly international institutions and organizations and non-governmental organizations and to those correspondents and information media which have supported, and continue to support, our people's uprising and struggle.

The National Council, in expressing its intense anguish over the continued detention of hundreds of our people's combatants in a number of Arab countries, vehemently deplores their continued detention and calls upon those countries to put an end to this irregular situation and to release the combatants in order that they may resume their participation in the fight and in the struggle.

In conclusion, the Palestine National Council affirms its complete confidence that the justice of the Palestinian cause and of the aims for which the Palestinian people is struggling will continue to enjoy increased support from honorable and free men throughout the world. It also affirms its complete confidence in victory on the road to Jerusalem, the capital of our independent Palestinian State.

STATE OF PALESTINE
DECLARATION OF INDEPENDENCE[1]
[1988]

IN THE NAME OF GOD, THE COMPASSIONATE, THE MERCIFUL:[2]

Palestine, the land of the three monotheistic faiths, is where the Palestinian Arab people was born, on which it grew, developed and excelled. Thus the Palestinian Arab people ensured for itself an everlasting union between itself, its land, and its history.

Resolute throughout that history, the Palestinian Arab people forged its national identity, rising even to unimagined levels in its defense, as invasion, the design of others, and the appeal special to Palestine's ancient and luminous place on the eminence where powers and civilizations are joined. All this intervened thereby to deprive the people of its political independence. Yet the undying connection between Palestine and its people secured for the land its character, and for the people its national genius.

Nourished by an unfolding series of civilizations and cultures, inspired by a heritage rich in variety and kind, the Palestinian Arab people added to its stature by consolidating a union between itself and its patrimonial Land. The call went out from Temple, Church, and Mosque that to praise the Creator, to celebrate compassion and peace was indeed the

---

1 November 15, 1988. Delivered to the United Nations on November 18, 1988, by Dr. Riyad Mansour, Deputy Permanent Observer and Chargé d'affaires of the Permanent Observer Mission of Palestine to the United Nations, and by Abdullah Salah, Ambassador and Permanent Representative of Jordan to the United Nations; *Interactive Encyclopedia of The Palestine Question*, accessed on January 25, 2024, online at: https://www.palquest.org/en/historictext/9673/palestinian-declaration-independence.

2 **Ed. Note:** The text of the State of Palestine's *Declaration of Independence* was translated into English by Edward Said.

message of Palestine. And in generation after generation, the Palestinian Arab people gave of itself unsparingly in the valiant battle for liberation and homeland. For what has been the unbroken chain of our people's rebellions but the heroic embodiment of our will for national independence. And so the people were sustained in the struggle to stay and to prevail.

When in the course of modern times a new order of values was declared with norms and values fair for all, it was the Palestinian Arab people that had been excluded from the destiny of all other peoples by a hostile array of local and foreign powers. Yet again had unaided justice been revealed as insufficient to drive the world's history along its preferred course.

And it was the Palestinian people, already wounded in its body, that was submitted to yet another type of occupation over which floated that falsehood that "Palestine was a land without people." This notion was foisted upon some in the world, whereas in Article 22 of the Covenant of the League of Nations (1919) and in the Treaty of Lausanne (1923), the community of nations had recognized that all the Arab territories, including Palestine, of the formerly Ottoman provinces, were to have granted to them their freedom as provisionally independent nations.

Despite the historical injustice inflicted on the Palestinian Arab people resulting in their dispersion and depriving them of their right to self-determination, following upon U.N. General Assembly Resolution 181 (1947), which partitioned Palestine into two states, one Arab, one Jewish, yet it is this Resolution that still provides those conditions of international legitimacy that ensure the right of the Palestinian Arab people to sovereignty.

By stages, the occupation of Palestine and parts of other Arab territories by Israeli forces, the willed dispossession and expulsion from their ancestral homes of the majority of Palestine's civilian inhabitants, was achieved by organized terror; those Palestinians who remained, as a vestige subjugated in its homeland, were persecuted and forced to endure the destruction of their national life.

Thus were principles of international legitimacy violated. Thus were the Charter of the United Nations and its Resolutions disfigured, for they had recognized the Palestinian Arab people's national rights; including the right of Return, the right to independence, the right to sovereignty over territory and homeland.

In Palestine and on its perimeters, in exile distant and near, the Palestinian Arab people never faltered and never abandoned its conviction in its rights of Return and independence. Occupation, massacres and dispersion achieved no gain in the unabated Palestinian consciousness of self and political identity, as Palestinians went forward with their destiny, undeterred and unbowed. And from out of the long years of trial in ever-mounting struggle, the Palestinian political identity emerged further consolidated and confirmed. And the collective Palestinian national will forged for itself a political embodiment, the Palestine Liberation Organization, its sole, legitimate representative recognized by the world community as a whole, as well as by related regional and international institutions. Standing on the very rock of conviction in the Palestinian people's inalienable rights, and on the ground of Arab national consensus and of international legitimacy, the PLO led the campaigns of its great people, molded in.

The massive national uprising, the intifada, now intensifying in cumulative scope and power on occupied Palestinian territories, as well as the unflinching resistance of the refugee camps outside the homeland, have elevated awareness of the Palestinian truth and right into still higher realms of comprehension and actuality. Now at last the curtain has been dropped around a whole epoch of prevarication and negation. The intifada has set siege to the mind of official Israel, which has for too long relied exclusively upon myth and terror to deny Palestinian existence altogether. Because of the intifada and its revolutionary irreversible impulse, the history of Palestine has therefore arrived at a decisive juncture.

Now by virtue of natural, historical and legal rights, and the sacrifices of successive generations who gave of themselves in defense of the freedom and independence of their homeland;

In pursuance of Resolutions adopted by Arab Summit Conferences and relying on the authority bestowed by international legitimacy as embodied in the Resolutions of the United Nations Organization since 1947;

And in exercise by the Palestinian Arab people of its rights to self-determination, political independence and sovereignty over its territory,

The Palestine National Council, in the name of God, and in the name of the Palestinian Arab people, hereby proclaims the establishment of the State of Palestine on our Palestinian territory with its capital Jerusalem (Al-Quds Ash-Sharif).

The State of Palestine is the state of Palestinians wherever they may be. The state is for them to enjoy in it their collective national and cultural identity, theirs to pursue in it a complete equality of rights. In it will be safeguarded their political and religious convictions and their human dignity by means of a parliamentary democratic system of governance, itself based on freedom of expression and the freedom to form parties. The rights of minorities will duly be respected by the majority, as minorities must abide by decisions of the majority. Governance will be based on principles of social justice, equality and non-discrimination in public rights of men or women, on grounds of race, religion, color or sex, and the aegis of a constitution which ensures the rule of law and an independent judiciary. Thus shall these principles allow no departure from Palestine's age-old spiritual and civilizational heritage of tolerance and religious coexistence.

The State of Palestine is an Arab state, an integral and indivisible part of the Arab nation, at one with that nation in heritage and civilization, with it also in its aspiration for liberation, progress, democracy and unity. The State of Palestine affirms its obligation to abide by the Charter of the League of Arab States, whereby the coordination of the Arab states with each other shall be strengthened. It calls upon Arab compatriots to consolidate and enhance the emergence in reality of state, to mobilize potential, and to intensify efforts whose goal is to end Israeli occupation.

The State of Palestine proclaims its commitment to the principles and purposes of the United Nations, and to the Universal Declaration of Human Rights. It proclaims its commitment as well to the principles and policies of the Non-Aligned Movement.

It further announces itself to be a peace-loving State, in adherence to the principles of peaceful co-existence. It will join with all states and peoples in order to assure a permanent peace based upon justice and the respect of rights so that humanity's potential for well-being may be assured, an earnest competition for excellence may be maintained, and in which confidence in the future will eliminate fear for those who are just and for whom justice is the only recourse.

In the context of its struggle for peace in the land of Love and Peace, the State of Palestine calls upon the United Nations to bear special responsibility for the Palestinian Arab people and its homeland. It calls upon all peace- and freedom-loving peoples and states to assist it in the attainment of its objectives, to provide it with security, to alleviate the tragedy of its people, and to help it terminate Israel's occupation of the Palestinian territories.

The State of Palestine herewith declares that it believes in the settlement of regional and international disputes by peaceful means, in accordance with the U.N. Charter and resolutions. With prejudice to its natural right to defend its territorial integrity and independence, it therefore rejects the threat or use of force, violence and terrorism against its territorial integrity or political independence, as it also rejects their use against territorial integrity of other states.

Therefore, on this day unlike all others, November 15, 1988, as we stand at the threshold of a new dawn, in all honor and modesty we humbly bow to the sacred spirits of our fallen ones, Palestinian and Arab, by the purity of whose sacrifice for the homeland our sky has been illuminated and our Land given life. Our hearts are lifted up and irradiated by the light emanating from the much blessed intifada, from those who have endured and have fought the fight of the camps, of dispersion, of exile, from those who have borne the standard for freedom, our children, our aged, our youth, our prisoners, detainees and wounded, all those ties to our sacred soil are confirmed in camp, village, and town. We render special tribute to that brave Palestinian Woman, guardian of sustenance and Life, keeper of our people's perennial flame. To the souls of our sainted martyrs, the whole of our Palestinian Arab people that our struggle shall be continued until the occupation ends, and the foundation of our sovereignty and independence.

Therefore, we call upon our great people to rally to the banner of Palestine, to cherish and defend it, so that it may forever be the symbol of our freedom and dignity in that homeland, which is a homeland for the free, now and always.

In the name of God, the Compassionate, the Merciful:

SAY: "O GOD, MASTER OF THE KINGDOM, THOU GIVEST THE KINGDOM TO WHOM THOU WILT, AND SEIZES THE KINGDOM FROM WHOM THOU WILT, THOU EXALTED WHOM THOU WILT, AND THOU ABASEST WHOM THOU WILT; IN THY HAND IS THE GOOD; THOU ART POWERFUL OVER EVERYTHING [...]"

Address to the Security Council of the United Nations on the Situation in the Occupied Palestinian Territories[1]

[1990]

Mr. Arafat (Palestine):

I greet my brother, the representative of the Republic of Yemen, the unified Arab State whose birth was announced a few days ago.

It is a source of great pride for me to be present today for the second time in a year and a half in this hospitable country, where I have already had the honor to address the United Nations, in order to speak with the voice of Palestine, and deliver the word of the Palestine Liberation Organization (PLO).

I should like, Mr. President, to thank you for having given me this special opportunity to undertake this mission on behalf of Palestine and the Palestinian people. While we consider this as a token of your deep understanding of the dangerous situation in our area, we also view it as an expression of sympathy for, and solidarity with, the Palestinian people, who are now being subjected to the ugliest oppression and terrorism while struggling for their freedom and for the implementation of the goals, principles and values consecrated by this international Organization.

When the Palestine Liberation Organization (PLO), with the support of the Arab Group, requested the convening of this urgent meeting of the Security Council, its request stemmed from the realization that the situation has reached an extremely dangerous and explosive point. No longer can hesitation be acceptable or verbal condemnation suffi-

---

[1] Ed. Note: Translated from the Arabic in the original document. Delivered at the 2923rd meeting of the UN Security Council, Geneva, May 25, 1990. Source: United Nations Information System on the Question of Palestine (accessed on January 25, 2024, online at: https://www.un.org/unispal/document/auto-insert-183279/).

cient. The situation now requires urgent action to enforce reverence for international legitimacy.

Last Sunday—"Black Sunday"—a heinous massacre was perpetrated against Palestinian workers who early that morning were in search of bread for their children. They had already been uprooted from their land by policies of the Israeli occupation and were forced to seek labor under the worst possible conditions of exploitation and repression.

Further, the massacre is being continued by the Israeli forces in the West Bank, the Gaza Strip and Jerusalem, accompanied by an outburst of Israeli racism against the Palestinian masses in the Galilee, the Triangle and the Negev. As a result of those policies, more than 25 Palestinian martyrs have fallen and more than 2,000 have been injured during the last five days. All this constitutes but one link in the chain of the Israeli iron-fist policy and Israeli racist practices against the Palestinian people, policies and practices which the international community, Governments and peoples have unanimously denounced.

It was not the insanity or derangement of an individual that was responsible for the Black Sunday massacre, as Israeli officials have claimed. The primary responsibility falls on the insanity and derangement of the whole system, a system which is haunted by mythical ghosts, by defunct illusions of racial superiority and by an obsession with expansion and invasion, stemming from the stupid arrogance of military superiority, in order to create a "Greater Israel."

I am addressing the Council while the wounds of my people are still bleeding and the graves of their martyrs are still exposed. Every moment, Palestinian children, women and men pay the price with their blood and their lives, faced with the organized Israeli machine of oppression and terrorism against our Palestinian people, who are struggling for a free and dignified life. During the 30 months of the brave *intifada* of the Palestinian masses against occupation forces saturated with hatred and aggression, the occupiers have been arrogantly waging a brutal war of extermination.

Over the past 30 months, 1,200 Palestinian martyrs have fallen under the bullets of the occupiers. More than 80,000 citizens have been injured as a result of various kinds of repression ranging from severe beatings, the breaking of bones and the use of rubber bullets and live ammunition to the use of internationally prohibited poison gases, which have caused more than 6,000 miscarriages and permanent handicaps to thousands of children, women and men, in addition to other kinds of terrorism and repression. Over those 30 months, the Israeli occupation forces have been waging a war of extermination on all fronts. Our people have been the victims of crimes prohibited by international law, divine law and moral and human values: from the war of starvation waged by laying siege to population centers, the destruction of the infrastructure of our national economy through continuing expropriation of land and water resources thereby devastating farms, and the imposition of huge taxes and attempts to collect them through terrorism and theft as happened in Beit Sahour and elsewhere, to the war of imposed ignorance which has led to the closing for three years of all educational centers in our country from kindergartens to universities.

The universities and most schools are still closed, as verified by reports and other documents available at the United Nations. This has been accompanied by the closing of many philanthropic, cultural and vocational institutions and by the opening, on the other hand, of mass detention camps and prisons for more than 85,000 detainees, scores of whom have been physically eliminated—in addition to deportations and house arrests. At the same time there has been an escalation of the policy of demolishing the houses of Palestinian citizens, by which the occupation forces have demolished, destroyed and shut down more than 2,000 houses during the years of the *intifada*, a policy which has left 10,000 persons, including 5,000 Palestinian children, homeless. All of this is in addition to burning and devastating 80,000 *dunams* of land and 188,000 fruitful trees, the application of collective punishment and the imposition of huge fines by the courts of the Israeli occupation. All this is being carried out with premeditation and racism on the part of the Israeli Government and the fanatic armed settlers against unarmed citizens in the Palestinian and Arab occupied territories.

The recently published report of the Swedish Save the Children organization states that 159 Palestinian children 16 years of age or younger were killed during the first two years of the *intifada* by prohibited terrorist methods, including internationally-prohibited gas bombs, as reports by two United States and Belgian medical teams have proved. That figure now stands at 256. The same Swedish report states that during the same period between 50,000 and 63,000 Palestinian children were injured and required medical treatment. Twenty-five thousand children, some six years of age or younger, were beaten and their bones broken. Further, 675,000 Palestinian children in the West Bank and the Gaza Strip were subject to curfews, with their attendant psychological and educational implications for everyday life.

B'Tselem, an Israeli human-rights organization, has reported that, out of 102 cases examined by them in which Palestinian children were killed, only one Israeli soldier was imprisoned—for a mere two months. That confirms the conclusions of the Swedish report, which shows the contempt of Israeli soldiers for the lives of our Palestinian children.

The Palestinian people expect the Security Council to shoulder its responsibilities to put an end to the Israeli occupation and to begin forthwith to adopt the necessary measures to protect the lives of the children, women and men of our Palestinian people and their property under occupation, especially in the light of the Israeli Government's refusal to abide by any United Nations resolutions, such as Security Council resolutions 465 (1980) and 605 (1987), which condemn and deplore Israeli practices and crimes against the Palestinian people and call upon Israel scrupulously to abide forthwith by the fourth Geneva Convention of 1949 relative to the Protection of Civilian Persons in Time of War.

The Israeli Government, not content with these crimes and this official organized terrorism against our people, has followed them up by bringing in new waves of Jewish immigrants from all parts of the world and by starting to settle them in the occupied Palestinian territories, including Holy Jerusalem, and other Arab territories in place of the Palestinian and Arab owners of those occupied lands, against whom Israel practices organized official terrorism and brutal oppression in order to drive them from their homeland and the homeland of their ancestors.

In addition, Israel has displaced Palestinian families. Within this very short period of the *intifada*, more than 256 families have thus far been expelled from their homeland. Settling new immigrants in the quarters belonging to the Greek Orthodox Church and the assault on the Patriarch of Jerusalem and other priests are part and parcel of the policies practiced by the Israeli Government, policies which were preceded and followed by aggression against Islamic and Christian Holy Places in Jerusalem and the rest of the Holy Land, places viewed as symbols of sanctity, love, peace and tolerance by Muslims and Christians throughout the world.

I have photographic and other evidence of the aggression against the Patriarch of Jerusalem; of the children, many of them nine years of age or younger, killed by Israel; of miscarriages caused by the use of poison gas, which is prohibited internationally. I shall leave these documents for the use of members of the Security Council.

In all it perpetrates and in its repressive, bloody actions and practices against the Palestinian people in the occupied territories, Israel considers itself to be outside the bounds of international responsibility which apply to all States of the world. Indeed, Israel—which was established by a decision of the United Nations—is the only State which ignores and challenges United Nations resolutions and which does not commit itself to implement them.

Israel even refuses to deal with the international Organization when it requests it to carry out its decisions and resolutions. It has now become necessary for the international community to take a stand on this subject and for the Security Council, and especially its permanent member States, to shoulder their responsibility to maintain international peace and security, to implement international resolutions, to end the occupation and to protect the lives of the Palestinian children, women and men under Israeli occupation, in order to arrive at a just and permanent peaceful political solution to the conflict in the Middle East through convening the International Peace Conference on the Middle East, under the auspices of the United Nations.

At a time when the international community is determined to build a world based on cooperation, fruitful dialogue and democracy, when the atmosphere of international détente is being enhanced and when the peoples of the world are preparing to welcome the coming century by underscoring the values of freedom, democracy and human rights, Israel and its leaders insist on clinging to their defunct racist and terrorist policies. Our peaceful initiatives, together with our approach and our *intifada*, represent a model that has been emulated and that has inspired many peoples struggling for freedom and democracy, peoples which have affirmed the harmony and congruence between the realities of our era and the direction of that model's principal course.

Members of the Council undoubtedly know that on 13 December 1988 in this hospitable country, in the name of the Palestinian people, I presented to the General Assembly the Palestinian peace initiative adopted by the Palestine National Council in Algiers on 15 November 1988, which was based on international legitimacy and resolutions and which was adopted by the Arab summit conference in Casablanca in May 1989.

That initiative also received the support of the summit of the Movement of Non-Aligned Countries, the African summit and the conference of foreign ministers of Islamic countries, in addition to that of many States in Western and Eastern Europe, the Soviet Union, China, Japan and the Scandinavian and other countries. The Palestinian peace initiative found support inside Israeli society and daily increasing support among Israeli democratic and peace-loving forces. It also had a positive influence among Jewish groups in Europe and the United States of America.

Basing itself on Palestinian priorities and rights which are in harmony with international legitimacy, the PLO has shown itself to be totally responsive and responsible. We remain flexible; we continue to approach flexibly and sincerely all international peace initiatives adopted by the United Nations, as well as other proposals, including the five points of the United States Secretary of State Baker. We have also reacted positively to the 10 Egyptian points and to the United States proposals conveyed to us by Mr. Sten Andersen, the Swedish Foreign Minister, on 16 September 1989. The PLO is still committed to its declared peace initiative and is ready to participate in arriving at a political solution through which the Palestinian people will be enabled to realize its legitimate national rights, including the right to return, to self-determination and to the establishment of an independent State of its own on its Palestinian national soil, on the basis of international legality and United Nations resolutions.

Regrettably, those peace initiatives have met with rejection and stubbornness on the part of the Israeli Government, which has escalated its iron-fist policy in order to move further from the peace process in the Middle East, thereby defying all international resolutions relating to the conflict in the Middle East, primarily General Assembly resolution 176/43 of 15 December 1988 relative to the convening of the International Peace Conference on the Middle East. In addition, Israel has ignored and refused to implement Security Council resolutions 242 (1967) and 338 (1973).

As for the city of Jerusalem and the Israeli decision to annex it and change its status, proclaiming it the capital of the State of Israel—which was unfortunately followed by a decision on Jerusalem by the United States Congress, encouraging Israel and its occupation, terrorism and crimes—Israel still refuses to carry out any international resolutions on the Holy City, including Security Council resolution 252 (1968) of 21 May 1968, General Assembly resolution 2253 (ES-V~ of 4 July 1967, which affirmed the inadmissibility of changing the status of the city of Jerusalem, Security Council resolution 476 (1980) of 30 June 1980, which declared null and void the measures taken by Israel to change the status of the city of Jerusalem, and Security Council resolution 478 (1980) of 20 August 1980 on the non-recognition of Israel's "basic law" on Jerusalem.

Israel continues to carry out the policy of settlement by expropriating the lands of the Palestinians, building Jewish settlements on those lands and changing the demographic nature of the occupied Palestinian territories, in defiance of Security Council resolution 452 (1979) of 20 July 1979, which stipulated that the Israeli occupation authorities should cease settlement operations in the occupied Arab territories, resolution 446 (1979) of 22 March 1979, which considered the Israeli practice of establishing settlements a serious obstruction to achieving peace, and resolution 465 (1980) of 1 March 1980, which called upon Israel to dismantle existing settlements and cease the construction and planning of settlements.

Recently Israel has exploited the conditions that have permitted opening the doors of immigration to Soviet Jews and Jews from Eastern European and other States, thereby transforming the right to emigrate into a political and colonial aim, as represented in forged immigration to Israel only, which deprives emigrants and those forged to emigrate of their right to choose their own destination. This constitutes a violation of the rights of those Jews. We would recall that the rights of any individual or people cease where the rights of other individuals or peoples— including the Palestinian people—begin.

Israel has endeavored by all means to close all doors but one to Soviet Jewish emigration, keeping only Palestinian land open for them. Israel has been helped in that endeavor by decisions made and obstacles raised by some States, especially the United States and Australia, within the framework of a special understanding and a fundamental and dangerous distortion of the concept of the right of emigration as stipulated in the Helsinki accords, transforming it to achieve the aggressive political aim of preventing the Palestinian people from living in their homeland and depriving Palestinian refugees of the right to return in order to settle new immigrants in the homeland to which the original owners have a right.

It is necessary for me to point out most responsibly that the issue of Soviet Jewish emigration to Palestinian lands represents a danger to the whole region, not only to the occupied Palestinian lands themselves. The threat extends to neighboring Arab States. Indeed, it has begun to threaten the Golan Heights and southern Lebanon' where bitter experience in the Middle East proves that Israel's greed and expansionist appetites know no limits.

I see it as my duty to point out that, most regrettably, the United States of America has given Israel unlimited support at all levels; this has encouraged Israel to continue its occupation and escalate its terrorist and barbaric practices against the Palestinian people, challenging the decisions of the international community and impeding all peace initiatives in the Middle East region, including the United States proposals themselves, quite apart from all other peace initiatives.

The United States, which raises the slogan of human rights, has totally neglected the Palestinians and their human rights and has ignored the comprehensive human and moral dimensions of the concept of human rights. This has encouraged Israel to persist in its barbaric practices against the Palestinian people in the occupied Palestinian and Arab territories, where Lebanese villages and Palestinian refugee camps are exposed to Israeli air raids, destructive bombardment and, in the South, occupation.

In view of the dangers in the surrounding Middle East region that arise from the continued Israeli occupation of Arab and Palestinian lands and Israel's escalation of State-organized terrorism and the war of annihilation against our people, with aggressive and expansionist threats against many Arab States, especially Iraq, Lebanon and Jordan, through Israel's continuous preparations for aggression and war, it is high time for the Council to shoulder its responsibility to implement United Nations resolutions relating to the Arab-Israeli conflict before it is too late. Through its practices, threats and war preparations, Israel is leading the entire region to a catastrophe whose danger is unprecedented in the light of the fact that the Middle East is among the regions where conventional, nuclear, chemical and biological weapons are stockpiled, which raises the prospect of a catastrophe which will go beyond the borders of the Middle East region to threaten international peace and security.

The dimensions of the danger threatening the prospect of peace in the Middle East are now visible every day. They are beginning to manifest themselves in mass killings, in increased escalation, in the tense situation which is leading the area to the brink of war, and in Israel's insistence on continuing its occupation of Palestinian lands, which only a few days ago Shamir officially declared to be "liberated and inherited lands."

The Palestine Liberation Organization, which affirms its strategic commitment to peace, submits to the Security Council the following practical steps which will realize the international community's consensus, transforming its resolutions into practice and inspiring confidence and hope with respect to the Council's role and effectiveness in achieving world peace, security and justice.

Before outlining those steps, I should like to bring to the attention of the Council a document concerning "Greater Israel" as depicted on the 10-agora 0 in. The document was published in the *Jewish Journal* in the United States on 19 February 1989. That document speaks of "Greater Israel," which is depicted on Israeli currency, and the map comprises all of Israel, all of Lebanon, all of Jordan, half of Syria, two thirds of Iraq, one third of Saudi Arabia up to the holy city of Al-Madinah and half of Sinai. The document contains a detailed map, with "Greater Israel" marked in blue.

The first step would be the designation by the Secretary-General of a permanent special envoy to work full-time on the peace process and engage in the contacts necessary to secure a peaceful, just and lasting solution to the Arab-Israeli conflict. Alternatively, the Secretary-General might himself undertake the duties of that mission.

The second step would be adoption by the Council of a resolution providing international protection to the Palestinian people to safeguard their lives, property and holy places in the occupied territories, under the flag of the United Nations and by means of international emergency forces, to supplement the United Nations observer force now stationed in Jerusalem, with the purpose of ending completely the Israeli occupation of our Palestinian land.

The third step is the adoption by the Council of a clear resolution—and the Council's assurance of its supervision and implementation—to stop settler immigration to the occupied Palestinian territories, a decision that will prevent completely the construction and expansion of Israeli settlements, military or civilian, in the occupied Palestinian lands, particularly in Arab Jerusalem, in implementation of the relevant international resolutions.

The fourth step would be for the Council to call the representatives of its permanent members to an immediate meeting to discuss the peace settlement and the peace process and to prepare for the convening of the

International Peace Conference on the Middle East, in implementation of international resolutions.

The fifth step is to start to adopt the necessary arrangements and preparations for the imposition of sanctions on Israel in accordance with Chapter VII of the Charter of the United Nations as a response to the crimes committed by Israel against the Palestinian people in the occupied territories and as a consequence of its breach and violation of the Fourth Geneva Convention of 1949 relative to the treatment of civilians in time of war, as well as for its refusal to implement the relevant international resolutions, for its deliberate defiance and its impeding of the peace process in the Middle East and, in particular, for its refusal to implement the Council's own decisions and resolutions.

The experience of the United Nations in imposing sanctions against South Africa has borne fruit in Namibia, where the heroic Namibian people have gained their independence through the New York Agreement, implemented under the auspices of the United Nations. It has also started to bear fruit for the people of South Africa, with the release of the militant hero Nelson Mandela and with the start of building peace and fulfilling the rights of the people of South Africa, far from racial discrimination and *apartheid*. In this context I should like to express our deep appreciation of the active and extremely important role of the Secretary-General, Mr. Perez de Cuellar.

Obligation and commitment to the human heritage and to the concepts of justice and righteousness to which that heritage has been dedicated require that the Council should decide to form an international investigation committee composed of members of the Council to investigate all the crimes against humanity that have been perpetrated by the Israeli Government against the Palestinian people.

While reaffirming that our choice of the path of peace is a genuine strategic alternative, we also affirm our right to continue our resistance and our self-defense until an end is put to the Israeli occupation. That is a sacred right guaranteed to us by the law of human rights, the Charter of the United Nations, international decisions and the will of the Palestinian people. The heroic people's *intifada* against the Israeli occupation of our country will continue until we wrest our right to freedom and national independence on our national soil.

Our people are committed to the issue of peace and to the initiative that I announced in the name of the Palestinian people a year and half ago before the General Assembly. Our people are determined to attain their political, national and human rights like all other peoples in the world. We are determined to do so because we are an indivisible part of the community of nations and of human society, with which we have participated in carrying the torch of culture, for it was in our land that the three heavenly religions were formed, flourished and lived side by side in harmony.

It is high time that [our] people enjoyed security, peace and independence. We are not asking for the moon. We are not asking for the impossible. It is high time for our children to live as peacefully as other children of the peoples of the world, far from fear, destruction and death. It is high time to stop the spilling of the blood of our people and for our flag to be raised over their liberated soil. It is high time for us to realize our freedom and for the curtain to fall once and for all, for the last time and forever, on the last racist, settler military occupation of Palestine, that holy land of our planet Earth.

198 AFTERWORD

Afterword
Disarming Empire[1]

Paweł Wargan[2]

The Israeli genocide in Gaza is not the first convulsion of the fading unipolar era—nor will it be its last. Tectonic movements not seen since the last great wave of decolonization are underway. The Western world, sustained for centuries by its capacity to rob humanity at the barrel of a gun, is losing its grip. As the forces rising against it grow in confidence, empire grows belligerent. We find ourselves in a moment of forking possibilities. Will the fascist violence unleashed against the Palestinian people today stand as a dark portent of the violence of Western imperialism towards all the world's workers and oppressed peoples tomorrow? Will people and planet expire in the final, desperate wave of exterminist violence unleashed by a capitalist order in decay? Or will this moment, so pregnant with clarity and resistance, generate the movement towards imperialism's demise?

In 1887, Friedrich Engels found himself tormented by similar premonitions. Humanity was edging towards a "world war [...] of an extent and violence hitherto unimagined," he wrote. This new war would usher in:

> famine, disease, the universal lapse into barbarism, both of the armies and the people, in the wake of acute misery; irretrievable dislocation of our artificial system of trade, industry and credit, ending in universal bankruptcy; collapse of the old states and their conventional political wisdom to the point where crowns will roll into the gutters by the dozen and no one will be around to pick them up; the absolute

---

1   Ed. Note: Originally published in *Peace, Land, and Bread* (online-only), November, 30, 2023, accessed on March 14, 2024, at: https://www.peacelandandbread.org/post/disarming-empire.

2   Ed. Note: Paweł Wargan is an activist, researcher, and organizer. He serves as the Coordinator of the Secretariat at the Progressive International and has published in *Tribune*, *Monthly Review*, and elsewhere.

impossibility of foreseeing how it will all end and who will emerge as victor from the battle.[3]

Although Engels believed that this war would bring about the conditions for the victory of the working class, his message was not optimistic. The new technologies of war so mercilessly tested in the colonies would, he predicted, soon be seen across the capitalist world. These armaments would be aimed at the stirrings of revolution sweeping across Europe. In the face of the military's new explosive power, the tactics of the militant proletarian movement would be rendered obsolete. What good is a barricade against an artillery shell, capable of tearing human bodies apart? Engels' answer to this looming threat was to advance a novel demand for the rising working class movement: disarmament.

Engels would not live to see the First World War, the brutality of which exceeded even his own dark predictions. But the agenda of disarmament persisted, with a budding new socialist republic picking up the mantle. In December 1922, the Amsterdam Trade Union International convened The Hague Peace Conference, inviting all forces "interested in the maintenance of peace"[4] to take part. Among the invitees were the trade unions of Russia. They dispatched the young Bolshevik Karol Radek to represent the October Revolution.

Radek reminded the workers of Europe of the great cost they had borne in the war, having bled out in their millions "for home and country." He implored them to build peace by breaking with the bourgeois architects of that violence. "You proletarians of the capitalist countries, you have no fatherland to defend," he said. "You must first conquer the land of your fathers." The task was pressing:

> [If] the working class does not rise before the cannon are mounted, it is much less likely to rise after martial law has been proclaimed, after all the demons of nationalism have been let loose, and the workers bound hand and foot.[5]

---

3   Engels, F. 1888. "Introduction to Borkheim." *Abstract*. First published as "Introduction" in *S. Borkheim, Zur Erinnerung fur die deutschen Mordspatrioten, 1806-1807*, Hottingen-Zurich. Accessed on January 25, 2024, online at: https://www.marxists.org/archive/marx/works/1887/12/15.htm.

4   Brandler, H. December 1922. "The Peace Conference of the Amsterdamers." *International Press Correspondence* 2, no. 113, pp. 946-947. Accessed on January 25, 2024, online at: https://www.marxists.org/archive/brandler/1922/12/peace-conf.htm.

5   Radek, K. January 1923. "Speech at the Hague Peace Conference." *International Press Correspondence*, 3, no. 1, pp. 4-5. Accessed on January 25, 2024, online at: https://www.marxists.org/archive/radek/1923/01/hague.htm.

On behalf of the nascent Soviet Union, itself embattled by a multi-frontal imperialist assault, Karol Radek put forward a 14-point resolution. Recognizing that "the abolition of war is only possible with the abolition of the capitalist system," the resolution called for the total disarmament of all "White Guard" organizations, including the fascists, and the evacuation of all foreign bases from Europe and from the colonies. It called on anti-war forces to organize in committees, bridging differences among them, but delineating their separation from the bourgeois imperialists. It called for the launch of an international "propaganda week [...] against imperialism, against the dictatorship of capital, and for the placing of power in the hands of the workers."[6]

The Soviet delegation's proposed resolution was rejected—a dark sign of things to come. But it remains salient for the questions that it poses: When must we begin organizing for peace? How do we organize? And what is the content of the peace that we are seeking? Today, humanity finds itself confronting horrors far beyond Engels' and Radek's imaginations. Having violently ended tens of millions of lives, imperialism now strikes at the very conditions of our survival. The planet stands at the brink of irreversible ecological change—driven predominantly by a handful of imperialist states[7]—and the threat of nuclear extermination hangs over our societies amid a New Cold War that has already claimed tens of thousands of lives on the battlefield. In this context, what is the genocide in Gaza but a warning against our resistance to imperialism's grim futurelessness?

Here, the Western ruling classes are unmasked. In their eager support for the genocide of the Palestinian people, figures like European Commission chief Ursula von der Leyen—herself the descent of wealthy slave owners and prominent Nazis—reveal a continuity in the Western colonial project. That project continues to be humanity's great burden. Since 1960, the old colonial powers of the Global North have drained $152 trillion from the Global South through structures of unequal exchange.[8] When these parasitic relations are threatened, imperialism responds with psychotic, untrammeled violence; the kind that exterminates a quarter of

---

6   Ibid.

7   Ghosh, Jayati, Chakraborty, Shouvikand, and Debamanyu Das. July-August 2022. "Climate Imperialism in the Twenty-First Century." *Monthly Review*, vol. 74, no. 3.

8   Hickel, Jason, Sullivan, Dylan, and Huzaifa Zoomkawala. 2021. "Plunder in the Post-Colonial Era: Quantifying Drain from the Global South Through Unequal Exchange, 1960–2018." *New Political Economy*, vol. 26, no. 6, pp. 1030-1047.

the Korean population, or over a million Indonesians, or two hundred thousand Guatemalans, or half a million Iraqi children, or a Gazan child every ten minutes. The sadism and dis-proportionality are necessary because of imperialism's central weakness: its inability to rule by consent. Leaps towards liberation are met with exterminist force.

The genocide in Gaza has brought these realities into sharp focus. Indeed, the Zionist state is so central to the imperialist project that Joe Biden once quipped that, "if there were not an Israel, we would have to invent one."[9] The existence of the Israeli state prevents regional integration and suppresses the self-determination of its neighbors—sustaining a zone of imperial extraction where states lack the power or unity to build an alternative, sovereign political project. Its importance degrades the imperialist states' pretensions to democracy, as they violently suppress opposition and reject the growing popular consensus for a ceasefire. Ultimately, Zionist violence itself finds echoes on the streets of imperial metropoles, where the weapons tested on a caged Palestinian population disperse protesters and police minorities. This is what Aimé Césaire meant when he said that fascism is colonialism turned inwards.[10]

The mass global movement of solidarity with Palestine that erupted in recent weeks reflects a dramatic process of radicalization and consciousness-formation. We see how readily the facade of liberalism is discarded. We see how readily the declining empire turns to fascism when threatened—that same fascism that is always deployed as the last defense against opposition to capitalist oppression and imperial domination. The historic task of our generation has become blindingly clear. To honor the Palestinian people, we must dismantle the entirety of this wretched system. Gaza's victory must be NATO's graveyard, and the EU's reckoning. It must collapse the global totalitarianism of the U.S. and never allow it to recover the prestige of its fraudulent claims to democracy. Empire must be swept away by the swelling tide of this moment. "Never again" can have no meaning other than this, because the staid logic of colonial and imperial domination—long ago rejected by humanity but sustained for decades with brute force—sits at the heart of the violence.

---

9 Dovere, Edwards-Isaac. 2013. "Biden: Always Israel's friend." *Politico*. Accessed on January 25, 2024, online at: https://www.politico.com/story/2013/09/joe-biden-israel-097586.

10 Césaire, Aimé. 2001. *Discourse on Colonialism*. New York: Monthly Review Press, pp. 36-37.

This requires that we transform this moment into a project of sustained resistance against U.S. imperialism—a global intifada that brings the war to all the fronts from which it is waged. It demands that we dismantle the weapons factories. It demands that we shut down the bases. It demands that we understand the economic logic underpinning imperialism's relentless advance. And it demands, above all, that we abandon the illusions that our aims can be achieved by collusion with the warmongers. There is no 'lesser evil' that can be voted into office, no reform that can sweep away this violence or mend the wounds it has inflicted. The system itself must go. Now is the time to build a global, anti-imperialist peace movement, bringing together all the nodes of resistance to the global military machine.

We confront a clear starting point. December 2, 2023 marked the 200th anniversary of the Monroe Doctrine—the United States' declaration of dominion over the Western Hemisphere. Over the past two centuries, that doctrine has gone global. Today, the U.S. operates a sprawling military and economic machine that spans the planet. Its hegemonic project echoes through visions of a "Global NATO" that polices all imperial frontiers. Through these infrastructures, the U.S. maintains a firm grip on the conditions of survival for nations and peoples around the world, even as its own population struggles to get by. As the global economic center of gravity shifts eastward, these crises manifest in increasingly extreme violence that seeks to arrest the stirrings of sovereignty everywhere.

In this moment, is ripe with resistance, the grim anniversary of the Monroe Doctrine must become our rallying cry. Every December 2nd must become a global day of action against imperialism, uniting workers, activists, and progressive forces around the world—from Korea to Colombia, Italy to the United States—to help form, coordinate, internationalize, and radicalize campaigns, movements, and direct action groups against U.S. imperialism and its military machine.

As Radek warned in 1922, the cannons are now being mounted everywhere. Military spending has exceeded $2 trillion annually, with the U.S. accounting for roughly 40% of the total. In South Korea, Japan, Guam, the Philippines, and across the Pacific region, we are witnessing a process of militarization unprecedented since the Second World War. U.S. warships are trickling into the Mediterranean, a grim warning to those who would seek to stop the Zionist genocide in Palestine. The cannons are being mounted, and the message is clear. No human cost is too great in the preservation of the imperial project. No law will be unbent.

No human right will be held sacrosanct. The cannons are being mounted, and we must disarm them before they bury us in their unrelenting warpath. Liberation from all rivers to all seas—this is the historic task of our generation.

Appendix
Historical Background of the PLO[1]

Leila S. Kadi

The significance of the armed Palestinian resistance is not to be regarded only in terms of a new and effective force in the social and political life of the Arabs. In addition to this there is the heroism of the men who have become guerrillas. There can be no doubt that these men have enkindled within the Arab world a new inspiration and a new awareness of the possibilities that exist for the Arabs. While the Arab world still bitterly remembers its third defeat at the hands of Zionism, these young men of Palestine go out to redress the balance, to restore Arab rights and pride.

These men, nearly all of whom are Palestinians, remember and fight because they want to return to the land—the land that is theirs and the land that is their patents'! In a random sample taken of 300 men of Al-Fateh who died fighting in 1968, it was found that their average age was 24 years six months, and 23 percent of them were born after 1948. The memory of Palestine is still strong in the hearts of Palestinians and, while that memory remains, Palestine is not lost to them.

Armed resistance, contrary to appearances, is not new to the Palestinian people. They have taken up arms against foreign rule since the British Mandate. In the following pages a condensed summary of the background to the present Palestinian armed resistance movement will be discussed.

---

1   **Ed. Note:** Originally published in Kadi, Leila S. 1969. *Basic Political Documents of the Armed Palestinian Resistance Movement*, PLO Research Center, Beirut. As of the publication of this book, there has recently been made available a new edition from Midnight Books Press, 2024. Kadi's essay has been included in the appendix to the present volume for the historical background it provides on the included political documents of the PLO, as well as for its clarity and its timelessness.

By 1936, the Palestinian people had enough of British occupation and a revolution broke out. This revolution represented the peak of the Palestinian struggle against both the British Mandate and Zionism. The 1936 revolution followed a long period of political struggle by the Palestinian people exemplified in memoranda of protest, demonstrations, strikes and attempts at dissuading Britain from supporting the Zionist movement.

The distinguishing feature of the 1936 popular revolution is that the traditional Palestinian feudal, religious, and bourgeois leadership had nothing to do with its outburst. The man who played a leading role in preparing for the revolution was Izz al-Din al-Qassam, a simple man who had contacted Hajj Amin al-Husseini requesting an appointment as a roving preacher to prepare for the revolution. Al-Husseini refused this request saying: "We are working for a political solution to the problem."

Such an answer did not discourage Qassam who went ahead and organized secret cells among the poor workers and peasants. On 14 November 1933, Qassam fought his first battle against the British forces in the Jenin area where he was killed. Although the Qassam movement was unable to achieve any of its major aims, it challenged the traditional family leaders before the people.

The second phase of the revolution started on 13 April 1936. Qassam's secret organizations renewed their operations from the rural areas and the revolution spread from the north of Palestine to the south. On 19 April, the city of Jaffa witnessed a massive popular uprising. The British forces reacted by blowing up whole quarters of the city. This action on the part of Britain prompted the "national committees" of the people to declare a general strike.

On 25 April, the national committees forced the Islamic Council (Hajj Amin al-Husseini), the Defence Arab Party (Ragheb al-Nashashibi), the Reform Party (Hussein al-Khalidi), the National Bloc Party ('Abd al-Latif Salah), the Arab Palestinian Party (Jamal al-Husseini), the Independence Party ('Awni 'Abd al-Hadi), to disband their political organizations and form the Arab Higher Committee to lead the people's struggle through a general strike and armed revolution. The above-mentioned leaders succumbed to the proposed radical measures under the obvious massive popular pressure generated by the Qassam's armed resistance movement.

When the British failed to crush the revolution or prevent it from spreading, they turned to the pro-British Arab rulers to use their influence to convince the Palestinian people to end the revolution and negotiate peacefully with Britain. The Arab rulers' response, headed by Nuri al-Sa'id, was positive. Sa'id visited Jerusalem on 26 August 1936, and asked the Arab Higher Committee to take all measures to end the strike and disturbances promising that the Iraqi Government would negotiate with the British Government to fulfill the legal demands of the Arab people of Palestine.

The Palestinian people rejected the principle of Arab mediation and carried on their armed struggle until the rulers of Trans-Jordan, Saudi Arabia, Iraq, and Yemen intervened and sent cables to the Palestinian people calling them to "keep quiet."

In spite of the popular rejection of Arab mediation, the Arab Higher Committee issued a statement announcing its approval of the principle of Arab mediation and urging the Palestinian people to end the strike and the disturbances as of 12 October 1936. With this statement the second phase of the Palestinian revolution came to an end. It clearly revealed the Palestinian people's readiness to adopt the method of armed struggle and reject the logic of negotiations with Britain by foiling the efforts of the Arab rulers to mediate between them (Palestinians) and the British Government who had refused to stop Jewish immigration into Palestine. Moreover, the second phase gave clear indications of the hesitation and continuous efforts of the traditional Palestinian bourgeois and feudal leadership to agree to any mediation to end the revolution and start political negotiations with Britain. The important element which was witnessed during this phase is the interference of the Arab rulers, who belonged to the same class structure as the Palestinian leaders, to impose their attitude on the Palestinian people.

The third phase of the Palestinians' armed revolution is marked by the assassination, on 27 September 1937, at the hands of the revolutionaries, of L. Andrews, Acting District Commissioner in Nazareth. The Arab Higher Committee issued a communiqué condemning this act in this phase the antagonism between the rural masses and the bourgeois feudal family leadership came out into the open. The British authorities reacted by escalating their acts of repression and terror. Members of the Arab Higher Committee were imprisoned, and others fled the country.

The people's revolution spread and was concentrated in the provinces of Nablus, Galilee, and the northern district. At the beginning of 1938 the revolutionaries were in full control of the villages of these areas where they had wide influence.

The weak point of the revolution was the absence of a unified politically aware leadership which could be responsible for coordinating military action between the different areas. As for the traditional feudal bourgeois leadership, some of its members were in exile while others were cooperating with the British authorities to destroy the revolution. The revolution suffered under some severe handicaps. First of all, there was the constant personal bickering for leadership by the bourgeois and feudal Palestinian parties and their attack on the revolution itself both in terms of condemning it before the Palestinian people and then by conducting negotiations with Britain. Then there was the lack of any proper military coordination on the different fronts. Thus, gradually the revolution became weaker and less effective. With the outbreak of World War II, the revolution came to an end. The reactionary traditional leadership continued its efforts to solve the problem through negotiations with the British Government. The latter sent commissions of enquiries and then issued the White Paper of 1939 which limited Jewish immigration and promised Palestinian independence in the hope of securing a calm situation in Palestine throughout the war years.

The occupying power imposed rigorous laws against the Palestinian people. It meant death for a Palestinian Arab to be found carrying a gun. This penalty, however, was not imposed on the Jews. Thus, during the course of the war, it was the Jews who were being armed often with British assistance, while the Palestinians were kept under surveillance.

The war period witnessed in Palestine an alliance between the traditional Palestinian leadership and the other Arab rulers who wanted the Palestinian people to terminate all violence against British rule.

By the end of the war the Zionists were ready to fight the now-unarmed Palestinians. The Palestinians were in no way ready to face the Zionist onslaught that was unleashed against them and the Arab armies that eventually came to their aid were too inefficient and ill-equipped. In addition, the Arab feudal and bourgeois regimes were primarily concerned with maintaining close relations with Britain and the United States of America. The Palestinian leadership in turning over the fate of the Palestinian people and their struggle to the reactionary Arab rulers went back to the same tragic course of 1936.

The year 1948 saw the establishment of the state of Israel and the Arab Palestinian people's loss of their homeland and dispersal.

The first reaction of the Palestinian people after this disaster was to resist any kind of rapprochement that would lead to a final settlement with the state of Israel. Examples of this opposition ate to be found in the following:

1. The publication in 1932 of a secret weekly bulletin Nashrat al-Thar by the Committee for Resisting Peace with Israel. This committee was mainly composed of students at the American University of Beirut (AUB). These same students were among the group that formed the nucleus of the Arab Nationalist Movement (ANM) founded by a Palestinian, Dr. George Habash. He obtained his degree in medicine from the AUB in the early fifties. After his graduation Habash practised in Amman for a few years. Then he devoted himself to the ANM and became one of its key figures. Nashrat al-Thar was very effective and had a widespread distribution among the Palestinians in the camps up to 1934. It played a role in uncovering various secret attempts to liquidate the Palestine problem on the basis of a final settlement with the state of Israel. Such a settlement could only mean that the Palestinians would remain forever after in a state of diaspora. The bulletin's effect was mainly among Palestinians in Lebanon, Syria, and Jordan, while its influence on thorn in the Gaza Strip was negligible.

2. During the years 1953-54 UNRWA put forward many projects aiming at the rehabilitation of the Palestinian refugees by constructing permanent residence units. They regarded these projects as having one aim, namely, the liquidation of their problem. Rehabilitation meant the end of their existence as refugees and their acceptance of the state of Israel as a *fait accompli*. This ultimately meant the loss of Palestine to them. In order to counteract the rehabilitation projects, the Palestinians launched mass demonstrations, organized general strikes, and destroyed many of the housing units set up by UNRWA, thus putting an end to such projects. The rehabilitation projects were put forward again by Dag Hammarskjöld in 1959 in the form of a plan for the integration of the Palestinians in the economic life of the Middle East. They opposed this plan by holding the Arab Palestinian Conference in Beirut in 1959. The rejection of the plan by Palestinians compelled the Arab governments to oppose it, thus forcing the UN to withdraw the plan.

3. Alongside the political struggle of the masses of the Palestinians, small Palestinian groups residing in the Gaza Strip, Syria and the West Bank took the initiative by undertaking commando action inside Israel. These commando raids, which penetrated deep into populated areas of Israel, prompted the latter to carry out a large-scale raid on Gaza on 28 February 1955. It also caused Israel to assassinate two commando leaders, Salah Mustafa and Mustafa Hafez. These guerrilla groups were not based on, connected to, or part of any political organization, but were trained and led by Egyptian army officers. These groups were disbanded after the 1956 tripartite aggression on Suez.

Politically active Palestinian groups considered that the Arab governments were mainly responsible for the 1948 defeat and thus they became affiliated to, and actively participated in national Arab parties such as the Ba'th and the Arab Nationalist Movement. These parties called for Arab unity which Palestinians believed was the road to a strong unified Arab state capable of confronting Israel and liberating Palestine.

With the establishment of the United Arab Republic, 22 February 1958, the Palestinians were convinced that they were on the brink of liberating Palestine. Historical developments proved them wrong. During the three years of unity the UAR Government attempted to build up popular Palestinian organisations such as the Palestinian National Union in Syria and Gaza. These organisations were unpopular and ineffective since they were imposed from above.

At the same time, in 1959, a secret monthly magazine of limited circulation Our Palestine (Filistinuna) began publication in Beirut. Our Palestine called for the Palestinization of the Palestine problem. This meant that the Arab governments should give the Palestinians a free hand to work for the liberation of their country. Later on, it became known that the sponsors of Our Palestine were the Al-Fateh group. This group came into existence out of the discussions of Palestinian students in the Gaza Strip who had suffered under the Israeli occupation of 1956 and were concerned with the problem of how best to win back Palestine admitting the Arab governments' inability to do it for them. Little by little, they became convinced that the Palestinians must take their cause into their own hands. Yasser 'Arafat became their leader.

'Arafat (his code name is Abu 'Ammar) was born in Jerusalem in 1929. His career, in a way, mirrors the history and thrust of the Palestinian commandos. He spent his early childhood in a house within a stone's throw of the Wailing Wall. When the Arab-Israeli fighting of 1948 ended 'Arafat found himself with his parents a refugee in Gaza. He managed to go to Cairo to study engineering at Fuad I (now Cairo) University, where he majored in civil engineering. As chairman of the Palestinian Student Federation he helped, in his own words, to "lay the basic foundation for our movement." While studying he also acted as a leader and trainer of Palestinian and Egyptian commandos who fought the British in the Suez area, served the Egyptian army as a demolitions expert, and fought against the British and French at Port Said and Abu Kabir in 1956. After a brief period as an engineer in Egypt he obtained an engineering job in Kuwait in 1957, where he stayed until 1965. Meanwhile, he travelled among the scattered Palestinians to recruit members for the organization. Soon cells were formed in Kuwait and among students in West Germany. The initial development was slow and went against the trends of the period. This could be linked to the belief that Arab unity was the only road to the liberation of Palestine, and any claims to unity boosted this belief. Thus, slogans and aspirations to unite under the leadership of President Nasser, made themselves felt strongly during the years 1957-1958, culminating in union between Syria and Egypt.

Between 1957 and 1967, talk about Arab unity reached its climax but, at the same time, rivalry between the various Arab governments became even more acute. But aspirations for Arab unity were so deeply held by the people that they constituted a reality which had to be taken into consideration. Also significant was the interaction and confusion of the various political movements: Nasserist, Ba'thist, Arab Nationalist, etc., regardless of their country of origin. In this context, the Palestinian national question was not a simple one, even more so because, through the idea of unity, the existence of Israel made it possible for many Arab governments to redirect popular aspirations towards external objectives and an outside enemy. Certain Arab states accused the militants of Al-Fateh of being agents of CENTO. One can relate such an accusation to the United Arab Republic and Tunisia's policies during the early sixties. President Nasser realized that the war in Yemen had dragged on for a much longer period than was expected and was thus costing the UAR treasury more than it could afford. This led to pressing internal economic problems which threatened the effectiveness and development plans of his regime. President Nasser was of the opinion that the industry and economy of the UAR should be more developed before embarking on a war against Israel. The UAR was of the opinion that Al-Fateh was trying to involve it in war with Israel at a time when Arab unity had not yet been achieved and the UAR's economy was not yet well developed. Thus, in his opening speech to the Second Palestinian National Congress which was held in Cairo on 31 May 1963, President Nasser declared: "We do not have a plan for the liberation of Palestine." Moreover, 1963 witnessed the first Arab leader who publicly declared that the Arabs should solve the Palestine problem by signing a peace treaty with Israel. Thus, the strictly clandestine character of various Palestinian resistance movements until 1967 was less due to the Israeli enemy than to the attitude of Arab states where Palestinian militants were often put under house arrest, thrown in jail or even worse. To this effect, Al-Fateh still remembers that one of its first partisans was killed in 1963 by the Jordanian army.

With the failure of the Syro-Egyptian union in 1961, the concept of unity as the road to the liberation of Palestine collapsed. Palestinians realized that the attainment of unity was an almost impossible task; and that they could not afford to wait until all of the Arab world was united. They started to talk of an independent Palestinian entity and action. As a result, more than thirty Palestinian organizations, most of which had only a small membership, were set up. This large number of organizations was ample proof of the Palestinians' desire to work seriously and independently for the liberation of their homeland. At the same time, it indicated that a strong effective organization was lacking.

The triumph of the Algerian revolution in 1962 gave more weight to the principle of independent Palestinian activity. The Algerians were able to recruit material and moral support from various Arab regimes and, through armed struggle, to attain their independence. Some Palestinians thus believed that they could adopt the same kind of policy if they took the initiative and maintained their freedom of action.

During this period Al-Fateh, which is the reverse initials of Harakat al-Tahrir al-Watani al-Filistini (Palestine National Liberation Movement), strove to create the nucleus of a political organization recruited from among the Palestinian intelligentsia. Since 1962 Al-Fateh has concentrated all its efforts on starting military action but was faced with the problem of the shortage of means to embark on such an activity. In 1964, Al-Fateh held a conference to discuss this question and the majority of the members voted for starting military action on 1 January 1965 in spite of the shortage of means. Those who opposed this decision proposed that military operations should be started under another name, rather than Al-Fateh, so that, in the event of failure, Al-Fateh might continue its preparations and its secret activities. The proposal was accepted, and it was agreed to use the name of al-'Asifah for the first military operations. Al-Fateh announced that it was al-'Asifah after the tenth military communiqué. Al-Fateh's leadership decided to continue using the name of al-'Asifah because it had become a historic name.

The first Arab summit conference, held in Cairo between 13 and 16 January 1964, was convened to discuss Israel's progress in its plan for the diversion of the waters of the Jordan River. The UAR was of the opinion that Syria, Jordan and Saudi Arabia were trying to involve it in war with Israel in order to stab it in the back. The UAR held that it would not let itself be pushed into a battle with Israel before the attainment of unity between all the Arab countries. Thus, President Nasser was suspected of having no intention of getting into war with Israel when the latter would start pumping water from the Sea of Galilee down to the Negev. Under these circumstances, President Nasser, in a speech delivered on 23 December 1963 on the occasion of the seventh anniversary of "Victory Day," said: "In order to confront Israel (which put a challenge to us last week, and whose Chiefs-of-Staff stood up and said 'we shall divert the water against the will of the Arabs, and let the Arabs do what they can'), a meeting between the Arab kings and presidents must take place as soon as possible, regardless of the strife and conflicts among them."

The conference was held, and at the end of its meetings issued a communiqué in which it decided to organize the Palestinian people to enable them to play their part in liberating Palestine and in determining its future.

The immediate background of this decision can be found in the 40th session of the Arab League Council held on 13 September 1963. At that session, the Council studied the problem of Palestine in a more constructive manner than usual by affirming the "Palestine entity" at the international level; by establishing the bases for action through the organization of the people of Palestine; and by making them assume responsibility for their national cause and the liberation of Palestine.

The first decision taken by the Council of the League was the appointment of Ahmad Shuqairi as the representative of Palestine at the Arab League. Shuqairi is a Palestinian lawyer who had been Assistant Secretary General of the Arab League; had later become a member of the Syrian delegation to the United Nations; and then became the delegate of Saudi Arabia to the UN. The Council also asked him to carry out consultations with representatives of the people of Palestine for the formation of a new general government in exile. Furthermore, he was asked to visit various Arab capitals to discuss the means which the Arab governments would place at his disposal for the fulfillment of this task.

Shuqairi began his tour of the Arab states on 19 February 1964, to discuss with Palestinians and the Arab governments the drafting of the Palestine National Charter and of the draft constitution of a liberation organization, on which the "Palestine entity" would be based. Shuqairi visited Jordan, Syria, Bahrain, Qatar, Iraq, Kuwait, Lebanon, and the Sudan. He met the then President of the Yemen Republic, Abdullah Sallal, in Cairo. His tour ended on 5 April 1964. Upon his arrival in Cairo, Shuqairi made a statement in which he announced that he had held about 30 conferences with the Palestinian people, during which he had met thousands of them. At these conferences he had captained the Palestine National Charter, and the basic system of the liberation organization.

On 28 May 1964, the Palestine National Congress, in which members of Al-Fateh participated, opened in Jerusalem. It unanimously elected Shuqairi as Chairman of the Congress. It was held under the supervision of the Arab League, and under the auspices of King Hussein, and attended by 242 Palestinian representatives from Jordan, 146 from Syria, Lebanon, Gaza, Qatar, Kuwait, and Iraq. The most important resolutions adopted by the Congress were the following:

a. Establishment of a Palestine Liberation Organization to be set up by the people of Palestine in accordance with its statutes.

b. Appeal to all Palestinians to form professional and labor unions.

c. Immediate opening of camps for military training of all Palestinians, in order to prepare them for the liberation battle which they affirmed could be won only by force of arms. The Arab governments were urged to admit Palestinians to their military academies.

d. Establishment of a Palestine National Fund to finance the PLO. The sources of revenue would include annual subscriptions, to be paid by every Palestinian over 18 years of age, loans and grants to be offered by Arab and friendly states, contributions to be collected on national occasions, and the revenue from issuing Palestine Liberation Bonds by the Arab League.

e. Election of Ahmad Shuqairi as Chairman of the Executive Committee of the PLO.

The second Arab summit conference, which was held in Alexandria from 3-11 September 1964, welcomed the establishment of the Palestine Liberation Organization. (It also fixed the obligations of each Arab state towards the PLO.) The conference endorsed the decision taken by the PLO Executive Committee to establish a Palestine Liberation Army to be stationed in the Gaza Strip and the Sinai Peninsula.

The creation of the PLO raised the hopes of the Palestinian people. It absorbed a number of the small organizations that had been set up earlier in the sixties. Al-Fateh, which was at that time operating only on the political level, clandestinely, and the Palestinian branch of the Arab Nationalist Movement (ANM), and a few other small organizations maintained their separate identity, in spite of the fact that they participated in the PLO national congress.

Up to this time Al-Fateh was the sole organization which called for the adoption of the principle of armed struggle as the only means for the liberation of Palestine. Furthermore, Al-Fateh believed that the Palestinians should start armed struggle irrespective of the reaction or plans of the Arab regimes. The Palestinian branch of the Arab Nationalist Movement called for coordination between the Palestinian armed struggle and the plans of the progressive regimes, mainly the UAR. The logic behind this thinking was to avoid a premature confrontation between Israel and the Arab states. They feared that Al-Fateh's action would force the involvement of the Arab states, and the UAR in particular, in a war with Israel. Yet despite this Al-Fateh embarked upon reconnaissance operations inside the occupied territories in 1963. On 14 July of that year Al-Fateh lost its first two casualties, 'Andah Swailem Sa'd and Salem Salim Sa'd.

In 1964, the Palestinian branch of the ANM formed a military group to undertake reconnaissance operations inside the occupied territories and to establish network and arms caches. This decision was adopted at a conference held in September 1964 that included representatives of all the Palestinian members of the ANM. The basic principles that were adopted at this conference were the following:

1. Armed struggle is the only way to liberate Palestine.

2. All secondary conflicts should be subordinated to the conflict with imperialism and Zionism.

3. The different revolutionary groups should be unified.

On 2 November 1964, the first casualty claimed by ANM—Khalid al-Hajj—was killed by the Israeli army in an unplanned clash. At that time the ANM refused to disclose the name of the man or to give any details about the circumstances that led to his death. This was done to avoid any hindrance of its preparations and to maintain secrecy.

On 1 January 1963, Al-Fateh's first communiqué was published in the Lebanese press announcing the start of its military activities in the occupied territories. At this early stage these activities were not clearly described for the reason that the Arab regimes and their mass media were tacitly opposed to the principle of Palestinian guerrilla warfare. The Palestinian people remained passive awaiting the Arab states, especially the UAR, to bring a favorable end to their problem. Al-Fateh was an isolated movement trying to prove that Palestinians could fight, could confront their own problems, and could escape the control of the various Arab states, especially Jordan which was hostile to any possibility of a change in the status quo.

Jordanian police checks on the refugee population made any political activity extremely difficult. In Cuban terminology, the Palestinian resistance began as a "foco," as a nucleus employing armed violence without any political preparation of the population it was trying to involve. But while the strategy of the "foco" as applied within the framework of class struggle has shown itself to be ineffective in Latin America, the armed nucleus of the Palestinian resistance, due to the military collapse of the Arab states, has been successful within the framework of a national movement. Naturally this strategy was imposed by the circumstances and by the nature of the national movement of which Al-Fateh is the nucleus.

The Arab regimes continued to oppose independent guerrilla warfare until 3 June 1967, except for Syria which found in Al-Fateh the embodiment of its slogan repeated since 1963 (without being applied), calling for a popular war of liberation.

The military grouping of the Palestinian branch of the ANM came to be known as Abtal al-'Audah (Heroes of the Return). It started its military operations in November 1966, under internal pressure from the members of the ANM who urged that the reconnaissance activities should be transformed into actual military operations. A few months after its emergence Abtal al-'Audah became associated with the Palestine Liberation Army (PLA) for financial reasons. Shuqairi welcomed this step because he wanted to bring the commando organizations under the control of the PLO in order to compete with Al-Fateh. The Palestinian branch of the ANM then formed another military group which carried out its first operation in the occupied territories a few days before the June war. This group was called Munazzamat Shabab al-Thar (Youth of Revenge Organization).

Another organization emerging prior to the June war was Jabhat Tahrir Filistin (Palestinian Liberation Front), headed by Ahmad Jibril and Ahmad Za'rur. Jibril is a graduate of the Royal Military Academy, Sandhurst, and a former officer in the Syrian army. Za'rur is a former officer in the Jordanian army. The organization is strictly military.

The Palestine Liberation Army (PLA) did not play an active role prior to 5 June 1967. Yet in the six-day war the PLA troops stationed in the Gaza Strip fought bravely against the Israeli forces.

The overwhelming defeat, in June 1967. of the Arab regimes took the Arab people by surprise. This defeat proved that dependence on the Arab governments and armies for the liberation of Palestine would lead nowhere. It proved that the idea of Arab unity, which was considered to be the road to Palestine, was far-fetched under existing conditions. The Arab masses were isolated and could not play their proper role in the war because the existing regimes feared their people—in case they armed and trained them—more than the enemy. Thus, the role of the people was limited to observing the defeat of their armies, the occupation of the whole of Palestine, Sinai and the Golan Heights. The Palestinians took it upon themselves to act, continue the war against the enemy, rally the Arab people to their side and make them play their proper role in retrieving Palestine, Sinai and the Golan Heights from Israeli occupation. Thus directly after the June war a number of conferences were held (in Damascus) in which representatives of Al-Fateb, Munazzamat Shabab al-Tbar, Abtal al-'Audab, and Jabhat Tahrir Filistin participated. The PLO was in touch with what was going on. The purpose of these conferences was to formulate a Palestinian response to the defeat The only formula that was approved was that of armed struggle. Nearly half of the Palestinian Arab people were now under the yoke of direct Israeli occupation. However, these meetings did not lead to any practical results; Al-Fateh renewed its military operations unilaterally in August 1967.

The other three organizations Jabhat Tahrir Filistin, Munazzamat Shabab al-Tbar, and Abtal al-Audab continued to hold meetings and agreed to merge together into the Popular Front for the Liberation of Palestine (PFLP). PFLP started its military operations on 6 October 1967 and the first military communiqué was published on 21 December 1967.

The re-emergence of several Palestinian politico-military organizations underlined the need to coordinate and unify their activities. This prompted Al-Fateh to call on 4 January 1968 for a meeting of all Palestinian organizations, including the PLO and PFLP. The conference was held in Cairo between 17 and 19 January 1968. The PLO and PFLP refused to attend this conference on the grounds that some of the organizations invited did not have a significant military or political weight. Nevertheless, Al-Fateh held the meeting at the end of which the Permanent Bureau for the Palestinian Armed Struggle was set up. This Bureau included, in addition to Al- Fateh, eight lesser organizations. It ceased to exist on the political level shortly after the convening of the fourth Palestinian National Congress, held in Cairo in July 1968. However, on the military level, the military wings of these organizations merged with al-'Asifab.

Early in September 1968, Jabbat Tabrir Filistm (Ahmad Jibril) seceded from PFLP and continued to operate on a limited scale under the name of PFLP—General Command. It designed for itself a new emblem to distinguish it from PFLP.

In February 1968, the Palestine Liberation Army (PLA) started its commando activities under the name of Popular Liberation Forces (PLF). Ulis is a commando organization operated under the auspices of the Palestine Liberation Army within the political framework of the Palestine Liberation Organization.

On 10 July 1968, the fourth Palestinian National Congress was held in Cairo and was attended by representatives of the different commando organizations, including al-Sa'iqah. Al-Sa'iqah is a Palestinian group which has very close associations with the Bath Party, ruling in Syria. The fourth National Congress was held in the absence of Ahmad Shauqairi,

who had been forced to resign from the presidency of the PLO after a long struggle between him and the majority of the Executive Committee backed by the rank and file of the PLA in Syria. Some other Palestinian organizations had played a role in the pressures which caused his resignation. They accused him of having single handed leadership harmful to the Palestinian struggle. They also believed that he subordinated the struggle to political maneuvering.

The Congress elected Yebya Hammouda as Acting President of the PLO Executive Committee. Formerly he had been president of the Jordanian Lawyers' Association, however, since 1957 he had been barred from Jordan because he was accused of being a communist. Hammouda was given the job of contacting the Palestinian commando organizations and holding the fifth Palestinian National Congress within a period of six months.

With the collapse of Arab military strength, the Palestinian guerrilla movement gained momentum and strength very quickly. This was most obvious in Jordan where there was no fast military build-up of the conventional armed forces as was the case in the UAR. The commando organizations armed themselves with great rapidity and in only 18 months, Al-Fateh, for example, was able to train thousands of combatants while, before the defeat, it had taken the same organization seven years (1958-65) to complete the structure of its first politico-military nucleus. Soon the commando organizations came to control the mass of the Palestinian population especially in the refugee camps in Jordan. With the battle of Karameh, 21 March 1968, the commando groups (and particularly Al-Fateh) emerged as undisputed leaders of the Palestinian population. Political education was intensified among the refugees with the aim of rediscovering their Palestinian identity. It was also about this time that the resistance was able to consolidate its military bases, the state of Jordan included, and to turn them into relatively secure bases, first of all in the Ghor mountains where a great number of fighters have been trained. The resistance movement, in short, asserted itself in the Arab world, obliged Israel to take account of its existence, began to mobilize the Palestinian population, and set up the beginnings of an administrative infrastructure.

The armed struggle, intended to win popular support, began to bear fruit. Soon, the impression made by the resistance on Arab public opinion overtook the influence of Ba'thism and Nasserism and imposed itself upon the mass of Palestinian. All this led even King Hussein to declare in one of his press conferences after the Karameh battle "we are all fedayin."

Under these quickly changing circumstances a potential conflict was developing between the resistance movement and the Jordanian regime. One manifestation of this conflict was the official acceptance by the Jordanian regime of the peaceful settlement of the Arab-Israeli conflict on the basis of the UN Security Council resolution of 22 November 1967. In contrast to this we have the firm and unambiguous rejection by the entire Palestinian resistance movement of this sort of settlement. Another manifestation of the conflict was the confrontation which occurred in October 1968 between the commando organizations and the Jordanian authorities. The commandos were anxious about rumors of contacts between Jordanian and Israeli officials for a peaceful settlement. This led Al-Fateh and PFLP to issue separate statements proclaiming their determination to carry on the struggle at all costs.

Al-Fateh issued a statement on 20 October asserting that it was not opposed to peace and stability in the area; what it did oppose was surrender and acceptance of the *fait accompli*. It rejected any attempt by the United Nations to find a peaceful solution on the basis of the UN Security Council resolution of 22 November 1967. Further it declared that it was determined to continue fighting at all costs.

The statement of the PFLP issued on 22 October 1968 accused the "reactionary Palestinian right" of selling out the true interests of the Palestinian people to "counter-revolutionary forces." It compared the proposed peaceful solution to the disaster of 1948.

It also asserted that these were critical moments for the Palestinians; and it was up to the liberation movement to resist with all the means at its disposal the Security Council's resolution, and to condemn outright any Arab country that adopted a hesitant attitude to the Palestinian problem. Any attempt by the "reactionary Palestinian right" to depict this attitude as an "interference in the internal affairs of the Arab countries" was part and parcel of the "reactionary Zionist imperialist" conspiracy to liquidate the Palestine problem.

The first open and serious clash between the commando groups and the Jordanian Government occurred on 4 November 1968. Tahir Dablan, a close associate of the Jordanian intelligence services, who had set up an armed group Kataib al-Natr (Battalions of Victory), provoked an incident with Jordanian security forces to provide them with a pretext for opening fire on the Palestinian organizations. Immediately the Jordanian Royal Guard took up positions in the streets of Amman and around three camps—al-Wahadat, Hussein and Schneller. They shot at the people there and several deaths resulted. In addition, they bombarded the arms and food depots belonging to Al-Fateh. A curfew was imposed in Amman by the Jordanian authorities. King Hussein urged Yasser 'Arafat to negotiate a compromise. Shortly afterwards a Palestinian emergency council was set up which, in principle, was composed of all the Palestinian unions, parties, organizations and armed groups.

This council included a bureau of military coordination which was dependent upon it. The Palestinian organizations were driven to tighten up their ranks by the political context as well as by the necessity of uniting to form a national force in the face of Israel. The palace made the various Palestinian movements sign an agreement of fourteen points which, among other things, stipulated that there should be coordination between the military forces of the Palestinians and the Jordanians and which called for the formation of a unified staff and prohibited commando operations south of the Dead Sea. The agreement served the purpose of restoring peace between the commandos and the regime and was never implemented.

The guerrilla groups issued a statement announcing that agreement had been reached between the two sides, but without giving any details. On Wednesday evening, Al-Fateh, in a broadcast from Cairo, had this to say in the wake of Jordanian events: "Al-Fateh does not accept to commit suicide with Arab bullets. The Palestinian organizations are alone competent to punish those Palestinians who deviate from the revolutionary line and we reject controls which, under slogans of 'coordination' and 'cooperation,' are designed to liquidate us." Al-Fateh went on to say that "Arab frontiers must remain open for our operations and we demand the immediate liberation of Palestinian revolutionaries detained in Arab prisons. The insecurity of Palestinian fighters inside Arab frontiers cannot continue and we cannot guarantee to remain quiet in the future. We shall not pay the price of a peaceful settlement and we call on all Arabs to disown the Jarring mission."

One of the most interesting aspects of the crisis was the attitude taken by Egypt. According to al-Abram of 7 November, the guerrilla organizations dispatched an open letter to President Nasser asking for his personal intervention to settle the crisis. Nasser, however, took the position that, despite his anxiety at what was going on, he did not wish to interfere for fear that his move would be misconstrued; also, Jordanian sovereignty had to be taken into account.

Meanwhile, in Cairo itself, President Nasser addressed a meeting of the Central Committee of the Arab Socialist Union with the following reference to events in Jordan: "Our stand regarding Palestinian resistance and commando action is one of complete support and assistance in their rightful struggle against Israeli occupation. The basis on which we must work is to maintain the unity of the Jordanian front and preserve the relations of confidence between the Jordanian people, government, army, and commando organizations, and also to support the unity of the eastern front."

Finally, on 10 November a decree was issued by the Jordanian Minister of the Interior to the effect that arms could only be carried by those given a special permit by the government. This decree was in blatant contradiction to the agreement concluded between the Jordanian authorities and the principal guerrilla organizations.

In accordance with the resolution adopted by the fourth Palestinian National Congress the PLO Executive Committee held several meetings with the different commando organizations. From these meetings a formula of representation for the National Assembly of the PLO was drawn up. This formula gave 33 seats to Al-Fateh, 12 seats to PFLP, 12 seats to al-Sa'iqah, 11 seats to the Executive Committee of the PLO, 3 seats to the PLA, 1 seat to the National Fund of the PLO, 3 seats to students', workers', and women's organizations, 28 seats to independents.

PFLP rejected the formula and refused to participate. It proposed to establish instead a front for all organisations to be formed on an egalitarian basis, i.e., one organization one vote. Al-Fateh, on the other hand, agreed to the formula and issued an important political statement a few days prior to the convening of the Congress. In this statement Al-Fateh announced its belief in the PLO as a general and proper framework for Palestinian national unity and said that it would participate in the conference and the PLO Executive Committee.

The fifth Palestinian National Congress was held between 1 and 4 February 1969 in Cairo. At the end of the Congress a new Executive Committee was formed headed by Yasser 'Arafat—official spokesman of Al-Fateh. The new Executive Committee was composed of four representatives of Al-Fateh, two of al-Sa'iqah, three independents, and one from the old PLO executive committee.

At the end of this Congress a statement was issued. It declared that the Palestinian cause was facing the danger of liquidation in the interests of Zionism and imperialism through the UN Security Council resolution of 22 November 1967. It further warned against everything that went under the name of peaceful settlements including the Soviet project to lay down a timetable to implement the Security Council resolution. It also rejected any Arab policies or international interventions which contradicted the Palestinians' right to their country. It objected to any form of tutelage over Palestinian affairs and particularly over the development of the rising Palestinian resistance movement.

The statement called on the Palestinian masses, in particular, and the Arab masses, in general, to mobilize all their resources and put all their forces at the disposal of the armed Palestinian resistance, and to consider that the Palestine liberation movement was part of the overall Arab revolution.

The statement went on to say that the aims of the fighters should be directed against one target only—the Zionist enemy. The fundamental conflict was with Zionism. All other internal conflicts should be shelved because they were secondary.

The statement warned against the "defeatist deviationists" who wanted to liquidate the Palestinian cause in favor of a spurious Palestinian entity subservient to Zionism and imperialism. Furthermore, the Congress drew up a plan to augment the effectiveness of the Palestinian resistance. This included, above all, a call for the unification of guerrilla action and financial resources, and the strengthening of the Palestinian Liberation Army.

Since this plan required additional finances, the Palestinians were called upon to give more money and the Arab states to meet all their financial commitments to the Palestinian Liberation Organization. It urged Arab states to facilitate the residence, work and movement of Palestinians found on their soil.

After the fifth Congress Al-Fateh announced that it would retain its organizational independence.

Towards the end of January 1969 an open conflict arose within the ranks of the PFLP. As previously mentioned, the Front had originally consisted of three separate groups which had agreed to operate together. These were Shabab al-Thar, all of them members of the Arab Nationalist Movement; Abtal al-Audah; and Jabhat Tahrir Filistine (i.e., Ahmad Jibril's and Ahmad Za'rur's group).

As mentioned before the Jibril and Za'rur group split off from the others, though it continued to use the name "Popular Front for the Liberation of Palestine," adding "General Command" to distinguish itself from the others. The split took place after the arrest of three of the Arab Nationalist Movement's leaders in Damascus: Dr. George Habash, Payez Qaddurah and 'Ali Bushnaq. Ahmad Jibril's group refused to condemn the arrest on the grounds that it might have been the result of party political disputes only. However, this, probably, precipitated the split and did not simply cause it.

Moreover, during the month of August 1969, PFLP General Command witnessed another split. The group led by Ahmad Za'rur called itself the Arab Palestine Organization, while Ahmad Jibril's group retained the name of PFLP General Command.

Meanwhile, the Arab Nationalist Movement as a whole was undergoing a sharp shift to the left. This did not happen with the same speed and decisiveness everywhere in the Arab world, but it became clear that with the internal splits taking place most ANM members were in the leftist camp, whose organ of expression is the Beirut weekly al-Hurriyab. It was only to be expected that this conflict should make itself felt in the Popular Front for the Liberation of Palestine. The conflict persisted until Dr. Habash returned to Amman after being freed from Damascus. However, the Front refused to participate in the Palestine National Congress under the pressure of the left-wing group.

On 10 February 1969, the Beirut weekly al-Hurriyab carried a statement by the left-wing faction of the PFLP (under the leadership of Nayef Hawatemah: a Jordanian and a graduate from the Arab University in Beirut, who joined the ANM in the fifties, and early in the sixties became one of its leading members) pointing out that at a decisive PFLP conference held in Amman in August 1968 the progressive-wing gained the day in its call for a revolutionary policy linked with the toiling masses. According to al-Hurriyah, although the moderates had ostensibly approved the conference proposals they had acted in a manner contrary to these proposals. For example, on 28 January 1969, they arrested three members of the progressive-wing in the cultural club of one of the refugee camps in Amman. Then five more were arrested in al-Baqa' camp, and six others in various places.

The progressives called for an immediate meeting of the coordinating bureau of the resistance which the moderates refused to attend. The bureau strongly condemned the arrests and sent a delegation to the moderates to ask them to release the prisoners. The request was turned down.

In a communiqué published on 15 February 1969, George Habash, leader of the moderate-wing of the PFLP, declared that while the front had been exposing the "reactionaries" and "petit bourgeois" and their luke-warm attitude towards the Palestine cause, while it had been challenging the Zionist enemy in the occupied territory and outside it, "opportunist pockets" had appeared within the Front's own ranks who sought to impede its revolutionary progress. These were a group of "adolescent cafe intellectuals" who subscribed to scientific socialism in name only.

On 24 February, the Beirut weekly al-Hurriyah officially announced that the progressive-wing of the PFLP had broken away and formed an organization to be known as the Popular Democratic Front for the Liberation of Palestine (PDFLP). The causes behind this split can be summarized as follows.

The Marxist group led by Nayef Hawatemah, who was behind the split, called for the breaking-off of all relations of subservience with the Arab regimes whether they were progressive or reactionary. Furthermore, this group strongly criticized the other Palestinian organizations, especially the PLO and Al-Fateh, on the grounds that, like the progressive Arab regimes, they were led by the "petit bourgeoisie" and its ideology, which had proved its failure in the 1967 defeat. The new Marxist group called for a long-term war of popular liberation against imperialism and Zionism. They also called for the establishment of a Marxist-Leninist party completely committed to the ideology favorable to the dispossessed peasants and workers (the Asian proletariat).

On the other hand, the majority of the PFLP, led by George Habash, while agreeing to the basic analysis of the Hawatemah group, believed in maintaining certain relations with the progressive Arab governments. These relations they see as necessary to secure financial and military support vital for the survival of PFLP and the resistance movement in general.

As for the Palestinian people, Habash maintained that the war with Israel is a national liberation war which requires the recruitment of the widest sections of the Palestinian people, a great number of whom are "petit bourgeois." Thus, to alienate and antagonize the "petit bourgeois" class would bring a heavy loss to the national cause. At the same time, Habash stressed that the leading cadres of PFLP should be in the hands of those who are committed to the ideology of the proletariat.

On 3 April 1969, the PLO Executive Committee issued a statement in which it stated that the PLO had established a new command for a number of Palestine guerrilla groups. It would be called the "Command for Armed Palestinian Struggle" (CAPS) and would include al-'Asifah, the Popular Liberation Forces, al-Sa'iqah, and the Popular Democratic Front for the Liberation of Palestine. The PFLP under George Habash has not agreed to participate in the Command for Armed Palestinian Struggle. The establishment of the Command was described as an "essential step towards the unification of commando activity and armed struggle." The Executive Committee took this decision because it was profoundly aware of how necessary it was that the Palestinian revolution should be unified in order to escalate and develop guerrilla activity.

The PLO had decided that from now on all reports of the operations of forces attached to the new command would be exclusively issued in the form of statements in the name of a military spokesman speaking for the new command, instead of the communiqués hitherto issued by each commando organization individually.

In addition to the above-mentioned Palestinian commando organizations, towards the end of 1968 the Egyptian daily newspaper al-Ahram announced that there had been in existence a resistance organization known as the "Arab Sinai Organization." This organization coordinates its activities with other Palestinian resistance groups in the Gaza Strip.

On 10 April 1969, the "National Command" (pan-Arab) of the Ba'th Party, backing the faction ruling in Iraq and opposed to the party regime in Syria, announced that they had formed their own commando organization called "The Arab Liberation Front."

The new organization was not intended to replace existing commando activity but to give it wider (inter-Arab dimensions). It is formed of Palestinians and nationals of various Arab countries who are members of the Ba'th Party.

On 10 April, King Hussein addressed the National Press Club in Washington. In his address, Hussein presented a six-point program for settling the Middle East conflict. He declared that he spoke for President Nasser as well as for Jordan. The program promised to end the state of belligerency, recognize the existence of the state of Israel, and guarantee Israel freedom of navigation in the Suez Canal and Gulf of 'Aqaba.

On 15 April 1968, the Popular Liberation Forces of the Palestine Liberation Organization, al-'Asifah, al-Sa'iqah, the Popular Front for the Liberation of Palestine (PFLP), and the Popular Democratic Front for the Liberation of Palestine (PDFLP) issued a statement rejecting King Hussein's six-point Middle East plan. The statement was distributed lifter a meeting held on 14 April to discuss what was termed as "the grave and dangerous situation through which the Palestine issue is passing due to plans being put forward, especially the latest Jordanian plan, which affects the fate of the Palestine issue and the future of the armed resistance to Israeli occupation."

The statement said that the five organizations decided the following at their meeting:

1. To reject the Jordanian plan in its entirety, and to reject also all plans for the liquidation (of the Palestine issue) as well as all solutions proposed earlier. The organizations have also agreed to a unified plan to face this serious situation.

2. To form delegations which would contact certain Arab countries seeking a clarification of their position concerning the proposed plans rejected by the resistance movement.

In spite of the existence of numerous differing commando organizations there is complete agreement among them concerning the rejection of a political settlement of the Palestine problem to which they do not fully agree. Finally, it should be noted that all these organizations have made it very clear on numerous occasions that their war of liberation is not directed against the Jews as such but against the Zionist state which has rendered the Palestinians a homeless and dispossessed people.

Yasser 'Arafat of Al-Fateh in his press conference held in Damascus on 28 October declared: "The Palestinian revolution is against Zionism and not the Jews. Our Jewish brothers, the sons of the Israeli sect ate Egyptians in Egypt, Syrians in Syria, Lebanese in Lebanon, Palestinians in Palestine. We welcome every free and honest person of any nationality and religion to work within the framework of our humanitarian revolution, which aims at liberating our occupied lands and establishing our Palestinian democratic state."

The Popular Democratic Front for the Liberation of Palestine (PDFLP) presented the following proposed solution at the sixth Palestinian National Congress held in Cairo between 1 and 4 September 1949: "The establishment of the people's democratic state of Palestine in which Arabs and Jews will live without any discrimination whatsoever. A state which is against all forms of class and national subjugation, and which gives both Arabs and Jews the right to develop their national culture [...] The people's democratic state of Palestine will be an integral part of an Arab federal state in this area, [...] hostile to colonialism, imperialism, Zionism and Arab Palestinian reaction."

The Popular Front for the Liberation of Palestine (PFLP) in its February 1949 Political, Organizational, and Military Report states: "The aim of the Palestinian Liberation Movement is the establishment of a national democratic state in Palestine in which both Arabs and Jews will live together as citizens equal both in rights and in duties. The state will form an integral part of the progressive democratic national Arab entity which lives in peace with all the progressive forces in the world."

www.ingramcontent.com/pod-product-compliance
Ingram Content Group UK Ltd.
Pitfield, Milton Keynes, MK11 3LW, UK
UKHW042003230426
12048UKWH00009B/520